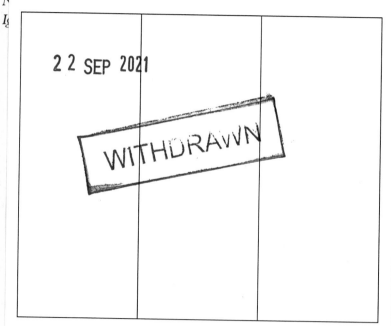

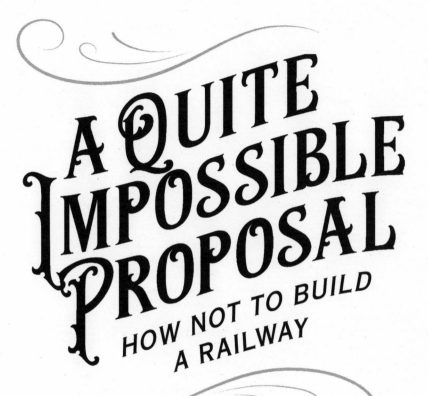

A QUITE IMPOSSIBLE PROPOSAL

HOW NOT TO BUILD A RAILWAY

ANDREW DRUMMOND

ORIGIN

First published in Great Britain in 2020 by
Origin, an imprint of Birlinn Ltd

West Newington House
10 Newington Road
Edinburgh
EH9 1QS

www.birlinn.co.uk

ISBN: 978 1 912476 88 6

British Library Cataloguing-in-Publication Data
A catalogue record for this book is available on request from
the British Library.

Typeset by Biblichor Ltd, Edinburgh
Printed and bound by Clays Ltd, Elcograf, S.p.A.

CONTENTS

ILLUSTRATIONS

PLATES

IN-TEXT MAPS AND PLANS

11.2 In 1898, the Hebridean Light Railway Co. drafted plans for a short railway which simply traversed Lewis from east to west, for the transportation of fish.

IN-TEXT ILLUSTRATIONS

2.1 Drawing (by Alexander Stuart Boyd, aka 'Twym') of the Napier Commission in session in Glasgow, 19 October 1883.

5.1 Sample page from the Book of Reference which accompanied the 1890 railway plans: items of interest at Ullapool.

Detailed maps and plans of the proposed railways may be viewed at: www.andydrummond.net/impossible

ACKNOWLEDGEMENTS

My thanks for assistance, advice and clues must go above all to Joan Michael of Ullapool, without whose encouragement, patience and local knowledge much of this book would be pure guesswork. I am seriously in debt to Jack Kernahan of Fortrose, who generously furnished me with the notes, plans and photos from his own researches into the Skye and Lewis railway proposals; and also to David Prescott of Dunblane for his enthusiastic, inspired and informed demonstration of how the Ullapool Railway might be built today. And then, in loose alphabetical order, to: Hugh Andrew for his suggestions on exploring the historical context; Dr Karen Buchanan of the Gairloch Museum, for her help on matters Aultbean; Andrew Cordier of Banchory for his calm explanations of unfathomable Admiralty charts; Peter Newling, for his kind sharing of Fowler family photographs and historical knowledge of the Braemore estate; David Spaven and John Yellowlees, gentlemen railway-encyclopaediae of Edinburgh, who kept my wheels on the correct rails; Gavin Strang, for his potted history of Lord Lovelace; David Sutherland, herring-history-man extraordinaire, for separating my red herrings and silver darlings; my editor Mairi Sutherland, whose stoicism has been exemplary; and finally to the ever helpful staff of the National Records of Scotland and the National Library of Scotland, in Edinburgh.

Should any of these people prove responsible in any way for my omissions and mistakes, then I will let them know quite forcefully. But the likelihood is small.

Andrew Drummond

INTRODUCTION

Be not deceived, nor yet disappointed: this is not a book about obscure
railway lines which were never built in a remote area of Scotland in the
late nineteenth century. If it were only that, the book would be very
short indeed. It would have scant relevance or resonance for the
present day. But what this book does concern itself with are the political and social events of the times and how these in combination
triggered several proposals to build railways to villages in north-western
Scotland, as well as on Skye and Lewis. Laid bare is an underlying story
of southern neglect of the Highlands and Islands and of blinkered
private interests. The history of the proposed railways – and especially
of the one between Garve and Ullapool – is not a pretty one. It is a tale
of exhaustive planning and shattered dreams. If there had been a
deliberate conspiracy to prevent such railways from being built, then it
is doubtful that the conspirators could have done a better job than was
achieved by a combination of government incompetence and the
treachery of private capital.

I first came across the Garve to Ullapool railway sometime in the last
decade of the twentieth century, and considered it fair game for a
lengthy piece of fiction – hence my novel of 2004, whose short title
was *An Abridged History*, though its full title was almost as long as the
railway itself. Happily, in that novel, the railway was built, and the good
people of Ullapool enjoyed an excellent transport service which
continues, no doubt, to this day.

In 2018, while considering a re-issue of the novel, I decided to look
more closely at the facts. Too many facts can get in the way of good
fiction, which is why I had been slightly less than attentive to them on
my first outing. Oddly, however, the facts turned out to be as

I

convoluted and unexpected as the fiction. Naively believing there had been but one attempt to build the Ullapool railway, I was aghast to discover that there were at least five, spread over a period of fifty-five years. And, worse, there were proposed railways all over the place. For all I know, there may well be others which remain to be uncovered. Twice, the Ullapool railway got within a whisker of being financed and built. 'Unfortunately,' in the understated words of one proposer, 'owing to a hitch at the last moment, the scheme was dropped for the time being.'

What stands out clearly from the various proposals is that the justifiable and vital task of improving transportation in the Highlands and Islands was a major struggle – against southern indifference, against bureaucracy, against geographical ignorance and, not least, against competing private investments. Commissions of inquiry came and went over the years, making solid recommendations in favour of improvements – and ultimately achieved nothing. There was a sound principle, expressed on several occasions between 1885 and 1920, that public transport at standard and reasonable costs should be viewed as the right of a British citizen in exactly the same way as a postal service at standard and reasonable costs was viewed as a civic right. While this principle might have appeared obvious to our ancestors, both sides of the equation have been eroded by late twentieth-century privatisation and competition. So much for one aspect of social progress in Great Britain.

You are invited now to dip into the archives, to dream of railways across the Isle of Lewis, across the misty Isle of Skye, between Garve and Ullapool, and to several other more obscure termini. Dream only – for, as yet, none of them exist.

MEASUREMENTS AND MONEY

Without any sort of apology, I have used imperial measures in the text: tons, pounds, miles, feet, yards and, where necessary, furlongs, chains and links. The modern reader can convert these according to her or his own taste. In the text, a reference to (e.g.) '100 feet' means 100 imperial feet – i.e. 30.5 metres. For those sadly unenlightened in the matter of imperial measures of length, be advised that:

1 foot = 12 inches, or 30.5 centimetres; 1 yard = 3 feet, or 91.44 centimetres; 1 link = 7.92 inches.

1 chain = 22 yards, or 100 links; 1 furlong = 10 chains, or 220 yards; 1 mile = 8 furlongs, or 1,760 yards, or 1.60 kilometres

I also talk blithely of acres:

1 acre = 4,840 yards² (or 160 square rods, poles or perches . . .) or 0.4068 of a hectare.

Thus, 21,000 acres is approximately 8,500 hectares.

And, in the spirit of completeness, for weights:

1 pound (1lb) = 16 ounces (16oz) or 0.45 kilograms; 1 ton = 20 hundredweights (cwt) or 1,016 kilograms; 1cwt = 112lb.

Currency in the past, of course, comes with its own foreign-ness:

One pound (£1) = 20 shillings (20s); 1 shilling = 12 pence (12d). One shilling therefore can be understood as 5 'new' pence. I have not succumbed to the temptation to talk of farthings and halfpennies.

How difficult can it be?

Well, slightly more difficult than strictly necessary. We will, in the course of our story, come across both 'crans' and 'barrels' of fish. It might be of help to you to know that a 'cran' was a measure equivalent to 37½ imperial gallons, or about 3 hundredweight of fish; whereas a 'barrel' contained 32 'English Wine gallons', which itself was 0.83 of an imperial gallon. Cling on to that difference.

Monetary values in 1890 would be worth – very, very approximately – one hundred times more in today's (2020) currency: thus, £240,000 in 1890 would equate to around £24 million today; £80 would equate to £8,000. Much the same ratio applies up until 1918. For 1945, multiply by about twenty, rather than one hundred. As an extremely approximate and purely indicative figure for the 1890s, the average weekly wage for an urban labourer might be in the region of £1; a sailor perhaps £1 13s (£1.65); a male teacher would be paid around £2 10s (£2.50) per week; and expenditure on the bare necessities of life might be around £1 to £1 10s (£1.50) per week.

NOTES

For the notes collected at the end of the book, the following guide:

- A reference suffixed with (e.g.) [NRS: GD40/16/39] refers to an item held by the National Records of Scotland, Edinburgh, under their catalogue reference (e.g.) 'GD40/16/39'.
- The majority of the references to the Napier Commission Report will be of this format (e.g.) – Napier Commission Report, Vol. 3, p. 1868, Q29040; the Q-reference indicates the sequential 'question and answer' paragraph on the relevant page.
- See the bibliography at the end of this volume for full details of each book or archival reference.

'A Right to Improved Communications'

Railways for the North-West of Scotland?

At the end of the First World War, a group of eminent civil servants put forward the idea that the inhabitants of north-west Scotland 'have a "right" to improved communications in the same way that they have a "right" to cheap postage'.[1] This rather bold sentiment reiterated what had been said several times before in connection with the development of railways in the remoter parts of Scotland. In 1891, for example, a Liberal MP in the House of Commons argued that

> In the Postal Service a letter is carried for 1d., but it may cost the Post Office 6d. to carry it. There is a loss to the Exchequer, but there is no charity towards the individual whose correspondence is carried; he simply enjoys the advantage of a system in common with the rest of the country. So will the people pay for the use of harbours and light railways as they do in other parts of Scotland.[2]

Interesting and arguably very sound ideas, which stand up to robust examination even today. But in 1891, such reasoning had a greater resonance. Railways at that time constituted the very lifeblood of transportation. There were no motor-cars or charabancs puttering along country lanes anywhere in the north of Scotland: on land, you either rode on a cart or – less likely – inside a coach, walked or – less likely – rode on a horse; if you were lucky, had far to go, could afford it and lived near a harbour, you could take advantage of the erratic steamer services provided by David Macbrayne, which would transport you to Glasgow or the islands.

But the logistics of travel were daunting: a Barra man stated in 1883 that if he wished to make a judicial complaint of any sort, he would have to travel to see the procurator fiscal in Lochmaddy – a journey of at least 50 miles to be made on foot, with two ferries intervening. It took about two days. When asked whether he would 'rather lose something than go on such business' he replied 'I would, by far.'[3] Before the completion of the railway from Fort William to Mallaig in 1901, one could catch a coach from Arisaig to the Fort, around 35 miles; that journey took seven and a half hours and it cost around 11s – easily half of the average weekly wage. After the coming of the railway, the journey time was ninety minutes and the cost about one-third. Similarly, for the 50-mile trip from Fort William to Kingussie in the central Highlands, you had to pay the coachman 14s 6d (second class; or 17s 6d if you could rise to first class) and put up with being jolted around for six and a half hours. Even short-distance travel required long and painful inner debate.[4] Towards the end of the First World War, many journeys in the remoter parts of the Highlands were still slow (the new-fangled motor-vehicles, a great rarity, could barely manage 8 mph), they were uncomfortable (sometimes one sat in the close company of live lobsters and calves) and they were expensive.

So railways constituted something of a revolutionary force – across the world – in the nineteenth century. In North America, the trans-continental railroads were effectively stitching together the United States and Canada. In Europe, railways were being laid down mile after mile to consolidate new or existing sovereign states. In Britain, the first half of the 1840s was characterised by 'railway mania', during which every town and county had its own building projects and competing lines. After the bubble of railway construction burst during the economic downturn of the second half of that decade, there was a short lull; and then came yet more railways across the land.

In Scotland, where things happened a little later, there was growth in both the central belt and Angus in the 1850s and 60s, largely driven by the need to move coal from mining areas to industrial towns and cities; the 1860s and 70s saw the building of railways up the central spine of Scotland (from Perth to Inverness) and into the north-east (Aberdeen and Elgin). Over this period, smaller railway companies were gobbled up by larger ones until, by the 1880s, the railway lines had almost all settled under the management of four huge companies – the Highland, the Great North of Scotland, the Caledonian and the North British. In the last two decades of the nineteenth century, these companies were anxious, on the one hand, to ensure that their rivals did not encroach on 'their' territory and, on the other hand, to milk as much revenue as possible from the routes that they controlled.

Such competition gave rise to some bizarre occurrences. On one day in December 1896, civil servants in London were surprised to receive no fewer than three rival proposals to build a railway between Fort Augustus and Inverness: one from the Highland Railway, one from the North British Railway and one from a tiny company named the Invergarry and Fort Augustus Railway (funded almost exclusively by the brewer Lord Burton, owner of the Cluanie and Loch Quoich estate). It was clear that neither of the two larger companies wanted Lord Burton to succeed – and one has to concede that the project to run a line up the side of Loch Ness to Inverness was a step too far for such a small outfit. It was equally clear that the Highland Railway did not want any rival coming within whistling distance of its citadel in Inverness; the Highland proposal therefore had the whiff of a 'spoiler' strategy. As we shall see, the company was not above getting permission to build a railway without any intention of going ahead with construction, the permission merely being used to block any competing attempt.[5]

While these railway companies tightened their grip over the Scottish landscape south and south-west of Inverness, the north-west of Scotland was largely left untouched. A desire for social and economic improvement was sweeping through communities in the northern counties and the western islands. Thus, while the Highland Railway was pressing ahead with plans to extend the Dingwall to Strome Ferry line all the way to Kyle of Lochalsh, and the West Highland Railway was ploutering its way muddily across the moors from Crianlarich to Fort William and ultimately Mallaig, the Scottish Office and Members of Parliament were being assailed with petitions from local communities advocating small branch lines to the north-west coast. We will look at these lines in more detail later, but let us list them here, to familiarise ourselves with the exotic nature of the proposals.

The southernmost project was the Achnasheen to Aultbea railway. This would branch off the Highland's Dingwall to Strome Ferry line at Achnasheen, 28 miles west of Dingwall. It would then proceed in elegant curves up Glen Docherty and over the hill to Kinlochewe, before following the south shore of Loch Maree to its western end (some interesting engineering work was required, inclusive of several viaducts that would today be worthy backgrounds to a Hollywood blockbuster about boy wizards). At Poolewe it would curve around the eastern shore of Loch Ewe to terminate just at the end of the pier at Aultbea. From here, so the plan went, connecting steamers sailed to Stornoway. This line was to be slightly more than 37 miles in length.

Slightly further north came the Garve to Ullapool railway. This was a line of 33 miles in length which, like the Aultbea line, would branch off from the Strome Ferry line; the junction would be at the village of Garve, 12 miles west of Dingwall (16 miles east of Achnasheen). It would proceed north-westwards along the same route as the modern A835 road, drop in precipitous manner to the head of Loch Broom and end up conveniently at the steamer pier in the centre of Ullapool – where, with a hop and a skip, the refreshed and rested traveller could also board a steamer bound for Stornoway.

Thirdly, the Culrain to Lochinver branch railway would start on the existing Far North Line operated by the Highland Railway Company, at the village of Culrain, which lies about three miles north-west of Bonar Bridge. The Far North Line had connected Inverness with Bonar Bridge in 1864, and with Wick and Thurso in 1874. From Culrain, the branch line would make its way up Glen Oykel (following the route of the present-day A837), head north up to Loch Assynt and ease its way into Lochinver from the north-east: a line of about 42 miles in total.

Furthest north, the Lairg to Laxford railway was to start at the village of Lairg, also a station on the Far North Line and situated about 8 miles north of Culrain. This line would reach the west coast by following the modern A838 road past Loch Shin and Loch More and then down the Laxford River, to terminate at the head of the sea-loch at Laxford Bridge – a place slightly less deserted then than now (but not much). A distance of around 37 miles would have been covered.

On the islands, things were more complex. For Skye, several proposals were in circulation, all for lines centred on Portree. Railways were proposed from there to Dunvegan and to Uig or Snizort in the west of the island (with one proposal even suggesting Trumpan, a tiny place now, tucked away near the top of the Vaternish peninsula). All of these would have connected with steamers to Lewis or Harris. Southwards from Portree, there were to be lines to Broadford and even Kylerhea or

Isleornsay, these connecting in imaginative ways to further transportation options on the mainland.

On Lewis, Stornoway was the obvious hub for lines extending in different directions – to Carloway on the west coast and to Ness at the top of the island, either via the township of Barvas on the west coast, or via Back and Tolsta on the east. From the west coast, there was no expectation of further sea connections even by the most fevered of imaginations: the railways would be primarily for the transportation of dead fish back to Stornoway. (Although, come to think of it . . . there was once a plan for Fort William to become a rival to Liverpool, the port of choice for transatlantic steamers to and from Quebec: the more northerly crossing would shave a day off a six-day voyage.[6] So why not, after all, Canada to Carloway or Stornoway?)

Between 1888 and 1893 these six proposals, along with the extension lines to Kyle of Lochalsh and to Mallaig, exercised the minds of locals, of journalists from the big cities and of politicians resident in far distant London.

But why, you might object, should these railways be of any interest to us now? The fact that only the lines to Kyle and to Mallaig were ever built suggests that Fate had taken a good hard look at the other proposals and found them wanting. Anyway, the Victorians had a thing about building railways, so no surprises here – it's just something they did. And are there not, in the words of a commentator of 1901, 'perfectly good carriage roads' on precisely the routes in question?

All quite valid points, until you remember that this is now, and that was then: a 'perfectly good road' was something of an oxymoron for the north-west Highlands at the end of the nineteenth century. For just a moment, picture life without basic transportation options: it is an uncomfortable image. Forget cars and buses and modern ferries. Forget bicycles and horses. Take a walk on the wild side of the Highlands and Islands even today, and then consider just how you could get your bare necessities to and from market without a decent road or a decent railway. Even by horse and cart, your journeys would take forever; by steamer, your options were severely limited. You would be cut off from even the most rudimentary centres of modern civilisation. Access to shops, doctors, schools, lawyers and officialdom would be difficult; in some cases it would be impossible. Your understanding of the outside world would be severely limited in breadth and in time.

So, to answer the central question of the importance of any railway in nineteenth-century Scotland, we need to appreciate that it was not just rails on sleepers. A railway had a social purpose. It could bring isolated settlements within comfortable distance of towns and cities, and it could underpin a developing economy. It allowed people to become part of a wider community and engage more fully with the political questions of the time. James Caldwell, the Liberal MP whom we quoted earlier, put it neatly:

> For what purpose is such a railway proposed? Not merely to improve the locality through which the railway will pass, but also for the purpose of bringing the fishing villages into speedy communication with the markets. That is exactly what we want, and no one who knows anything about the North of Scotland will deny that that district is sadly in want of development. We simply ask that we should be treated as part of the United Kingdom. We do not want exceptional treatment. We ask that if poverty exists in Scotland it shall be dealt with.[7]

Railways as a cure for poverty: it is an assertion which demands closer investigation. In the pages which follow, we will traverse more than a hundred years of clearances, evictions and land-wars. We will contemplate the tragedy of the commons of Ireland. We will gaze upon land-owning hypocrisy, governmental myopia and charitable cruelty. We will stumble across caravans of political gentlemen and their hangers-on, and we shall be impressed by the sight of Royal Commissions sailing around the north and west of Scotland. Before we reach the first episode of the campaign to build a railway to Ullapool, we shall have been caught up in millions of barrels of fish and saluted the herring-eating peoples of the Baltic lands. We will consider forests that were not forests and improvements that failed to improve. We will hear the voices of the dispossessed. We will detect the whiff of revolution on the islands and witness the military occupation of Skye. We will do all of this, because the story of the railways of the north-west cannot be properly understood in isolation from the wider historical background.

2

'We Must Speak the Truth to All Men'

The Condition of the People of the Highlands and Islands

At the risk of filling our pages with the pronouncements of just one man, we quote once more the words of James Caldwell, the Liberal Unionist MP for Glasgow St Rollox.

> In Scotland there is only one thing which a man may do. He may not beg, he may not steal, he may not commit suicide, he has no legal right to relief. The only thing he can lawfully do is to die from starvation.[1]

Mr Caldwell could be accused of over-egging the facts; but in that period, for many of the people living on the west coast of Scotland and on the islands, his was by no means a fanciful summary. The poor who tried to wrestle a living from the land and the sea suffered from modern-day versions of the biblical plagues, albeit without the locusts: a relentless cycle of hunger and poverty, rent rises and evictions, emigration and migration. Whenever they sought help, it came with a sting in the tail. Whenever they protested, their voices were drowned out. Whenever they thought they had swum clear of the tidal race of penury, another wave crashed over them and sucked them back down. They had nothing, because the land they had once farmed was now the property of others.

THE THEFT OF THE LAND

'One Absorbing Monopolising Class of Landlords'

In 1883, the Napier Commission was sent out into the wilds of north-west Scotland by a government made slightly nervous by recent events there. We will examine this commission and its works in more detail later, because it was quite extraordinary that such a group of gentlemen should actually talk and listen to ordinary people. The Commission very thoroughly investigated the conditions of crofters and landowner-ship in the region. All of the evidence collected – both oral and written – was recorded for posterity in five enormous volumes; these statements provide us with a very clear view of society and the economics of the time and the place. In a typical example of evidence presented to the Commission, the crofter Donald Campbell of Barra made the following statement on behalf of the people of his township; it was a fair summary of the century so far.

> They complain that they are kept down for the last sixty years with high rents, their little holding is made smaller, and deteriorating from having been long cropped, so that they are not now worth cultivating. They cannot support themselves but by their earnings elsewhere, only they lose their time by working after it and about it, and although they are constantly engaged with it, they are not able to make a livelihood out of it for themselves and their families. They are in that condition for the last sixty years. There are today twenty-six families where there were only twelve fifty years ago. They are very badly off . . . Very stormy winters prevailed, and our chief means of support, the potato, has been precarious ever since the potato disease . . . During winters such as these, perhaps the people of the place would have no means of support except shell-fish. [The proprietors] wished to deprive us of the shell-fish . . . They sent away most of our relatives to America thirty-five years ago. They pulled down the houses over their heads and injured them in every possible way. They valued the brutes higher than the men whom God created in his own image, and were more gentle with them.[2]

'We must', concluded Donald Campbell, 'speak the truth to all men.' He had just provided a thumbnail sketch of the intolerable conditions of life common in the western Highlands and the Islands. Crofters and fishermen were living in small townships which were packed tight beyond sustainability, only permitted to work land that was unworkable from the beginning or was now exhausted, forced to seek a living away from home or even on another continent. And all this was a result of the land policies pursued by the ruling class of Great Britain for over a century.

The nineteenth century in the northern and western Highlands and Islands is tragically associated with what came to be known as 'the Clearances'. And the clearing of tenants from large areas of land reached its peak in the first half of the century. But this was merely the end result of a long period of decline that began well before 1745, as the traditional clan chiefs were sucked inexorably into the cycle of wealth and ruin of the southern British economy. Ancestral lands were slowly parcelled up and sold to cover disgraceful debts. After 1745, the process accelerated, and the largely self-sufficient rural economy began to be geared towards the production of goods capable of sale in a wider market. The principal export was soda ash, a substance derived from the burning of kelp seaweed, to be used in the production of glass and soap. Over the years, the west-coast communities also engaged in cattle-rearing, whisky-distilling and fishing, and, as global conditions demanded, in that most useful task of all – providing fighting men for the British army and navy. But after the end of the Napoleonic wars, kelp-processing succumbed to more efficient European alternatives and fighting men were no longer in demand. The people of the Highlands were required to stay at home and scratch a living from whatever land they might have at their disposal. All of this put a great deal of pressure on the land. Migration to the central belt of Scotland, or emigration to the British colonies, began to increase. Sometimes the internal migration was purely seasonal, and sometimes it was only short-term, for a year or two. The fisheries on the east coast, the farms in the south and the factories of the central belt all attracted these temporary migrants. A potato blight in 1846, while not as devastating as that which hit Ireland, exerted further pressure on the crofters and cottars (the landless rural poor) of the region.

At around this time, the availability of cheap and extensive estates began to attract the attention of wealthy industrialists and bankers from England, or those returning to Scotland having made their fortunes abroad. Following on from the instructive and encouraging example set by the Marquis of Stafford and his wife (later the Duke and Duchess of Sutherland),[3] large tracts of land were swept quite clear of their original inhabitants and laid out as extensive sheep farms. In the early decades of the century, landowners were able to undertake these cleansing operations with impunity, assured that the political and legal establishment would not lift a finger to assist the victims. (Even William Wilberforce, who, along with Thomas Clarkson, did so much to abolish slavery, was persuaded to ignore the inhuman treatment of the poor much closer to home.)[4] Such people as were evicted from their homes in the glens, where they had free access to decent arable and pasture land, were offered entirely unsuitable crofts on rocky parts of the coastline, leaving the sheep to enjoy the fruits of centuries of husbandry.

The Sutherland events, although deservedly infamous, were by no means the most cruel of the clearances. Quite appalling actions were taken against their tenants by the owners of land in other parts of the Highlands and Islands. In the 1830s and 1840s many of the larger estates were formed from smaller parcels of land acquired in stages, the purchasers most frequently being men who had made huge amounts of money in colonial plunder or in the more domestic varieties of human exploitation: mining, brewing and manufacturing. Landowners such as these were by no means averse to continuing the clearance of land under the more acceptable guise of 'improvements'. In some cases, rather than remove people from their land by brute force, those landowners who could afford to do so would pay for emigration passages, weeding out the poorest and least productive tenants, slowly but surely freeing up the land for other purposes. On the Lewis estate of Sir James Matheson, for example, the strategy was to clear the west coast – where kelp-gathering had once been a traditional source of income – and move tenants either to distant countries or to the east coast of the island, where they could (it was faithfully promised) engage in fishing. The western side of the island thereby vacated was turned over to sheep and deer.

Other landowners were less concerned about the ultimate fate of their evicted tenants, unless it affected their ability to make money out of their estate. When, at the very end of the eighteenth century, the numbers of people taking passage to North America threatened to depopulate large tracts of land where kelp could be harvested, the landowners agitated for legislation which placed obstacles in the way of unfettered sea-passage across the Atlantic. This resulted in the Passenger Vessels Act of 1803. This Act set a high minimum cost of passage and limited the numbers which could be carried aboard a ship: no bad thing, given the utterly appalling and often fatal conditions in which people were forced to live below decks for weeks on end. Nominally, therefore, the legislation was a humane act. As a secondary argument, the promoters of the legislation (led by the Highland League) also suggested that unrestricted emigration would cause severe manpower shortages in the army, at a time when Britain was gearing up for yet another war against the French.

The Act being passed, the outflow of kelp-gatherers and cannon-fodder was stemmed. But when, twenty-five years later, the kelp industry had collapsed and young men were no longer required to line up and die for their country, the landowners suddenly discovered that their estates were cluttered with impoverished tenants and labourers. This perceived overpopulation soon led to agitation for the Government to assist people to leave the country; this necessitated, of course, the repeal of the Passenger Vessels Act, which duly occurred in 1827. So much for compassion.[5] As the century progressed, many of the Highland and Island landowners exerted themselves to rid their land of the burden of a growing population. But it was a task fraught with risk: those people who could afford to emigrate and were willing to do so were often younger and more hardy, which meant that they would also be the most likely to provide the muscle to 'improve' the land at home and thereby contribute to the wealth of the estates. Generally speaking, though, no tears need be shed for the land-owners. There was never a stagnant market for buying land in the Highlands and Islands.

The land reform campaigner John Murdoch summed it up with these words:

Under the land laws established in England by conquest and trans-planted into Scotland by fraud, the property and power of the country are being concentrated in the hands of the one absorbing monopolising class of landlords. The estates and farms get larger and larger, and the country is depopulated, to the same end of aggrand-ising this class.[6]

John Murdoch deserves far more attention than he has so far received in Scottish history; over several decades he was an indefatigable champion of land reform, before, during and after the short existence of his weekly newspaper *The Highlander*. Although it would be a step too far to describe him as a revolutionary, he was unequivocally radical in his proposals and not a man to back down from an argument. During the summer of 1883, when the Napier Commission was making its way around Scotland seeking the views of crofters and landowners, John Murdoch followed on behind – and sometimes went ahead – mopping up those people who had missed the opportunity to give evidence to the Commission. He finally caught up with Lord Napier and his colleagues in Glasgow in October 1883 and proceeded to give them two days' worth of his views, in the most polite, most intransigent and most rousing terms.

> The first thing wanted in the Highlands is the revival of the spirit of the people. The second, the calling forth of their intelligence, common sense, and enterprise. The third, definite legislative protection from interference with them by such petty deputies of absentees and aliens as have kept them so long in a state of slavish uncertainty and fear.[7]

When asked whether he would like to 'do away with landlordism', he replied simply: 'Decidedly.'

In the middle years of the century, the lot of the poor became even worse. From about 1846 onwards, over a period of almost ten years, potato crops were killed off by *Phytophthora infestans*, more commonly known as potato blight. This originated in Central and North America and was brought to Europe in 1844, where it almost immediately ravaged crops in the British Isles and across northern Europe. The devastation was most severe in Ireland, where, it is calculated, more than a million people died directly or indirectly from starvation. In Europe, while the effects were not so catastrophic, deaths occurred in the tens of thousands, with the Low Countries and Prussia being the worst affected; this crisis in a basic food staple is plausibly considered to be a prime cause of the revolutions of 1848 in France, Germany, Italy and beyond. Closer to home, in the Highlands as in much of the rest of Scotland, the potato had become the daily diet of the poor. This reliance on one cheap food was largely due to the changes in land tenancy – people being moved to tiny crofts with poor soil, where it was impossible to grow anything other than the potato.

The Westminster government intervened during the middle years of the century to alleviate the poverty and near-starvation caused by the lack of arable land and the potato failures. It could scarcely ignore the crisis. But its attitude to the victims tended to be punitive rather than supportive.

THE POOR LAWS

'Prevent Assistance from Being Productive of Idleness'

Donald Fraser of Glenelg gave evidence to the Napier Commission; he was himself an evicted crofter, but now worked as a schoolteacher, a registrar and an Inspector of the Poor, supervising poor relief. His statements provide a succinct sketch of the state of the townships in the western Highlands. For the people of Glenelg parish, life was precarious: the locality was undergoing rapid depopulation due to 'a good many [being] put out of their holdings'; there was no work, and the fishing in Loch Hourn was unpredictable. And around seventy-five of the Glenelg population of 1,600 were paupers. When asked, 'Has the condition of the people improved since you came here?' Fraser replied: 'I think it is rather the reverse. I find that we require to give a larger allowance to our paupers than when I came here. They live very largely upon their neighbours – the crofters – who are not in a position to assist them.'[8]

Fifty years before Napier, the paupers in England and Wales had benefited from the wisdom of their political masters in the passing of the Poor Law Amendment Act of 1834. Although designed to reform provisions for the management of the poor, the Act simply set up institutions which were equally open to abuse – as we see in, for example, the novels of Charles Dickens – and moreover transferred the problems of the rural population to the larger cities, where disease and abject poverty already held sway. These Poor Laws, like later ones in Ireland and Scotland, were designed to place a firm grip on the poor, remove beggars and similar vagabonds from the streets of the cities and roads of the countryside, and put a halt to the 'moral degradation' arising from abject poverty. The poor of Ireland were little better off than their English counterparts, since the Irish Poor Law Act of 1838 was modelled closely on the English one.

Scotland had to wait another decade for similar legislation, the Poor Law (Scotland) Act being passed in 1845. The only advantage to being poor in Scotland rather than in England was that – in theory at least – those refused assistance had the right of appeal. In practice, however, this right amounted to very little. Some measure of patriotic protection was offered as well: there was provision in Clause 77 for the removal of English and Irish (and, indeed, Manx) paupers back to their countries of origin, if they had been resident in Scotland for less than five years. The English legislation had a reciprocal clause for Scottish repatriation. Interestingly, the Irish laws had no such clause, leading one later commentator to remark drily that this was 'probably because it was thought that the Irish guardians would have no use for such power'[9] – no pauper in their right mind would cross the sea and seek a living in Ireland.

The figures for poor relief in Scotland are quite striking: between 1846 and 1850 – 1847 being the year being when the potato blight was at its worst – the amount of poor relief dispensed doubled (from £295,000 to £581,000).[10] The money to fund poor relief came from the rates; it is perhaps no surprise that crofters, frequently among those requiring relief, paid one shilling per pound of their rental towards relief, but that owners of sporting land paid no rates on the acreage of that land. The 1841 census put the population of Scotland at 2.6 million. In 1846, 2.6 per cent of that population were registered as 'poor' and 1 per cent received assistance; by 1848, the latter figure had risen fivefold (to 126,684 individuals). The number of paupers 'removed' to England and Ireland peaked in 1848 at around 13,700, and then fell back to around 6,000 per annum and were no longer of any concern to the Scottish inspectors of the poor.

What was quite clear from the policies of the Poor Law Commission was that it was never going to be charitable. The Assistant Secretary to the Treasury, Charles Trevelyan, who oversaw the Poor Laws in both Scotland and Ireland, pointed his officials firmly in the right direction:

Next to allowing the people to die of hunger, the greatest evil that could happen would be their being habituated to depend upon public charity. The object to be arrived at, therefore, is to prevent the assistance given from being productive of idleness and, if possible, to make it conducive of increased exertion.[11]

Following this very clear instruction, the Central Board of Management of the Fund for the Relief of the Destitute Inhabitants of the Highlands, founded in 1847 for the purpose of distributing moneys largely donated by churches and private citizens (the Government was not going to be seen funding any such thing), was very much against handouts: those who wanted relief would have to work for it, frequently in conditions not dissimilar to slavery. And there are today still very tangible traces of what was achieved by the labour of starving men in the north-west of Scotland: the 'Destitution Roads'. The longest of these was the one running along the south side of Loch Maree, past Gairloch and up to Braemore – what is now the A832. There was another from Lairg to Laxford, now the A838. Rather conveniently, both of these roads provided much improved access to the huge estates belonging to Mackenzie of Gairloch on the one hand, and the Duke of Sutherland on the other – and all free of charge. Idleness turned to very good effect, their lordships would have agreed.

The Poor Law in Scotland provided some assistance but fell far short of addressing the underlying cause of the problems, which was not the lack of seaweed, potatoes or fish, but the hugely inequitable conditions of landownership. Evictions and migrations had not ceased; the crofters and landless cottars continued to become poorer; the landowners continued to become richer and to build extravagant homes, and very occasionally used their wealth to engage in estate improvements (we use the term both in its literal sense, and in its usage by the Duke of Sutherland). But what did change, slowly, was the attitude of the country's newspapers and more principled MPs, who at last began to question the appalling conditions of the rural poor; in this burst of conscience, they were almost certainly prodded along by the activities of land reformers and by events in Ireland. One result of the agitation among the professional classes was a floodlight on the later clearances whenever they occurred; these tended to be of much smaller scope, but attracted much wider adverse publicity. One example, close to Ullapool, was Alexander Pirie's eviction of twenty-three families in the Loch Broom area in 1879, of which we shall hear more later.

CROFTERS, TACKSMEN AND OTHERS

'Extraordinary Privation'

It is perhaps worth pausing here to remind ourselves of the general economic and social status of the vast majority of people in the Highlands and Islands. A definition of the hierarchy of land-tenancy was provided by a gentleman writing in 1856 about the Scottish Poor Laws; we quote his definition below, as it is both revealing and flawed:[12]

> The population of these districts [the Highlands and Islands] chiefly consists of three classes, each holding land directly from the proprietor. The *'Crofters'* are persons occupying lands at a rental not exceeding 20*l*. [£20] a year, and are by far the most numerous class. The *'Tacksmen'* have leases or 'tacks' generally paying a rent exceeding 50*l*. a year, and in point of circumstances are the most considerable of all the classes. Intermediate between these is another class paying rent of between 20*l*. to 50*l*., and who not having leases are not 'Tacksmen' and not liking to be classed with the 'Crofters' are called *'Tenants'*. Besides these three classes, who hold land directly from the proprietor, there is another called *'Cottars'*, who are numerous on some districts and who either do not hold land at all, or hold it only from year to year as sub-tenants.

Although this is a concise enough definition, the author mistakenly supposed that all crofters paid rent directly to the landowner; in fact, they generally paid rent to the tacksman, and one can see, from the discrepancy between multiple rents received of £20 each and one paid out of £50, just how much a tacksman stood to profit. Our commentator's Victorian view of the population clearly pokes through when he mentions 'cottars' almost as an aside and most definitely apart from the 'three classes'; cottars certainly out-numbered crofters and tacksmen and those rather posh 'tenants'. He writes further that, whereas earlier the ordinary people had their own 'runrigs' and shared common grazing, rotating their management of the arable lands on a regular basis, a change came 'in the present century' which led to 'crofters', as they were now called, receiving a fixed allocation of land, usually small, which had to make do for themselves and their children. The gathering of kelp for a couple of months a year supplemented the family income. The crofter (our informant supposes) thus 'lives, or rather did live, in a rude kind of abundance, comparatively idle, and knowing little of the daily toil by which labourers elsewhere obtain a livelihood'. The words 'or rather did live' give the game away.

Thirty years later, Lord Napier and his commission had the daunting task of fixing the crofter/cottar problem. When their massive report was published in 1884, even they were a little vague about the difference between a crofter and a cottar:

> By the word crofter is usually understood a small tenant of land with or without a lease, who finds in the cultivation and produce of his holding a material portion of his occupation, earnings, and sustenance, and who pays rent directly to the proprietor. The term cottar commonly imports the occupier of a dwelling with or without some small portion of land, whose main subsistence is by the wages of labour, and whose rent, if any, is paid to a tenant and not to the landlord. The crofter is a small farmer who may live partly by the wages of labour; the cottar is a labourer who may have some share in the soil. But these definitions are deceptive, for there are crofters who are sub-tenants under tacksmen, and there are many cottars who pay rent to the owner. The distinction between the two classes is more easily felt and understood than delineated. Nor is a strict definition necessary. For the purposes of this inquiry and report we limit the class of crofters to tenants paying not more than £30 annual rent, but we are unable to fix any point in rental below which the crofter descends into the cottar class.[13]

What this tells us is that the distinction between a crofter and a cottar was quite unclear to a group of men tasked with improving the lives of crofters and cottars; it could not be defined by activity, income, rental or anything measurable; hence Napier's arbitrary figure of £30 rent. Perhaps the people whom Napier interviewed were a little clearer about their own status: of 775 interviewees, well over half defined themselves as crofters (384) or cottars (36); and of these, more than a third also stated that they pursued an additional trade – 'crofter and mason', 'crofter and post-master', 'cottar and fisherman' and so on (there was even one 'crofter and missionary'). But the distinction was important: it can be argued that the Napier Report's lack of clarity about the difference between crofter and cottar led to faulty legislation at a later date.

It should be remembered that the rent was not restricted to rent for a piece of land; typically, a crofter would pay additional sums according to the number and type of animals he kept on his croft. During the course of a rather tetchy interview with the Napier Commission, William Gunn, the factor for the Cromartie estate near Ullapool, stated that supplementary rates 'for cows were from 7s to 10s each; young cattle, 4s to 6s each; sheep 1s 6d to 2s 6d each; horses, 15s to 20s each'.[14] One of Gunn's tenants had earlier that day complained bitterly that he had to pay an extra £1 for every additional horse, regardless of where the horse was to be grazed; since he was already paying around £3 as a basic rent, a horse cost him an extra 33 per cent.[15] But a horse was essential if any improvement was to be made either to the land or to the overall quality of life. And on top of all that, a crofter had to pay rates to the county council.

Crofting was a relatively new form of land management, arising in the second half of the eighteenth century.[16] It replaced, as the above definition suggests, an earlier form of community-based tenancy, where much more of the available land was utilised in common and where the good and less good parcels of arable land were shared equally amongst the residents of the adjacent township. As a system, crofting was introduced in order to ensure that 'improvements' took place, by shunting the people of the more open townships into smaller, clearly delineated crofts which were most frequently – and quite deliberately – laid out too small to provide a living on their own: other employment needed to be found. And so, as if by magic, there was always a ready supply of labour to harvest kelp or man fishing boats, and so increase the income of the landowner. Crofting, then, emerged from the practice of clearing estates. Under more sympathetic governance, it might have led to a positive move towards the establishment of a peasant class on the European model; but in the way it was implemented in Scotland, it became the framework for oppression, poverty and – ultimately – the emptying of the land. As our Victorian Poor Law analyst explains:

Those who emigrated were for the most part the better description of tenants and crofters, whose lands were then in most cases let for sheep-farming, by which higher rents were obtained – yet adding at the same time to the disproportion between population and employments, and by consequence tending to depress the condition of the bulk of the people; and thus to render them less capable of bearing up against extraordinary privation, whether arising from failure of crops, the inclemency of the seasons, or any other cause.[17]

DISEASE, NUTRITION, HOUSING AND DEATH

'Grossly Insanitary Conditions'

Alexander Fraser MB, of Edinbane, provided the Napier Commission with a report on the health of the people of Skye. Prefacing his remarks with the observation that, if the people did not live their days so much in the open air, things would be a lot worse, he reports

a good deal of scrofulous disease, and also a good deal of lung disease, and a large proportion of eye disease . . . This year, eye diseases from want of food – ulceration of the cornea and so on; scrofulous complaints, and abscesses connected with diseased bone.[18]

He attributed all this to the abysmal quality of housing, the nature of the food and the lack of proper clothing. Worst affected were children who 'have not sufficient milk. There is no grass at present for the cows to make milk with.' On the same theme, Roderick McMillan, grocer of Portree, stated that

the want of grazing for cows and the want of ground for potatoes is felt very much . . . The land surrounding Portree is practically in the hands of two individuals, none of whom will give grazing to the village people . . . The consequence is that the milk supply for the village is exceedingly scarce and very dear; and the children suffer in their health through the scarcity of milk.[19]

The comments of these two men were echoed throughout the body of evidence to the Napier Commission; clearly, the health of the average person in the Highlands and Islands was piteous. The root cause, once again, was the lack of land.

This dire situation was one which the Napier Commission did not address directly, and as a result, such conditions continued for another three decades. We are indebted to the report issued by the Dewar Committee of 1912 for a glimpse into the grim living conditions faced by crofters and cottars alike. Sir John Dewar was the elder son of the founder of the whisky blend; he and his Highlands and Islands Medical Service Committee were asked by the Treasury to consider 'how far the provision of medical attendance in districts situated in the Highlands and Islands of Scotland is inadequate' and come up with some proposals. Yet another glaring social problem, yet another committee. Fortunately, Dewar and his colleagues did not have to look far or investigate deeply to discover how 'inadequate' things were. Put simply and concisely:

> The bulk of the people are, over large sections of area, in very strait-ened circumstances, especially at certain periods of the year, and are consequently unable to pay for medical attendance even when the fee, having regard to time and distance, is quite inadequate to compensate the doctor. Ready cash is a rarity with the ordinary crofter; and the amount is at most so small that when he has provided for the necessaries of life and paid his rent and rates he has, as a rule, little or nothing left to pay the doctor.[20]

Here were conditions of penury, chronic ill-health and malnutrition. The Committee had, without any difficulty whatsoever, determined that the physical condition of the population of the north and west of Scotland was in a bad way. But why else, one might ask, would the government of the day have sent out their commission? They had been told thirty years earlier and they knew now what would be found: malnutrition, poverty and chronic medical deprivation. 'The general trend goes fully to substantiate the conclusion to which the enquiry has led us, and that is that in many parts of the Highlands and Islands the medical attendance on the bulk of the people is insufficient, even when measured by the wholly inadequate standard of medical treatment that long neglect and privation have established in the popular mind.'[21] The population was being crushed from two directions – firstly, from having very sparse medical facilities, and secondly from living in rural slums:

So long as dwellings in so many parts of the area continue in grossly insanitary conditions, so long will the local conception of medical requirements be crude, and the treatment of disease more or less . ineffective.[22]

Lewis in particular was singled out for criticism of housing in whose damp and sunless interiors tuberculosis, typhus and whooping cough ran riot.[23] And then there was under-nourishment:

Another relative fact, and one of serious import in connection with our enquiry, is the character of the food consumed, especially by the children. For example, we were told that in South Uist it is rarely that any of the produce of the croft, with the exception of potatoes, is used for food. No meal is ground, the surplus sheep and cattle are sold for urgent cash, every egg is bartered for shop commodities, and the milk supply is insufficient, especially in winter. The excessive indulgence in over-brewed tea, especially by children, is deplored by several witnesses.[24]

The drinking of tea had for some time been a concern of gentlemen sent into the Highlands. It was a valid concern, not so much because of the tea, but because of what tea replaced: milk. The recognised cause of this was the need to conserve what little milk a cow produced, either for any calves or for sale. Sir Alexander Matheson's factor, in his contribution to the Napier Commission thirty years earlier (1883), had been quite certain about the effects, but had taken a slightly different approach. When asked how to improve the state of the poor, rather than the desirable answer 'by giving them the glens', he instead replied, without any trace of embarrassment, 'By continuing to take the fine solid food the old people used to take, and throwing away slushes of tea. They are destroying the nervous system and that causes the complete degeneration of the present race. Unless they go back to the old system of food, the race of the Gael will soon become as extinct as the Gael.'[25] Not that he felt that the extinction of the race was necessarily bad; he volunteered his view that 'it is one good thing that the bloods are mixing up'.

What Sir Alexander's factor did not seem to appreciate was that the lack of 'fine solid food' was caused primarily by the lack of decent land on which to grow crops or graze cattle. And it was not a problem easily resolved: in 1912, one witness to the Dewar Commission, John Maclean of Coigach, was able to state that: 'I cannot give you an idea of the yearly income of a crofter in my district, but I can tell you this – that there are crofts in my district where the income of the croft would not pay the herd boy.'[26]

The lack of nutritious food and decent housing was one huge problem; insufficient access to medical care was another. In one parish on Lewis there was a single doctor for a population of 7,000, which prompted the Committee to throw up its hands: 'That such a condition of affairs as we found in Lewis should exist within twenty-four hours of Westminster is scarcely credible.'[27] National Health Insurance had been introduced across Britain in 1911 to fund free medical care, but this only benefited people who actually had employers. The bulk of the population in the north-west Highlands and the Islands – crofters and cottars – had no employers to speak of. Additionally, the rural medical profession was disastrously underfunded and underequipped, and beset by 'difficulties of locomotion and communication'[28] – which meant that less accessible parts of the region remained without adequate medical care of any sort. One measure of this was that in Coigach near Ullapool, in the period 1901–10, 94 per cent of all deaths were 'uncertified', meaning that the deceased had not seen a doctor 'for some time' prior to death.[29] (By contrast, the equivalent figure for the rest of Scotland was 2 per cent.) But necessity, as they say, is the mother of invention:

> The most populous district of the parish, viz., Coigach, is 25 miles distant from his [the Lochbroom doctor's] residence in Ullapool, but it is much nearer Lochinver, where the doctor of the adjacent parish of Assynt resides. The doctor of Lochbroom told his neighbour that as he was nearest he was free to practise in Coigach, and he continued to do so till that parish doctor left and his successor wrote the Assynt doctor accusing him of breach of professional etiquette.[30]

And remember: this was a report issued just before the First World War. As we have seen, conditions were no better in 1890. Perhaps a railway would improve communication and access to medical care? Sadly, that question was never asked.

WHAT HAD HAPPENED IN IRELAND

'Skyemen Are Imitating the Irish'

Alexander Nicolson was a native of Skye and the Sheriff of Kirkcud-bright; this fortuitous combination of provenance and profession saw him duly appointed a member of the Napier Commission. When the Commission visited Barra, Nicolson had an exchange with a crofter named Michael Buchanan, who complained that some 'gentlemen' in Castlebay

> called us privately – but I was within hearing – Fenians, and we were not very well pleased to hear ourselves called Fenians. We do not like the name. *Sheriff Nicolson* – Have your ideas been in any way influenced by what you have heard from Ireland? – Not in the least. I am not an Irishman, nor have I imbibed their notions.[31]

But the Sheriff had a bee in his bonnet about Irishmen; a few months previously, he had even gone to the extent of publishing an 'Address to the People' in Gaelic, upbraiding the rebellious people of Skye:

> What dreadful news is this that has come to us about you? . . . I am very sorrowful today . . . Skyemen are imitating the Irish, and making themselves objects of derision and of dread . . . Nothing will come of it but trouble and shame.[32]

It is unlikely the Skyemen were much chastened by this 'Address'. Indeed, some of the evidence subsequently given in front of Nicolson at the Napier sessions is suggestive of mischievous provocation. John Mackenzie, Kilmuir crofter, declared heartily that 'we were hearing of good news from Ireland. We are very much inclined to turn rebels ourselves in order to obtain the same results,'[33] while John Gillies, crofter of Uig, approached it more subtly: he complained of 'want of sufficient land to support [our] families and that at a reasonable rent, as the place could afford. We are wanting that we should be treated as we hear other parts for the country are treated.' Which other parts of the country, he was asked? 'I refer to Ireland.'[34] Even more galling to Sheriff Nicolson was the opinion of Hugh Macrae of Portree that 'All that is necessary to remedy this sad state of matters is a redistribution of the land, giving each family as much arable and pasture land as will keep it in comparative comfort, and then to apply the principles of the Irish Land Act by fixing fair rents and giving security of tenure. Nothing short of this will allay agitation, restore contentment, and satisfy the just demands of the people.'[35]

One can readily imagine Mr Nicolson's heated state of mind at the end of these sessions with the Skyemen.

It is quite clear, from some of the parliamentary debates and newspaper editorials concerning the Scottish Highlands and Islands during the 1880s, that the ruling class was haunted by the spectre of 'Fenianism'. General Burroughs, argumentative landowner in Orkney, had enraged himself with the thought that delegates to the Napier inquiry 'want to go in, I think, like the Irish and get judicial rents and fixity of tenure and all that sort of thing'.[36] In Edinburgh, *The Scotsman* worked itself and its readers into a nervous froth, seeing Irishmen under every Skye bed: of the 'the crofter agitation in Skye', it warned darkly that 'rumours of a somewhat disturbing character are being received from remote districts of the island. It seems that the connection between the disaffected crofters of the Braes and the Irish National Land League is closer even than has already been indicated.'[37] Worse, 'two gentlemen' were being sent to Skye from the 'Central Land League of Great Britain', one of them the radical Edward McHugh, the other the campaigner John Murdoch, both described inaccurately by the newspaper as 'Irish Agitators'. (Rather undermining its own scare-mongering, *The Scotsman* judged that the Central – properly 'National' – Land League 'consists of only a few obscure persons of no influence or importance whatsoever'.) As it was, McHugh was politely ignored by the crofters of Skye – which did not prevent a Skye factor from declaring that the cause of commotion in Skye was 'Irish Land League literature'.[38] A more nuanced view was adopted by the land reformer Alexander Mackenzie of Inverness: 'I think Irish influence was attempted, but I do not think it was at all required. I think the people had all made up their minds before anybody from Ireland went among them; and I think the people are more resenting this Irish interference than otherwise.'[39]

Not only were the dreaded Irish agitators slinking around Scotland, but innocent Scots fishermen were being seduced in Ireland. Several witnesses from Skye stated that their trade as fishermen frequently took them and their families to Ireland. Peter Macnab of Waternish replied to the question 'To what places do they [the young] generally go? – Glasgow and Greenock, and the young men go to the east coast fishing and Ireland. I have a son in Ireland just now at the fishing.'[40] And from Ireland, it seems, came great news. It is small wonder that a significant number of Napier witnesses – especially from Skye and Lewis – cited the precedents of Irish land legislation; for, as we shall shortly discover, land reform in Ireland was far more advanced than it was in Scotland.

But we can interpret Sheriff Nicolson's phrase in another way: the Skyemen were indeed imitating the Irish, since the conditions of their daily existence were very similar to those of the poor people of Ireland. If there was one place in the British Empire which was comparable to the north and west of Scotland in terms of poverty and deprivation, it was just across the Irish Sea. We must not forget that until 1922 Ireland was just another part of the United Kingdom, albeit one that was much exploited, usually misruled and frequently betrayed. The similarities between Scotland and Ireland were easy to see: poverty, recurring hunger, land clearances and evictions, rack-renting, emigration, neglect, disease and ill-health. It is far beyond the scope of this book to examine nineteenth-century Irish history in any detail; but a swift summary is required to highlight many parallels and some critical differences.

Firstly, and most infamously, there was blight and famine. The Potato Blight which emerged in 1845 hit Ireland's poor hardest of all, causing by most estimates at least one million deaths directly from starvation or indirectly from illness and disease cutting a swathe through a starving people – and this loss was from a total population of just over eight million. It was a tragedy of unimaginable proportions, and one which struck forcefully on those who observed it from close at hand or from across the Irish Sea. Famine had not been seen in England since the 1620s, nor in Scotland since the 1690s; and yet here it was, in a close and constituent part of the kingdom. In the six years from 1846 to 1851, one person in eight died. Although the blight affected much of northern Europe, including Scotland, it has been calculated that 'only' 100,000 people died elsewhere. Nothing so terrible on this scale had been seen in Europe since the Black Death. Even under normal circumstances, a large part of the population in Ireland was already practically destitute for two or three months over any given winter, with no access to grain, meat or fish. The destruction of their potato crops – all that lay between them and starvation – tipped chronic deprivation into cataclysm. While such huge mortality was not uncommon in British India in the nineteenth century and was doubtless regarded as a lamentable side-effect of being foreign, the Irish famine so near to the centre of the British Empire stirred consciences, from Queen Victoria downwards. Efforts were made to supply food and aid: in the first year of the crisis, Peel's Tory government in London arranged for the importation of a huge amount of corn from America; but in 1846 and onwards, when the Whigs were in power, no such relief was forthcoming.[41] The attitudes of government officials, Poor Law administrators and landowners from 1846 to 1851 resulted in little being done to save the lives of hundreds of thousands of people. Where relief was given, it was common practice to demand forced labour in return; the Treasury official Charles Trevelyan wrote in 1850 of the Irish tragedy: 'The famine, the poor law, and the encumbered estates commission have given a new stimulus to the principle of individual exertion as contrasted with the old habit of depending upon the government.'[42]

The population of Ireland had increased from around 2.5 million in the 1750s to 8.2 million in 1841; by 1914, it had dropped back to 4.4 million – almost half the population had emigrated in the period 1851 to 1901, mostly to the United States.[43] As emigrants established themselves across the Atlantic, reports of relative prosperity, and sometimes funds to assist in passage, were sent back home: there would be no stopping their friends and relatives from following. The bulk of those who left were the young, with between 20 per cent and 30 per cent of people under the age of thirty-five leaving the country.[44]

Such a drain on the able-bodied led to a surprising consequence: instead of rural land becoming more available, it became scarcer. This was a result of consolidation: as one small tenancy was abandoned, or became unworkable from a lack of labour, it would be taken back by the landlord and put to other uses; a number of smaller pockets of land would be consolidated into one larger farm, and turned into a cattle ranch of adequate size. It was rather like a typical Highland Clearance, but without the annoyance of a complaining tenantry. Between 1841 and 1851, the number of small holdings of up to 15 acres halved from 563,000 to 280,000, while those above 15 acres rose in number from 120,000 to 290,000.[45] This, of course, did not affect the least productive land on the west coast – land just as poor and unproductive as that on Scotland's western seaboard. A commissioner of the Congested Districts Board later described the counties from Donegal down to Kerry as containing half a million souls who might be divided into 'two classes, namely, the poor and the destitute'.[46]

Against this background there was, in nineteenth-century Ireland, a significant increase in what was termed 'agrarian crime': in 1832, for example, there were 242 murders, more than 300 attempted murders and countless acts of vandalism and arson in a rural setting.[47] These troubles continued throughout the following decades, culminating in the 'Fenian' movement which flourished from 1858 to 1870; this was a movement seeking independence for Ireland, using violent means as necessary. The conditions of the rural poor in Ireland also led directly to forceful agitation on the whole question of landownership; this agitation burst forth regularly in acts of public disorder and violence, especially during the decades of the 'Land War' (1870–90), but in almost every year between 1600 and 1922 that you care to examine. In these later years there was also the relentless growth of a Home Rule parliamentary party, led by men such as Charles Stewart Parnell, whose goal was achieve Home Rule through the ballot box and legislative means. The Home Rule movement, the Fenian escapades, the random acts of violence and decades of civil disobedience – all arose largely from the issue of landownership and land usage.

In the 1870s and 1880s, the campaign for land reform resulted in several pieces of legislation, which we shall survey shortly. In 1879, the Irish National Land League was founded by Parnell and his colleagues with the aim of reducing 'rack rents' – i.e. those that annually equalled the total value of the rented property, or were otherwise exorbitant – and 'to facilitate the obtaining of the ownership of the soil by the occupiers'.[48] In the 1880s, the rural economy was devastated by more bad harvests, leading to another spike in emigration and to a sharp upturn in the non-payment of rents.[49] Many rents had by then been fixed at an agreed level for a period of fifteen years; but when harvests failed, rents became unpayable – tenants had no money and no hope of ever having any. The non-payment of rents and the resulting evictions added to further emigration, which in turn led to a crisis in landownership: with a huge reduction in income from rents, some landlords were obliged to sell up and remove themselves to more modest surroundings.

In the face of agitation both in the Irish countryside and in Parliament (where Irish Home Rule MPs were slowly gaining ground), the various governments took action in the later decades of the nineteenth century. Several Acts aimed at land reform were shuffled through the two Houses at Westminster by Liberals and Conservatives alike. Some were more effective than others.

There was, in the northern part of Ireland, something known as the 'Ulster Custom'. This essentially gave tenants the right to remain on their holdings as long as they did not fall into arrears, and to pass on their tenancy to another – for example, a son. It was a custom that had no legal basis, and did not in any case apply across the south of Ireland – at least not until 1870, when the Landlord and Tenant (Ireland) Act was passed in Westminster. This Act specifically legalised the 'Ulster Custom' and applied it to the whole of Ireland; however, the definition of the 'custom' both inside and outside Ulster was left appallingly vague, and it was up to arbitrators to determine what was 'custom' and what was not.[50] The Act prescribed compensation for improvements up to £150, as well as for crops in the ground, on quitting or eviction; it set up courts of arbitration to resolve disputes, and permitted the sale of a holding to another tenant. As a first attempt to resolve the underlying land question, it was acceptable, and it served as a model for Scotland. But further steps were demanded.

In 1881, the Land Law (Ireland) Act ensured that rents were to be fixed for fifteen years; commissions would be set up to arbitrate on fair rents; no tenant paying rent could be evicted; and tenants were able to sell their tenancies on the open market. This Act was followed in short order by the Arrears of Rent (Ireland) Act of 1882, which made tenants with accumulated arrears only liable for one year of their arrears, with the Government paying half of the remaining balance. Subsequently, almost every parliamentary session between 1870 and 1900 produced yet another piece of legislation designed to reduce the burden of arrears and facilitate the purchase of holdings by tenants.

It was almost as if the British government was trying to create a satisfied and stable peasant class.

To chivvy things along, in 1891 the Congested Districts Board was established, whose remit was to improve the conditions of life in the western counties (compulsory purchase powers were added in 1903); in the thirty years of the Board's existence, it managed to buy up almost

1,000 estates and transfer land totalling 3 million acres to small farmers.[51] All this culminated in the Irish Land Act of 1903, which made it extremely simple for tenants to purchase their holdings and all but impossible for landowners not to sell – the Government, in the guise of a Land Commission, would pay the vendors a 12 per cent bonus on top of the selling price. By 1920, some 11 million acres of land was thereby transferred to former tenants. Considering that the total acreage of Ireland is twenty-one million acres, that is not a bad result.

The Irish legislation did not go unnoticed on the west coast of Scotland. When Donald McNeill of Braes on Skye was asked at the Napier inquiry, '[I]f the landlord was prepared to give additional arable ground, and the additional common pasture, would the existing crofters be able to cultivate it and stock it?', he replied, 'That depends greatly if the legislators would give us the same kindness as they showed the Irish.'[52] Even in douce Kingussie, a land reformer named Duncan Lawson maintained that crofters

> all agree that a Bill on the principle of the Irish Land Bill would give them what they want. The Scottish peasantry ask indignantly why should a law be framed so as to give so much to Ireland and so little to Scotland? Is it because the Scotch are a law-abiding people, and the Irish, alas! too often the reverse? Is our respect for the laws of our country to be used against us, to bind us down to a life of servitude?[53]

John Maclean of Waternish was slow but steady in his approach to the same issue: 'Do you know what has been done in Ireland for the improvement of the people? – I do not know. I have not heard. I am not hearing so much about that now as I was hearing before. I think they are getting better now. We hope it will all be better of the Commissioners' arrival here. If we are the worse of it, it will be a bad business.'[54] A bad business, indeed.

Leaving aside the land question, it was also recognised in London that communications – specifically railways – were of social and economic benefit to Ireland. Between 1850 and 1880, an average of 60 miles of new track were laid every year across the island. The railways were built for a variety of reasons, but one argument that will become familiar to us was that they would benefit the fishing industry. However, there were other recognisable advantages to having railways penetrate the rural districts of Ireland, such as navvies with money to spend locally, journeys to the larger towns and cities being made in hours rather than days, and 'shop goods' being available in the smallest village.[55]

One thing to fix in our minds, when we come to examine similar proposals for the west of Scotland, is that the government in London freely financed the railways in Ireland: between 1871 and 1882, the State provided almost £1 million in finance for the building of new lines. After the passing of the Light Railways (Ireland) Act of 1889, more than 300 miles of new light railways were constructed with government subsidies of up to 85 per cent. (This Act was cited by the design engineers for the Achnasheen to Aultbea railway, as a model of how railways could be built quite cheaply). And all this despite the fact that most of the lines were actually owned and operated – as in the rest of Britain – by myriad small local companies. Railway loans were regarded as a kind of 'public works', much like land reclamation or drainage.

All these various pieces of legislation, all these concessions for Ireland, are significant because they were later used as templates to be applied to the intractable problems of the Highlands and Islands – although largely in watered-down and less effective form.

From this necessarily superficial review, we can see that Ireland offered some suggestive comparisons to the situation in the Scottish north-west in the 1880s. Both places suffered from deprivation, starvation and emigration; both had a population perpetually on the edge of penury; in both places, the aspirations of the rural poor had been slowly strangled by the inequity of landownership; in both places, government remedies were frequently applied with a consummate lack of empathy; in both places, the people were beginning to fight back – although in this respect, Ireland was streets ahead of Scotland, having been in an almost incessant turmoil of violence and counter-violence for nigh on three centuries. Anxious not to touch off anything resembling a concerted uprising or give encouragement to 'Home Rule', successive London governments slowly reformed the conditions of landownership and improved the rights of tenants in Ireland. This was one difference from Scotland. And the Great Famine had made another difference: the surviving Irish poor and their representatives looked on the 1840s as a period in which the Westminster government was tested and found wanting. Bitter resentment nourished the politics of the succeeding decades, which in turn led to more concessions from London. The over-arching policy of the Government was to ensure that Ireland remained part of the United Kingdom. In the 1880s, in a sort of early Brexit meltdown, the Liberal Party itself was ripped apart by factional differences over Home Rule, leading ultimately to the downfall of Gladstone's government in 1886. The policy of 'constructive unionism' was one pursued by both Tory and Liberal administrations alike: it was more snappily known as 'killing home rule with kindness'. However, although it created a broad class of peasant-farmers, it was a strategy which ultimately failed. In Scotland, by contrast, while little fires of civil disobedience were flickering around the islands, no 'home rule' tendency had been detected: placatory legislation on a large scale was not deemed essential.

But now, in the 1880s, much to Mr Nicolson's chagrin, the Skyemen began to imitate the Irish.

CROFTER REBELLION AND CIVIL DISOBEDIENCE

'Contumacious Crofters'

Given the overwhelming problems of the crofters and cottars of the Highlands and Islands, the unchallenged powers of carrot and stick wielded by their landlords and the relative isolation of many communities, it is perhaps no surprise to find that efforts to resist were few and far between. It can be argued, however, that effective resistance to oppression only emerges in a period when conditions for the oppressed have recently improved, and are showing signs of declining again – and this is what happened in the 1870s and 1880s. These years saw a steady upturn in the fortunes of such crofters as had managed to stay on their crofts and eke out a living from fishing, farming and seasonal migration, often supplemented by money sent back home from emigrants. Additionally, the men and women of the islands were in this period beginning to see something of the world while working in the East Coast fishing communities, in the cities and slums of the central belt of Scotland or on the fishing boats that harvested the seas off the coast of Ireland. Such contact with the outside world raised expectations and questions. The events and concessions in Ireland were beginning to impact on the Scottish consciousness.

Thus it was that, in the early part of the 1880s, acts of open resistance became commonplace. This came as a nasty shock to landowners and government alike. It is not the place of this book to examine these manifestations of disobedience in any detail. That has already been done by authors such as James Hunter, Roger Hutchinson and Tom Devine in their excellent studies of a gripping and inspiring period in Scottish history – of the withholding of rents on a massive scale, of acts of trespass, of destruction of enclosures, of temporary land-grabs, of squatting, of illegal deer-hunts, of all the things which had become common in Ireland and for which, until then, there had been no energy in the islands. And it was principally in the islands that these events took place: most famously on Skye and Lewis, but just as much on the Uists, Benbecula, Barra and further south on Tiree and other smaller islands.

The Free Church minister of Kilmuir on Skye, John McPhail, submitted written evidence to the Napier Commission. 'As a rule,' he wrote of his parishioners, 'the people are moral, quiet, respectful to superiors, and law-abiding. Yet I have been of late led to think that there may not be many steps between such a desirable condition and one of disorder and lawlessness.' He referred to the notorious cases of Braes and Glendale, but also to the mood in Kilmuir. 'There have been combinations of people against payment of rent . . . This course was followed from the idea that they had serious grievances for which there was no remedy, but by placing themselves in an attitude of opposition to those in authority . . . I feel sure', he concluded darkly, 'that a little more strain and a little more agitation would soon fan them into a state of wild confusion. This is a matter requiring the serious consideration of those who have the responsibility of governing our country.'[56] Such were the thoughts of a sober churchman living in the middle of a crofting community.

The 'Battle of Braes', on the east coast of Skye, took place in April 1882, when local men let their sheep graze on land that had earlier been taken from their community. A detachment of fifty burly Glasgow policemen, sent to quell the uprising, was beaten back by the men and their families. *The Scotsman* newspaper was moved to report on the 'Disturbed State of the Island' in awful detail, identifying the 'cause of the agitation . . . in the defective nature of the crofter system . . . It is not so generally known, however, that the means by which the agitation has been brought about are due to a large extent to the machinations of the Irish Land League.'[57] Gratifyingly, those few men who were eventually arrested at Braes and carried off to prison found plenty of popular support as they were marched through the streets of Inverness, where 'the crowd increased to several hundred, and lustily booed the policemen'.

The events at Braes were swiftly followed, at the start of 1883, by turmoil in Glendale on Skye's west coast – once again, direct action by crofters protesting against the privatisation of grazing land was met with police action. To the horror of the readers of *The Scotsman*, 'no sooner did the constables enter the glen than they were attacked in a cowardly fashion by an overwhelming party of about 400 men and women, knocked down, beaten and severely bruised . . . A medical gentleman has been despatched from Inverness to attend to them.'[58] Understandably, no local medical gentleman was going to risk his local standing by treating the men in blue. The stand-off lasted three weeks, with the police being continually hunted down and harassed; the situation was eventually resolved by the arrival of the gunboat *Jackal*. Aboard was Malcolm MacNeill, Poor Law commissioner for northwest Scotland, who used his skills in the Gaelic language to persuade 'four contumacious crofters' to surrender and stand trial in Edinburgh (a better class of booing crowds there, as it turned out).[59] In a laudable act of defiance, the accused men elected to make their own way to the capital, rather than travel aboard the *Jackal*.

The Skye uprising was a hard one to quell – even in November of 1884, twenty-nine policemen, 250 marines and a handy assortment of naval gunboats were obliged to make their way to Portree and Dunvegan to establish a military occupation of the north of the island lasting six months, all in the name of keeping the peace. And back in Braes, too, events were still rumbling on as late as October 1886, when – yet again – the gunboat *Jackal* with marines on board had been sent as a precaution during the serving of eviction notices. (On this occasion, Alexander Macdonald, a crofter served with a summons over arrears of £3 12s 1d, was heard to address the sheriff-officer with these words: 'You are strong just now . . . but the day is close on your heels when you will be very weak; and our poor-law government will soon be far down.')[60] On the Duke of Argyll's Tiree in late July 1886, seventy-five 'ejectments' were to be enforced, but the process did not go smoothly on 'that Land League-ridden island' (thus *The Scotsman*), with the result that a large detachment of 250 marines and fifty policemen had to be sent out from Oban to serve the eviction orders, only to be met and beaten back by a decidedly hostile reception.[61]

That the events on Skye, Tiree and elsewhere were moving the focus from the merely socio-economic to the political is beyond doubt, and it was soon time for a political organisation to emerge from the troubled scenes. In February 1883, the Highland Land Law Reform Association was established, the precursor to the Highland Land League of 1886, and was very effective in campaigning for reforms. From this body emerged the parliamentary candidates known collectively and popularly as the 'Crofters' Party', which, while independent, was in essence a left-wing grouping inside the Liberal Party; had any kind of Labour Party been in existence at that time, it is likely the Crofters would have been allied to it. One of the leaders of this group, Dr Gavin Clark, had once even been a member of Karl Marx's International Workingmen's Association.[62]

Benefiting greatly from the increased franchise provided under the 1884 Representation of the People Act, five out of six Crofters' Party candidates were returned to Parliament as MPs at the end of 1885 (the sixth won his seat at the second attempt). Their constituencies covered most of the north of Scotland – Argyll-shire, Inverness-shire, Ross and Cromarty, Caithness and Wick – and they took 54 per cent of the total of votes cast. Significantly, in all six constituencies where they stood, they stood against an official Liberal Party candidate (one should not make the mistake of regarding the Liberal Party as anything like its later twentieth and twenty-first century equivalent: there was sometimes very little to distinguish it from the Conservative Party). The Crofters' Party did not, alas, survive as an independent organisation for long, the MPs burying themselves inside the mainstream Liberal Party before the end of the century; but for a while it stood proud as the first British political party with a large popular and grass-roots support. At its founding conference in September 1886, the Highland Land League stated that it campaigned for:

> the restoration to the people of the land and of the right to distrib-
> ute, to value and to regulate the same; the prevention of eviction and

depopulation; the doing away with all game, forest and fishing monopolies and class privileges; the fair and free administration of justice in the Highlands by men fully versed in the language of the country.[63]

It was no mere accident that John Murdoch, the moving spirit behind the Land League, was also invited to preside over the first meeting to prepare for the founding of the Scottish Labour Party in 1888. For the actions of the contumacious crofters did not take place in a vacuum. All over Europe, more radical forces were once again making their voices heard. This was a logical extension of the revolutions in France and the USA, of the later revolutions of 1848, of the Chartist movement in Britain, and – dialectically, indeed – of the rapid rise of heavily industrialised capitalism. And then, in the mid 1870s, Great Britain, along with much of Europe and the United States, fell into the grip of an economic downturn known as the 'Long Depression'. For Britain, this lasted from approximately 1875 to 1895, and its effects were felt in a reduction in industrial output, the collapse of the odd bank (in Scotland, for example, the City of Glasgow Bank in 1878) and increased competition from Europe and the United States. One other result of the downturn was that landowners felt the necessity of squeezing their tenants even more efficiently, to offset financial losses to their investments in industry and banking.

During this period, the urban working class of mainland Britain was beginning to make its voice heard in the trade unions (even in quiet Dingwall, a strike of the town's apprentice plumbers was threatened in April 1892),[64] in working men's associations and through the medium of their representatives returned to Parliament under the banner of the Liberal Party – a trend greatly accelerated by the Representation of the People Act, which resulted in Scotland in 60 per cent of the male population having a vote. And in August of 1888, the Scottish Labour Party was founded in Glasgow under the leadership of Keir Hardie, calling for, among other things, 'graduated income tax; free education at all levels; control of the liquor trade; 8-hour day legislation; national insurance for working people; wage arbitration courts; legislation providing houses; land reform with a tax on large landholdings; nationalization of the railways, banks and mineral rights; and abolition of the Monarchy'.[65]

But even without the nightmare of an organised working class, these events in Skye – agitation, civil disobedience, general Irishness, political campaigning, MPs in Westminster – were quite enough to set nerves jangling in London. Westminster reaction was uncommonly rapid.

3

'Our Trusty and Well-Beloved Commissioners'

The Napier Commission and the Crofters' Law

Exactly two months to the day after the start of the Glendale events, the Government on 22 March 1883 put together a commission of inquiry into crofting and crofters. The ruling class was clearly rattled. In the warrant summoning the Napier Commission into existence, there was a sense of urgency: 'Our further will and pleasure is that you . . . do with as little delay as possible report to Us . . . upon the matters referred to you.' 'We' – i.e. Queen Victoria speaking through the Home Secretary, Lord Harcourt – desired her commissioners to 'forthwith issue to inquire into the condition of the Crofters and Cottars in the Highlands and Islands of Scotland, and all matters affecting the same'.[1] The 'trusty and well-beloved' gentlemen tasked with this hasty investigation were as follows:

- Francis Napier, the 10th Lord Napier and 1st Baronet of Ettrick, was a career diplomat and briefly Viceroy of India. He owned the Merchiston estate in south Edinburgh (now the site of part of Napier University – named after his illustrious mathematician ancestor) and a much larger country estate at Thirlestane in the Scottish Borders.
- Sir Kenneth Smith Mackenzie, the 6th Baronet of Gairloch, was also Lord Lieutenant of Ross and Cromarty, and the hereditary owner of 170,000 acres of land in the county, centred around the village of Gairloch.
- Alexander Nicolson was a Gaelic scholar, a Scottish legal expert and Sheriff-Substitute of Kirkcudbright. He was for

several years inspector of schools for the Western Isles, and strongly argued for the teaching of Gaelic in schools. In his spare time, he was a pioneering climber of the Skye Cuillins. The son of the proprietor of Husabost on Skye, he was also noted for that aforementioned 'Address to the People' of April 1882, lamenting that Skye men were emulating the Irish.

- Donald Cameron of Lochiel was the Conservative MP for Inverness-shire between 1868 and 1885 (in the 1880 election he held on to his seat with a majority of twenty-nine over Sir Kenneth Mackenzie). He married in 1875 the daughter of the Duke of Buccleuch, one of the largest landowners of Scotland. His Highland residence was in the estate centred around Achnacarry, at the east end of Loch Arkaig. He stood down from his seat in 1885, and in that year's election it was captured by . . .

- . . . Charles Fraser-Mackintosh, a champion of Gaelic, a lawyer and urban land-developer. He was elected as Independent Liberal (in subsequent years, simply Liberal) MP for Inverness Burghs, a seat he held from 1874 to 1885. In 1885, he was elected Crofters' Party MP for Inverness-shire: it was a three-cornered fight against a Conservative and a Liberal – the latter being (yet again) the aforementioned Sir Kenneth Mackenzie. Fraser-Mackintosh later found a home in the mainstream Liberal Party, and was fittingly defeated in the 1892 election by a 'proper' Crofters' Party candidate He had made his money in building houses in Inverness and bought the Drummond estate in the south of the town.

- Professor Donald Mackinnon was a native of Colonsay, and Professor of Celtic Languages and History at Edinburgh University from 1882 to 1914. He was reputed to be sympathetic to the crofters' cause, and his knowledge of spoken Gaelic was certainly useful for the Commission's taking of evidence.

- The Secretary to the Commission was Malcolm MacNeill, Esq., a son of the Laird of Colonsay, Poor Law commissioner for north-west Scotland, and later Chairman of the Local Government Board of Scotland. This was, of course, the same man who had been sent by gunboat to cool the contumacious hotheads of

Glendale in January 1883. His uncle, Sir John MacNeill, was in the 1850s a very vocal supporter of emigration.

In short, the commission investigating the stand-off between crofters, cottars and landowners contained three major landowners, the sons of two others, and one man with a small land-holding interest. Such a state of affairs should not come as a surprise. Let us just be content that one member appeared to have no connection to land-ownership. Slightly less forgivable was the fact that two of the gentlemen (Mackenzie and Cameron) were actually looking into matters that touched on their own estates and localities; however, some measure of decorum was observed when Mackenzie excused himself from the interviews which took place in Poolewe on his vast Gairloch estate.

Figure 2.1 Drawing of the Napier Commission in session in Glasgow, 19 October 1883, by Alexander Stuart Boyd, aka 'Twym'. From left to right: Nicolson, Mackenzie, Napier, MacNeill, Cameron, Fraser-Mackintosh, Mackinnon. (*Quiz* magazine, 26 October 1883)

When the Commission convened in Glasgow in the autumn of 1883, a newspaper reporter was dispatched to describe for avid readers the six members of the panel. He did so admirably:

Well, the chairman, Lord Napier, is a benevolent looking old gentle-man, with a dreamy pair of eyes and a slight *burr* in his speech. Sir Kenneth Mackenzie is a half sailor-looking man of dark complexion, speaking with the slightest possible suspicion of an aristocratic lisp. Sheriff Nicolson has rather a solemn face, and his shaven cheeks give him quite a stage appearance. His accent is decidedly nasal and the eyeglass pressure well down his nose tends to exaggerate this characteristic. The bald head and refined appearance of Lochiel suggest more the Lowland gentleman than the hardy Highland chief; but with the Cameron tartans waving about him in his native wilds no doubt he will be quite the Cateran. Mr Fraser Mackintosh, M.P., might be a venerable professor, while Professor Mackinnon is a stout, good-humoured smiling gentleman with a strong Highland pronunciation suggesting the keeper of a mountain hotel, and the secretary of the Commission, Mr Macneill, would pass for a soldier, such is the militariness of his heavy moustache. Altogether, the Commissioners seem a weighty body of men, the chairman having the reputation of being an indefatigable worker, being willing to prolong the sittings to all hours, and the grievances of the crofters are bound to meet with proper consideration at their hands.[2]

If the composition of the Commission was not a great surprise, what it proceeded to do was certainly an eye-opener. For probably the first time in British history, a government commission actually set out to listen to ordinary people, to record their thoughts and grievances and to take the time to conduct an extensive investigation. The bare statistics of the Commission's activities give some measure of what was achieved. Two sets of forms were sent out to every single landowner in the north of Scotland, asking for detailed information about their land use and the names, ages and rents paid by their crofters and cottars; 775 interviews were conducted, and every interview was carefully minuted and reproduced; ninety-nine additional written statements were received and also recorded; 46,750 questions were asked of the interviewees. A total of 3,375 pages of evidence were published in four volumes; the written statements occupied a further 512 pages of the fifth volume, which also contained the Commission's conclusions. The report and conclusions run to 111 pages and the 'dissents' of three of the Commissioners to a further twenty-six pages. Interviews were held at sixty locations (including, rather astonishingly, the remote islands of St Kilda and Foula), on seventy separate days. The Commission was on the road – with several interruptions, unavoidable or planned – between early May and the end of October, and there was a minor mopping-up operation in December.

(One of the interruptions occurred on 7 June, when the Navy yacht put at their disposal, the HMS *Lively*, ended up on the 'Hen and

Chickens' rocks just off Stornoway; no one was in any way hurt, the seventy-eight-member crew, their seven illustrious passengers and a motley selection of newspapermen all being taken off safely, if damp. In a court-martial three weeks later, the captain and his lieutenant were severely reprimanded and dismissed from their ship.[3] By then, regrettably, there was no ship: the stranded *Lively* was battered to pieces in a storm on the very same day that the court-martial took place in Devonport. This disaster did not prevent the Commission from getting on with business: the gentlemen pursued their investigations on Harris and Lewis for a further week. The Admiralty was unable to provide a replacement ship immediately; the Commission was due in Lerwick on 18 June, but only after a delay of almost four weeks did they manage to reach Shetland. The mishap also proved frustrating for Lord Napier, who had, on 6 June, been advised of his mother's death in Melrose, and who had planned to take the *Lively* back to the mainland to travel south. However, alternative travel arrangements were made for him, possibly involving, yet again, the *Jackal*; and the last few days of the Commission's work on Harris and Lewis were conducted without its eponymous chairman.)

Significantly, the Commissioners' very first port of call was Braes on Skye, where they interviewed a dozen locals on 8 May. The decision to start there speaks volumes. And two weeks later, they were in Glendale, that other locale of seething rebellion. From Skye, they continued to Barra, Uist, Harris and Lewis; after the careless episode with the *Lively*, they boarded a steamship named *North Star*, at vast but unavoidable expense to the Home Office, and set off for Shetland and Orkney; next they proceeded down the north-west coast, from Kinlochbervie to Ullapool and as far as Arisaig; out to Tiree and Mull; back to Lochaline, then up to the east coast of Sutherland; finally sitting in Inverness, Glasgow and Edinburgh; and, as a hurried afterthought, a day out at Tarbert on Loch Fyne, on 26 December. The range of the journey was, for that time, quite staggering – which did not prevent the Duke of Argyll from complaining pettishly that 'They went in a steam vessel; they landed at certain points of the coast; they retired to the nearest church or schoolhouse; they sat with open doors; everybody could make what complaints they pleased; but they never visited the localities.'[4] Curiously, the campaigning land reformer John Murdoch found himself criticising the Commission (he called it 'our yachting commission') for exactly the same reason: that they never saw for themselves how the best land had been fenced off from the communities.[5]

A statistical analysis of the professions of those interviewed proves rather revealing – almost two-thirds were crofters, cottars, or pursued manual trades:

Crofters/cottars	420	(152 of these also had other trades)
Fishermen	19	
Other manual	52	
Church ministers	59	
Teachers	14	
Landowners	27	
Factors/agents	58	(i.e. representatives of landowners)
Other non-manual	69	(bankers, lawyers, clerks, rich idlers, etc.)
Not declared	59	

Women were not entirely absent; there was a grand total of five in the above, with their occupations given as 'wife' or 'widow'.

Many of those who turned up to submit evidence had been delegated to do so by their local communities. Some of them never had the opportunity to give evidence (sessions managed to average about a dozen people per day). Evidence ranged from brief complaints about 'too much rent', to long and detailed statements prepared in advance and read out. Frequently, the statements made by crofters, cottars and fishermen demonstrated great eloquence. Regardless of their status and contribution, all were subjected to questions from the attendant commissioners (a statistical average of sixty questions per interviewee). A reasonable number of those giving evidence were church ministers, both 'Wee Free' and 'Kirk': by and large, their evidence was not at all supportive of the landowners. Teachers were, on the other hand, rather under-represented, perhaps fearing for their continued employment.

There was one procedural matter which no one seemed to have addressed until it was too late. The evidence was taken in open session, where no one's identity was concealed. The later report provided a verbatim account of all that was said, and by whom. Some of the specific complaints raised early in a session (by, for example, a crofter) were later in the same session put before subsequent interviewees (for example, that crofter's landlord or estate factor). Indeed, if we are to go by the evidence of *The Scotsman* newspaper's reporting of the interviews on St Kilda,[6] which replicated almost all the words exchanged two days after the event, the nineteenth-century equivalent of Twitter was broadcasting all the sessions almost live: the good ship *Lively* had had plenty of space for reporters. In these circumstances, it was clear that (a) some people would not say all that they wished to say, for fear of reprisals; and (b) other people could and would take reprisals. And sure enough, the very first witness heard by the Commission, Angus Stewart of Braes, requested an assurance that he would not be evicted as a result of giving evidence;[7] the Commissioners stated that it was impossible to give any such assurance; the crofter drew the logical conclusion, and walked out. The very next interviewee was his landlord's factor, who professed himself greatly insulted that a suggestion of reprisals could even be contemplated, before grudgingly promising that he would 'in no way visit anything upon' the crofter; Mr Stewart then returned to give his evidence.

But later, as one might expect, there were consequences. Two crofters on Mull wrote to Napier in late 1883, complaining that they had been served eviction notices as a direct result of giving evidence to the Commission. Angus McInnes complained: 'There was no promise required from Mr Allan [the landowner] that the delegates would not suffer at his hands . . . for giving evidence as to the usage of these settlers and crofters by their successive several landlords of Tobermory.'[8] McInnes's only crime had been to complain publicly that his rent was too high. A neighbour of McInnes was also served notice of eviction – even though, despite having been elected as a delegate to give evidence on behalf of crofters, he had never actually had the opportunity to do so. His only crime was to have been delegated. In both cases, the landlord claimed that these tenants were in arrears, but evidence to the contrary was presented to Napier. To his credit, Napier wrote to Allan asking for an explanation – but it is unlikely that his intervention did much good. Questions were also asked in Parliament on these cases, and representations were made to the Lord Advocate, who of course washed his hands of any responsibility.

In Orkney, things were even worse. When one crofter sought an assurance that 'our proprietor will injure no person for giving their evidence', the said proprietor, the apoplectic General Burroughs, sitting just a few feet away, stormed that 'I am not prepared to do so. It is contrary to human nature, that I could treat a man who spoke of me so inimically as one or two have done here, in the same way as other men who are friendly disposed.' When challenged by the panel, he blustered away repetitiously, before declaring in bullish manner that 'My intentions would be for them to go away . . . Is the property mine, or is it not mine? If it is mine, surely I can do what I consider best for it?' And sure enough, the crofters in question were shortly thereafter evicted, causing a great uproar in Orkney and beyond.[9] That a land-owner – and not just one – could contemplate defying a Royal Commission in Victorian Britain says much.

Nevertheless, this was a government commission of inquiry that actually went out and toured the land, listened to ordinary people and documented their complaints. In modern times, this might be described as a 'consultation'; in those days, it was a miracle. Such, then, was the disquiet of the Westminster government as a result of the rebellions on Skye.

The Napier Report was issued with immoderate haste in late April of 1884, less than twelve months after the Commission had first set out. It was immediately the subject of much debate in both Houses, and across Scotland, for the rest of the year and beyond. The report summarised the crofters' complaints as follows:

> Undue contraction of the area of holdings; undue extension of the area of holdings; insecurity of tenure; want of compensation for improvements; high rents; defective communications; withdrawal of the soil in connection with the purposes of sport. To these we may add, as contributing in our opinion to the depressed condition of the people, defects in education, defects in the machinery of justice, and want of facilities for emigration. The fishing population [complain of] want of harbours, piers, boat shelters and landing-places; inability to purchase boats and tackle adapted for distant and deep-sea fishing; difficulty of access to the great markets of consumption; defective postal and telegraphic intercourse.[10]

As a list of the things that could possibly be broken, this one is hard to beat. It really is all-inclusive – everything from rents, tenure and justice, through to education, health and economic opportunity. Much of this certainly was the result of more than a century of sheer neglect by landowners and government; but just as much resulted from the policies actively pursued by the landowners – clearances, moving entire townships to rocky shorelines, corruption of the justice system, arbitrary rent increases. Given the sheer weight of evidence amassed, it was hard for anyone to deny the problems (although the Duke of Argyll did his best).

The Napier Commission's solutions to these problems were outlined across several pages: we give the main points below.[11] The underlying argument of the report was that, although crofters, cottars and fishermen were not numerically significant, every effort should be made to maintain them as a social group, for the general good of both country and Empire. Fishing in particular was a skill that should not be allowed to go to waste. The economy would benefit:

The crofting and cottar population of the Highlands and Islands, small though it be, is a nursery of good workers and good citizens for the whole empire. In this respect the stock is exceptionally valuable. By sound physical constitution, native intelligence, and good moral training it is particularly fitted to recruit the people of our industrial centres, who without such help from wholesome sources in rural districts would degenerate under the influence of bad lodging, unhealthy occupations, and enervating habits.

This last argument seems a little self-defeating: if the wholesome residents of rural districts are shifted to degrading industrial centres, do they themselves not then fall prey to 'bad lodging, unhealthy occupations, and enervating habits' – or could they somehow, miraculously, rise above such degeneration?

Those who did remain in the rural setting should be able to expect security of housing, in the spirit of the times:

There is a general desire that the labouring man in every sphere of activity should be invested with a greater share of substantial possession, and be attached by deeper and more durable ties to the soil of his country . . . This great object is being partly realised in Scotland among the elite of those workmen engaged in urban industries . . . It is in the Highland and Islands . . . that occupancy may perhaps be most readily converted into property.

And no Victorian sympathy for the salt of the earth would be complete without a nod to military recruitment: 'It is not only in regard to fishing that the crofting and cottar population have a peculiar value. They constitute a natural basis for the naval defence of the country, a defence which cannot be extemporised.' And so it was to be thirty years later, as graveyards and stark war memorials across Scotland now testify. Emigration was also strongly recommended as a method of relieving the pressure on the land; this recommendation was made despite the fact that the majority of crofters – when asked – were against it: 'first', reported the Commission of the crofters' aversion, 'those who go abroad encounter serious risks, and have continuous difficulties to contend with there; and secondly, that while emigration has always been spoken of as a panacea for the ills of those that remain, it has ever left them just as they were'.[12]

Others, thinking more creatively, were all in favour of emigration – just as long as it was the sheep-farmers who emigrated, and the crofters who remained and took back their fields.[13]

Such aversion by the potential emigrants, however, cut little ice with the Commission – indeed, it was suspected that 'the prevailing land agitation' was influencing the naysayers. The only concession was to suggest that entire families, and not just able-bodied individuals, should be encouraged to emigrate, thereby ensuring that the sick, the elderly and the very young did not remain behind to clutter up the land and be an economic burden.

And lest the reader becomes impatient about the lack of mention of railways thus far, we should note that the report alluded to several proposed railway lines:

The question of extended railway communication remains to be considered. This is the principal requirement of the fishing population of the western coast . . . During the herring season special steamers are run from Stornoway to Strome Ferry, but white fish from the north and west of Lewis cannot be despatched fresh to market . . . A similar line from the remoter parts of Lewis to Stornoway . . . would be of equal benefit to the Long Island.'[14]

In this same passage, there was a strong recommendation that (a) the Dingwall to Strome Ferry line should be extended to Kyle of Lochalsh and (b) there should be a railway from Inverness to Fort William, and from Fort William to 'near the head of Loch Nevis' (i.e. Mallaig). A dose of realism was present in these remarks: the branch line to the western sea from Fort William 'would not pay interest on the outlay; and if left to the unaided efforts of railway companies, it might be indefinitely postponed, leaving the Highland fisherman, as at present, half idle . . . Under these circumstances, we are of opinion that Government . . . might step in and grant financial assistance.'[15] All very sensible and – in the remark concerning indefinite postponement – prescient; it would take another decade for the competing private railway companies to wrestle these proposals either into reality, or into the side-grass.

To round off the report, Napier summoned up a killer argument: the haunting spectre of Fenianism and socialism.

> The last argument which we shall adduce in support of our views on this subject, is the argument of public expediency. The Highlands and Islands have recently been at some points the scene of agitation, and even of disturbance. Acts of violence have occurred on the occasion of the delivery of legal summonses regarding the occupancy of land, and the enforcement of lawful claims on the part of the proprietors have been delayed or impeded by apprehensions of opposition . . . Collisions between proprietary rights and popular demands are to be deprecated, for they leave behind them lasting traces of resentment and alienation . . . The dissatisfaction of the small tenants in regard to their position is of native origin, but it is fomented by external influences. The land movement in the Highlands, even if it were not spontaneously maintained by the people themselves, would be aroused to further action by other forces: it is impelled by the democratic and social aspirations prevalent among various classes at home.

All of which should suggest strongly to Her Imperial Majesty that something needed to be done, and done urgently. There was plenty of precedent: if legislation had been made in the past 'for the benefit of workers in plantations, in mines, in factories, and in ships, it may be invoked for other industries with equal justice'.

The three fairly lengthy 'dissents' at the end of the report were from Mackenzie, Cameron and Fraser-Mackintosh, expressing their personal disagreements with some of the conclusions, or the detail thereof. Fraser-Mackintosh – who, we will recall, was shortly to become a Crofters' Party MP – was quite clear where he stood in relation to landownership:

> Re-occupation by, and re-distribution among, crofters and cottars of much land now used as large farms will be beneficial to the State, to the owner, and to the occupier. Until this is done, much as I deplore the present position of congested districts, I must view with jealousy [i.e. mistrust or anger] State-aided emigration.[16]

For his part, the Conservative MP Cameron of Lochiel suggested that a crofter, being assisted by the State to acquire a 12-acre croft and work it largely as a sheep-farm, ought to be able to support himself and his family on an annual income of £32 per annum – that is, 12s 4d (62p) per week – from which to feed family (with food over and above what he was able to grow at home), pay for any hired help and purchase seed. 'I am convinced that there is hardly a crofter of energy and ambition who is either possessed of £100, or who hopes by labour to make up that sum within three years, who would not gladly accept a farm and take his chances of success on the terms above indicated.'[17] Lochiel did not trouble to suggest quite where all the 12-acre pieces of land were to be found. The State ought to provide suitable loans, on fixed credit terms, to give such dynamic crofters a leg up. He ended on an upbeat note:

> Should the Legislature see fit to give effect to the above and to the other joint recommendations of this Commission, I myself entertain the sanguine hope that the present depression and discontent among the inhabitants of the Western Highlands and Islands will pass away, and that the future which is in store for them may be replete with the elements of independence, contentment, and prosperity.[18]

Remarkably, the MPs of Westminster – doubtless uplifted by Cameron's vision of an idyllic future – did decide to take positive action. Gladstone's government swiftly cobbled together a Bill which, it was promised, would be nothing other than a Scottish version of the Irish Land Act of 1881, with all that that signified. Parliament began to debate it in May 1885. As was to be expected, landowners were neither keen nor hopeful: our Duke of Argyll (the son-in-law of the 2nd Duke of Sutherland) even going to the extent of suspending drainage operations on his estate on Tiree, on the basis that he might lose his lands: 'I am sorry,' he told his tenants, 'I cannot do that, till I see what Parliament is going to do with my freedom of contract with you.'[19]

But no sooner had the parliamentary debate begun than the Government collapsed; and it was only after a new Liberal government was elected in early 1886 (and the new Crofters' Party MPs had taken their seats) that the wheels were once more set in motion. The Crofters' Act was passed in June 1886, the details of which we shall examine below; although it did not lead to 'independence, contentment, and prosperity', it was a step in the right direction. The speed with which this legislation was framed and passed also marked out the Napier Commission as something unique in British government up to that time. For all its flaws – in membership, procedures and conclusions – it was something of a watershed in the long and often depressing history of the Highlands and Islands.

SOME CHANGES IN THE LAW

'Quarrying, Mining, Hunting, Shooting and Fishing . . . '

The Crofters Holdings (Scotland) Act received royal assent on 25 June 1886. It was short and sweet, covering two major subjects: firstly, the provision of security of tenure for crofters; secondly, the establishment of a Crofters' Commission as independent arbitrator between crofter and landowner.

On security of tenure, the law now stated that a crofter could not be removed from his croft except under a small number of specific conditions: non-payment of rent for more than two years, sub-letting, property neglect, by becoming bankrupt, or selling liquor. A crofter could bequeath a tenancy to his legal heirs. Rents were to be agreed between landowner and crofter, and fixed for seven years; all subject to optional appeals by either party to the Crofters' Commission. On renunciation of a tenancy, the crofter was to be compensated for any improvements he had made. These four clauses alone constituted something of a revolution. Provision was also made to allow crofters to band together and apply for extended holdings from, for example, neighbouring sheep-farms. There were a number of concessions allowing the landowner to quarry, mine, remove timber or peats under or from a crofter's holding, with certain restrictions and compensations; similar provisions allowed for the landowner to pursue without obstruction the time-honoured activities of 'hunting, shooting and fishing' on a croft, in pursuit of 'game or fish, wild birds, or vermin' – all a little reminiscent of feudal hunting rights. In a nod to Irishmen, this particular section of the Act is lifted directly from Section 14 of the Landlord and Tenant (Ireland) Act of 1870.

For the Crofters' Commission, there were to be three commissioners, one of whom had to be able to speak Gaelic, and one to be an experienced advocate at the Scottish bar. They could appoint suitable valuers, assessors, clerks, local officers and so forth to help them carry out their duties. They were to make an annual report on their activities to Parliament. Their duties were largely to act as intermediaries in disputes, fix rents and determine whether any available land could be reassigned or leased to crofters. This available land, however, specifically excluded land used as 'a deer forest, or a grouse moor, or other sporting purpose' – in fact, a huge proportion of disputed land. Separate paragraphs in the Act permitted a parallel 'Fishery Board' (which had already been established in 1882) to provide loans to crofters and fishermen in crofting parishes for the purchase or repair of gear and boats, 'for the benefit or encouragement of the fishing industry'.

But there was one problem. The Napier Commission had failed to distinguish clearly between a 'crofter' and a 'cottar'. The text of the Crofters' Act made a brave attempt to do so:

> Definitions: In this Act, 'crofter' means any person who at the passing of this Act is tenant of a holding from year to year, who resides on his holding, the annual rent of which does not exceed thirty pounds in money.[20]

A 'cottar', on the other hand,

means the occupier of a dwelling-house situate in a crofting parish with or without land who pays no rent to the landlord, as also the tenant from year to year of a dwelling-house ... who resides therein, and who pays to the landlord therefor an annual rent not exceeding six pounds in money, whether with or without garden ground, but without arable or pasture land.

In short: a crofter pays an annual rent of between £6 and £30; a cottar pays less than £6, or none at all. This 'crofter' is the subject of this Act; that 'cottar' is not. As a result, both the cottar and the poorer sort of crofter were left without any protection or rights under the new Act. Charles Fraser-Mackintosh, in his dissent from the Napier Report, had argued for the cut-off figure to be set at £4: he was overruled. The higher figure was something which came back to haunt the Highlands and Islands.

That was one problem; but there was an even larger one. Gladstone had earlier suggested that the new law regarding crofters would incorporate the provisions of the Irish Land Acts. To some degree it did: security of tenure, compensation for improvements; as we have noted above, one relevant paragraph was lifted verbatim from an Irish Act. But what the Scottish Act did not address at all was the possibility of crofters being able to repossess lands taken from them in the earlier part of the century. And there was no mention at all of more land being made easily available to them. The new Crofters' Party MPs attacked the limited proposals in the House of Commons, one stating that 'the remedies you propose you will increase, instead of diminish, the disease', while another made it quite clear that his constituents were not amused: 'I have received hundreds of Resolutions informing me that I shall never be elected for Ross-shire again, because I do not go in for rejecting the Bill. That is the case with all of us. All the Crofter Members are endangering their seats by going in for this Bill.'[21] All of which was, of course, advice not heeded by the legislators; this too came back to haunt both the landowners and crofters.

Two problems, and one peculiarity: this Act was very specifically designed only for the northern counties of Scotland. Although there were tenant-farmers all across the Scottish Borders and up the east coast into Aberdeenshire and Moray, they were excluded from the Act. Paragraph 19 stipulated that 'the Crofters Commission after due enquiry shall ascertain what parishes or islands or districts . . . within the counties of Argyll, Inverness, Ross and Cromarty, Sutherland, Caithness, Orkney, and Shetland, are crofting parishes . . . this Act shall apply [only] to the parishes included in the determination'. It left many of Scotland's crofters without any legal rights. Indeed, this clause could make it possible for some northern parishes not to be affected by the Act either.

But: it was progress of a sort.

THE EXTENT AND PROBLEM OF DEER FORESTS

'Customers of Public Houses and Smugglers'

One thing which neither Napier nor the Crofters' Act addressed was the deer forest. It is a curious term: when used with the prefix 'deer', the word 'forest' rarely means that there are a lot of trees. Rather it refers to a vast acreage of heather, bog and rock, a wilderness where rich gentlemen and the occasional no-nonsense lady could go out and shoot stags. Napier and his colleagues encountered complaints about deer forest at almost every stop on their itinerary and were, even before they set out, well aware that the deer-forests constituted a huge can of worms. It was therefore odd that they should airily brush aside deer forests as something not problematical.

Early in the nineteenth century, Scottish landowners were keen to increase revenues from land which they classed as overpopulated and underused. This they did by turning huge areas of land – both arable and grazing – into sheep-farms. Potential profits were high, especially if the land was in the hands of skilled sheep farmers, usually from the Borders. But this monoculture had a sting in the tail: sheep, unlike cattle, are choosy eaters and excreters of nothing very useful.[22] Thus, after several decades of assiduous munching by sheep, much of their grazing land was degraded and overgrown with heather, bracken and patches of sterile bog. When that happened, there was little else the landowner could do, if he did not wish to sell his estate, but let the land return to nature and take up shooting. Thus there was a turn in the second half of the century towards transforming the land into 'deer forest'.

A further impetus towards the creation of deer forests came in the 1880s, when the price of wool plummeted in the world markets due to imports from, for example, Australia.[23] Sheep-farming in the Highlands was no longer the profitable enterprise it had once been; making money from the oligarchs of the south, on the other hand, was just such an enterprise. Deer forest was formed either on higher ground (land above the 1,000-foot contour lines, which was largely useless for any other purpose), or on land previously used by crofters, or from lower-lying sheep-farms which no longer paid their way, or a bit of all three. And sometimes, to replace the sheep-farms which were now deer forests, crofting land was converted to new sheep-farms.

As part of their investigations into the situation of the crofting communities, the Napier Commission of 1883 sent out blue forms for estate-owners to fill in. The forms asked for acreage and rents on different types of land on the estates, and a comparison of the 1883 figures against those of 1853. From the forms returned, and discounting the estate-owners who either did not have the information or were unwilling to make public statements, it is quite plain that deer forest was generally converted from large farms – the 'large farms' themselves, of course, historically created out of common grazings and smallholdings. Appendix 1 at the end of this book shows a sample of the returns from significant landowners, from which we can see very clearly how the sheep-farms became deer forests.

It was fortunate that the Napier Commission had collected these figures, for it had to field not a few complaints about deer forests. The very first witness heard, Angus Stewart of Braes, was asked naively whether he had received any assistance from the landowner in building his cottage. 'May the Lord look upon you!' he laughed in pitying tones, 'I have seen myself compelled to go to the deer forest to steal thatch – to steal the wherewith to thatch our houses.' (There was an interesting twist to Stewart's tale – 'I had to go in the daytime for this purpose, and was caught by the gamekeeper, and I had to give him part of what I had – for the purpose of thatching his own house.')[24] The deer forests, then, contained resources of fundamental value to local people, but were off limits: deer and their habitat were a valuable asset. No surprise, then, that the forests were a major bone of contention.

The Reverend Roderick Morison, Church of Scotland minister for Kintail, was most eloquent about deer forests in his written submission to Napier.[25] 'Glen after glen is being cleared of its shepherd families, who are replaced by one or two solitary game watchers . . . who are usually the idlest of people pretending to earn a living, and the best customers of the adjacent public houses and smugglers.' Kintail was in the middle of a huge swathe of deer forests (250,000 acres in total, 'stretching from coast to coast') which had been leased by Walter L. Winans, an American sportsman and millionaire. From all reports, Winans was a particularly unpleasant individual – one Highlander remarked of him mildly: 'Well, I don't think that the people wish him to live for ever.'[26] And he was a particularly unpleasant sort of trophy-hunter, too – his idea of a good day's shooting was to herd as many deer as possible into some impasse in the hills and then blast away at them with dozens of rifles. (A court case on this unsportsmanlike behaviour was brought against him in Edinburgh in 1892 by the Mackenzie estate.)[27] His gamekeepers and gillies were noted for being strangers, well-paid and aggressive: one witness to the Napier Commission cited an occasion when a Glasgow naturalist was innocently collecting insects at the edge of one of Winans' deer forests, only to be accosted by a keeper who chased him back to the road, issuing violent threats – 'it was very nearly coming to the greatest battle we ever had in Strathglass for an age – the battle of the midges'.[28]

The Reverend Morison surmised that local people employed as gillies, keepers and so on 'are not unlikely to prove, in course of time, a very troublesome and difficult element in the social fabric' – one detects here, perhaps, the minister's personal experience. There was no benefit to the local economy: 'The large sums of money paid as rent are chiefly taken away from the Highlands and expended in London and elsewhere, a very small portion being spent on local improvements or works likely to give employment to the people.' Vermin (foxes) come out of the deer forests to attack sheep, deer and game or eat up crops; sheep straying into the forests are lost and frequently destroyed by gamekeepers. Mr Morison concludes, in words worthy of some of the reddest of Red Clydesiders, as follows:

> It will no doubt be said that to interfere with the rights of property is to undermine the very foundations of society. To me it appears that those who endanger those rights are those who make them intolerable by a free and enlightened community. It may I think be boldly said that all rights, customs, monopolies, and privileges that tend to the manifest injury of a country and its inhabitants, must and

ought to – and eventually shall – fall before the increasing intelligence and advancing power of the people.

Despite the Reverend Morison's impassioned call to arms, it cannot be said that the Napier Commission considered deer forests a big problem. Its report declared that no arable land had ever been taken to form deer forests, that they had no adverse effect on local employment and that adjacent farming land was unaffected, an argument based on the premise that deer forest land – despite the evidence laid out in the blue forms – was already unusable for anything else. Nonetheless, their report did suggest that some 'management' improvements could be made: better fencing, compensation for crop-damage and so forth.

This recommendation gradually filtered through to yet another commission sent to the Highlands in 1892, known as the 'Deer Forest Commission'. The Napier Report did, however, publicise for virtually the first time some statistical information about deer forests:[29] according to the latest figures available then, almost two million acres of land was registered as 'deer forest' across the whole of Scotland, in 109 estates; of that, 565,358 (28 per cent of the national total) was in Ross and Cromarty, within forty-two estates. In Sutherland, for comparison, there were only four estates – all belonging to the Duke – with deer forest totalling almost 150,000 acres. The vast majority of all these forests began at heights below 1,000 feet, and many extended upwards beyond 2,000 feet.

One word of caution is required here and throughout: even with the rosiest of rose-tinted spectacles, the western Highlands cannot be considered as a land of plenty simply awaiting the attentions of the energetic crofter. Considerable acreages, either on higher ground or projecting out of the jagged coastline, would never be good for very much. At worst, such land was simply hostile; at best, it could perhaps be used for the grazing of sheep, deer and goats; but certainly not for growing oats or rearing cattle. What cottars, crofters and land reformers were pursuing, however, was the right to land which was indeed arable or grazable, stolen land which had once been managed by the communities. Deer forest tended to be a combination of the usable and the unusable land, and that combination is where the controversy was centred.

What is quite remarkable is that the acreage of Scotland covered by deer forest actually grew, and dramatically so, in the decades following the Napier Report. In answer to a parliamentary question put by J. G. Weir MP in March 1908, the Scottish Office issued a table of statistics of deer forest acreage in the northern six counties (Argyll, Inverness, Ross and Cromarty, Sutherland, Caithness, Orkney and Shetland – the northern isles, however, had almost no deer forest to speak of). The table lists every registered forest with its owner and acreage, and notes any increases since the previous audit. Incorporating those previous counts, we can summarise the figures as follows, highlighting – for the particular area of interest of this book – the numbers for Ross and Cromarty:[30]

TABLE I SCOTLAND'S DEER FOREST ACREAGE

Year	Acres of deer forest in six counties	Percentage of total land area (approx. 9 million acres)	Acres of deer forest in Ross and Cromarty	Percentage of total land in Ross and Cromarty (approx. 2 million acres)
1883	1,709,892	19.0	647,883	32.3
1898	2,287,297	25.4	795,545	39.8
1904	2,920,097	32.4	972,829	48.6
1908	2,958,490	32.8	965,579	48.2

In 1912, according to statistics taken from the Valuation Rolls for the whole of Scotland, the Ross and Cromarty acreage had slipped slightly to a mere 935,154 acres. The county of Sutherland now had 436,322 acres of deer forest – three times the amount of 1883, of which the vast majority was owned by the eponymous Duke. Mr Weir MP kept probing year after year, and was not averse to accusing the Government of gross inaccuracies; in a slightly evasive and singularly unhelpful reply, the Secretary for Scotland stated that 'short of an actual survey, it would be impossible to make up a really accurate return, and, as to usefulness, when made would be quite incommensurate with its cost . . . The Secretary for Scotland is not prepared to grant any Return such as asked.'[31]

Usefulness, cost and inaccuracies notwithstanding, the pattern is clear: in the twenty-five years following the first audit, the acreage of deer forest in the north of Scotland increased by an astonishing 73 per cent, and by 1908 in Ross and Cromarty this now accounted for half of all the available land. There were a number of reasons for this increase. Partly, it had much to do with the degradation of the land on large sheep-farms. Partly also it reflected the growing taste of the British ruling class to go out and shoot things, with landowners regarding this opportunity as a profitable one for social networking, as well as for their pockets. And partly it may be supposed that the Napier Report's effective endorsement of deer forests encouraged the landowners to extend the forests, as a way of placing another obstacle between communities and their land. And the corollary is clear: over a period of twenty-five years, land taken for sheep-farms was not being handed back willy-nilly to crofters. One might easily conclude that nothing much had changed since 'the yachting commission' was out.

At the end of 1892, Gladstone's Liberal administration set up another Royal Commission, this time looking into the whole question of deer forests, to determine if any such land could be returned to crofter cultivation, and generally make it appear that the Government was doing something helpful. This was the Deer Forest Commission, and it held sixty-four public sittings in various parts of the country and took evidence from landowners, crofters, cottars, fishermen, factors and law agents; its members also took the trouble to inspect in person the lands in question. They worked in collaboration with the Crofters' Commission, which had been set up six years earlier. Crofters initially had high hopes – until, that is, they realised that the Commission had no compulsory powers to take possession of the land and re-distribute it.

The procedure for redistribution was firstly to 'schedule' deer forest land into three categories: marked in yellow on the Commission's maps, Category 1, which represented land suitable for new croft holdings; pink, Category 2, which was for land which could be used for grazings for neighbouring crofters; and brown, Category 3, which was land suitable for larger holdings, at rents greater than £30 per year – far more than the average crofter could afford. In their report of 1895, the Deer Forest Commission had scheduled (i.e. coloured in on their maps) slightly less than 1.8 million acres;[32] despite which, by 1904, there were fifty-two new deer forests totalling an additional half-million acres. A question was then asked in the House of Commons about this discrepancy.[33] The Lord Advocate's reply must inevitably disappoint – between 1896 and 1904, only 411 acres of arable land and 12,206 of pasture land had been assigned to crofters, of which total a miserly 907 acres had been clawed back from deer forest.[34] As if in justification, the Lord Advocate also chose to 'inform the Hon. Member that the Crofters Commission have no power to form new crofters' holdings or moderately-sized holdings'.

In 1897, James Caldwell MP in the House of Commons attacked the Deer Forest Commission's performance to date. He took as an example the recommendations for North Uist, where 2,000 acres of rough grazing and 140 acres of arable land had been identified for distribution to eighty-two crofters. The result? 'The proprietors failed to give any land for such purposes. This, notwithstanding the fact that the report of the Commissioners showed there were 1,529 acres of old arable land gone out of cultivation, and more than 8,000 acres of pasture land.'[35] Thus it was not at all unusual to discover that, even though deer forests had irrefutably been established on land taken from crofters and townships within the previous hundred years, the owners of that land felt under no obligation to pass it back to the crofters. And the Crofters' Act of 1886 made this perfectly legal.

Despite the manifest toothlessness of government bodies, the owners of deer forests were a little reluctant to co-operate. In 1913, the Scottish Office found itself obliged to engage in increasingly pointless correspondence with the Duke of Argyll's chamberlain on the matter of assessing the acreage of some of the Duke's deer forest. The Duke simply refused to provide any updated figures, considering it to be no one's business but his own. Finally acknowledging defeat, the statisticians had to re-use 1908 figures for these estates. This particular set of national statistics did, for the first time since 1883, include estimates of the acreage which lay below the 1,000-foot contour, considered to be a point below which there might be an argument for other land-usage.[36] From a review of the figures which were provided, it is fair to conclude that the majority of deer forests did indeed begin considerably below 1,000 feet, particularly in Ross and Cromarty. Alas, more often than not, the column reserved for this figure against each estate contained the disheartening comments 'not known' or 'uncertain'.

So much for the empowerment of commissions.

THE IMPORTANCE OF THE FISHERIES

'The Vigilance Committee of the Inhabitants of Stornoway'

For all that crofting and rights of tenancy were high on the agenda, the Napier Commission considered that the mainstay of the rural economy of north-west Scotland was not cultivating potatoes and oats, nor sheep-farming, nor even the shooting of deer. It was fishing. 'Taken as a whole, the population into whose conditions we have been making inquiry derive a larger annual income from the sea than they derive from the land.'[37] Notwithstanding Napier's pronouncement, the evidence suggests a more nuanced picture. On the one hand, Hugh Morrison of Finsbay on Harris stated that fishing 'is what has always supported us, and not the land';[38] and John McDiarmid of Scalpa on Lewis said: 'The whole of the population – cottars and crofters – have to pursue the fishing . . . and they have to be out summer, spring and winter, and live in bothies, and sometimes as far as Uist. Then everyone that can go to the east coast fishing goes there – to Wick.'[39] On the other hand, the members of the Napier Commission were not averse to leading their witnesses: Finlay Mackenzie of Ness was asked: 'You have told us that the only way to put the people right in your opinion is to give them more land. Is there anything else you think would benefit the people here?' and he replied dutifully that 'I am thinking they would require to get a remedy by the sea – to assist them with boats and nets to carry on the herring fishing, as the ling fishing now is a great failure.'[40] Murdo Macdonald of Meavaig on Lewis stuck to his guns, however: 'Of late years, fishing has fallen back. It is far away from the land. We can have no living without the land, and plenty of the land which our fathers had – twenty townships in possession of one bed-ridden man, and hundreds of us without as much as we can say that we have a right to.'[41] A man of similar views was Murdo McLean, fish-curer of Lewis: 'I considered the fishing a secondary consideration. Land is the first, if the people are to be elevated in any shape or form.'[42]

But regardless of how the crofters themselves thought of fishing as a solution to their problems, it was in fact the mainstay of their precarious existence. The North Atlantic teemed with fish at that time. And fish fed a nation. It also fed a huge export trade – fish, in particular herring, taken from Scottish waters in the Atlantic and the North Sea was at a premium in northern Europe, partly because there was an earlier fishing season in the Atlantic than elsewhere. The Europeans who had eaten their way through the previous year's harvests were prepared, in the early part of the year, to pay good prices for herring.

That the fisheries were important had been recognised long before Napier; in the late eighteenth century, the newly established British Fishery Society under William Pulteney built a number of fishing ports which had varying degrees of success – Tobermory on Mull (1787), Ullapool (1788) and Wick (1805). Over the course of one hundred years, however, the conditions and dynamics of fishing and boat-ownership had changed dramatically. By the 1880s, fishing was still only a part-time and under-funded occupation for communities on the west coast, but a full-time profession on the east. So the power in Scottish fishing lay almost completely with the East Coast fishing fleets – operating out of Wick, Peterhead, Fraserburgh, Aberdeen and further down the coast into Fife, East Lothian and Eyemouth. From the east coast, fish could readily be brought to the southern markets – railways ran from all the main ports. Although there were some fishing boats owned and operated by the people of Lewis and Harris, the men from the east controlled a mature and rewarding industry, and their larger boats – a few already steam-driven – meant that they did not restrict themselves to their home waters. Early in spring, herring was to be had in plenty on the west coast, and the bigger boats made their presence felt there.

The harbour of Stornoway, which had been redeveloped and extended in the 1860s (but only after a protracted struggle between the people of Stornoway and the owner of Lewis, Sir James Matheson – more of which later),[43] was capable of accommodating hundreds of boats and processing their catches. But it was a harbour jammed with East Coast boats. West Coast men found themselves having to leave their own small boats in some secluded inlet and sign up as fishermen and deck-hands on the larger ones. It caused no end of acrimony. During the latter half of the century, it was common practice for crofters and cottars to make their way, largely on foot, to the East Coast ports, to earn what they could on the boats fishing in the North Sea; in many years, a good living was to be had there, money which certainly helped to pay the rent of the croft. Women and girls, too, would frequently make their way to the ports such as Wick and make money in processing the catches; sometimes the women earned more than the men.[44] And since the East Coast herring season was slightly later than the West Coast one, it was possible to follow the fleets around the coasts and make a decent wage for half the year. Not only did fishermen migrate in season to the east coast, but it was common – at least in Skye – for men to head to the coast of Ireland to pursue a living there.

To give some idea of the extent of the fishing industry at the time of our proposed railway lines, we need look no further than the massive 660-page 'Ninth Annual Report of the Fishery Board for Scotland', which was published at the end of 1890.[45] It contains everything you could plausibly need to know about marine fishing in Scotland, and then some. Since it was an annual report, there are plenty of others to study, but we shall take 1890 as our average year.

(Before we look at the figures, please knuckle down to a minor lesson in recondite units of measurement. This report – and others like it of that era – talks of fish being measured in crans, barrels and hundred-weights (cwt). As a general guide, crans were used to measure the fish being offloaded from a fishing boat, and barrels were a measurement of fish having been gutted and prepared for onward shipment to market. Hundredweights also came into it, usually (but not always) after the fish had been dried. A 'cran' contained 37½ imperial gallons (one gallon = 160 fl.oz = 4.54 litres); thus a single cran was also 170.48 litres; or 3.5 cwt of fish. A 'barrel', on the other hand, contained 32 'English Wine gallons' (one such = 133 fl.oz = 3.77 litres); thus a single barrel contained 120.64 litres, or 2.5 cwt. It was reckoned that a single cran might contain about 750 herrings; a barrel could contain around 800–900 herrings;[46] the difference lay in discarded bones and guts. If the units of measure-ment confuse, let us put it more simply: a cran was a large basket with raw fish; a barrel was a bit smaller, and full of gutted fish. With that explanation, be content.)

In 1890, the total weight of all white fish (cod, haddock, ling, etc.) landed in all of Scotland was recorded with some precision: 5,864,488¼ cwt, having the value of £1,623,346. For herring, the numbers stacked up at 1,137,246½ crans (3,980,363 cwt), with a value of £827,072. Employed in the fishing industry were 47,150 fishermen and boys, and a further 62,122 men and women during the herring seasons. 14,352 boats were registered for fishing, of which still a very small number (118) were the modern 'beam trawlers' capable of sweeping up huge nets of fish: almost all of these new trawlers were from ports on the east coast, and none at all had their home-port in Stornoway.

On the west coast, 283,093 crans of herring were landed (a 30 per cent increase over 1889), of which almost half were landed in the Stornoway district: this 'district', for Fishery Board purposes, stretched from Ness at the top of Lewis down through the Long Isle as far as Barra Head. Of this harvest, Stornoway cured enough herring to fill 125,039½ barrels, representing an increase over the preceding decade of 65 per cent. (One can be sure of these figures if the odd half-barrel has been counted.) The Fishery Board was pleased to announce that this was an 'exceptionally successful season' in Stornoway. In a delicious cocktail of unlike units of measure, it was reported that here 604,837 cod, ling and hake were cured, of which 23,120 cwt were dried and 221 barrels pickled; 4,000 cwt of the dried fish went to Ireland, the rest being destined for Scotland and England. The total value of herring processed in Stornoway in 1890 amounted to £129,625, with a negligible amount for cod and haddock, lobsters and the like. In pounds sterling, hundredweights, crans or barrels, this was big business.

The equivalent figures for the Loch Broom district pale by comparison. 'Loch Broom' was defined as the entire coastline from Kinlochbervie in the north, through Lochinver and Ullapool, down to Red Point near Gairloch in the south. Here there were only 602 boats, mostly of the small inshore variety, and just under 2,000 men involved. Their 1890 fishing season was pithily described as 'indifferent', only 280 boats going after herring, and a shade over 3,000 crans being landed. This difference between the Stornoway and Loch Broom districts is important – the contemporary argument for railways was mostly about the forward transportation of fish landed in the Outer Hebrides, not simply on the mainland's west coast.

But, as we have noted before, the power in the fisheries lay not with Lewis fishermen, but with the East Coast crews. Of 1,500 boats registered in the Stornoway district, two-thirds were based in Lewis and Harris, the remainder in the Uists and Barra; but significantly, only a quarter of those were any larger than 30 feet in length and well over half were tiny boats, less than 18 feet long, quite unsuited for off-shore work. Of the Lewis boats, few were based in the town of Stornoway itself – the two largest 'fleets' were at Scalpay in the south-east and Carloway in the west. Most, therefore, were crofters' boats. What the local population contributed to the fishing was labour – the men crewed the fishing boats while the women processed the catch. According to counts taken by the Fishery Board in 1890, some 9,400 local people were employed in fishing and processing, with an additional 700 or so East Coast fishermen present during the season. In addition to those people employed in close personal contact with fish, there were also around 1,600 people employed in the western islands in the transportation of wood and hoops for barrels, in importing salt and in the carrying trade.

(If there is one other statistic which bears witness to the significance of fishing in the Western Isles, it is the tragic one cited by the Napier Report: that 'during the last thirty-five years not less than 293 Lewis fishermen were drowned at sea'.[47] In 1890 alone and for Scotland as a whole, 143 died at sea while engaged in fishing, eighteen of them on the west coast; a storm on 25 June took fifty lives around Wick.)

Clearly, during the fishing season, this entire commercial enterprise was vast. And for the crofters and cottars of Lewis, it was virtually the only way in which a living was to be made: either using their own boats or signing up on others, either gutting and packing in the local herring-stations or seasonally migrating to the east coast to do the same job there. It should be noted in passing that men from the Long Island regularly took themselves off to serve on Irish fishing boats in the 1880s and 1890s. And it was there that they found themselves washed over by Irish ideas as much as by Irish salt water.

Exports from Stornoway were impressively high: 61,372½ barrels (there's that half-barrel) were shipped off to foreign parts. Two-thirds of the total went to St Petersburg, the remainder to the Baltic ports of Germany – Königsberg (now Kaliningrad), Danzig (Gdansk), Stettin (Szczecin) and Hamburg. Although there was competition from Dutch herring-fleets, the Scottish industry had the advantage that fish was generally both caught and cured within a 24-hour period and was therefore of higher saleable quality. Much of the fish exported to the Baltic ports ended up in Russia. And all this in 1890, despite unwelcome protectionist measures from the Russian Imperial government, which necessitated 'strong representations' by Her Majesty's Ambassador to St Petersburg. So there were ships sailing directly from Stornoway to foreign parts with the processed catch (there is even mention of a ship sailing from Stornoway to the Black Sea port of Odessa with cured herring). Exporting was the easy bit; there was more of a problem with shipping fish to the much closer industrial cities of the British mainland. And that problem was railways – or the lack thereof.

In May 1889 John Anderson, secretary of the Callander and Oban Railway, reported to the Secretary for Scotland on the volume of fish being transported through the only two rail-heads on the west coast – Strome Ferry and Oban.[48] His report was decidedly downbeat, since it was his belief that a lack of proper shipping and rail infrastructure was holding back a boom in fishing. In 1888, he reported, 3,265 tons of fish came through Oban, and 4,810 through Strome. But there had been no great increase in these tonnages over the preceding decade. The duration of the rail-journey of a fish to London he put at around thirty-three hours, regardless of whether it was through Strome or Oban (or even, he predicted, for it was not yet built, the Mallaig connection). Anderson noted that in recent years, steamers had been sailing straight from Stornoway to places like Fleetwood (near Blackpool) to offload for the great cities of England, rather than pay railway freighting charges – which averaged about 3s 10d per hundredweight to London. But direct sea transport also meant an extra day in the journey.

Anderson was not an optimistic man – not only were local people not benefiting from the fishing; but: 'The working man in this country is unfortunately not a great eater of fish, preferring a chop or ham and egg for breakfast, or butcher meat for dinner.' Our only hope lay in the healthier eating habits of the Baltic nations and, maybe, should the Secretary for Scotland consider it, government subsidies for more steamers to Oban.

A Glasgow-based fish merchant and curer, writing to the Scottish Office two years later, was slightly more precise about the difficulties.[49] Working backwards from a deadline of 5 a.m. at the Billingsgate fish market in London, he stated that all West Coast fish had to be loaded onto the delightfully named 'Scotch Passenger Fish Train', which arrived in London at 3.50 a.m. To achieve this meant that fish had to leave Stornoway at 7 p.m. (thirty-three hours earlier) for Oban; or they could leave Stornoway at midnight to catch a later train at Aultbea. Either way, it was a lengthy journey for a dead fish.

*

There were two fishing lobbies on the Isle of Lewis: that of the fisher-men themselves, who struggled to eke out a living with their own boats or signed up with the East Coast fleet; and that of the fish-curers of Stornoway, whose business it was to gather in the harvest of the seas from as many boats as possible, as early in the season as possible. (Mr Anderson of Oban maintained that the fish-curers in Barra and Lewis were mostly 'English'.) The curers had a strong grip on the local fishermen, dictating prices and financing or providing boats and gear. It was in the curers' interests to maximise the fishing harvest; this meant striking deals with the East Coasters, as well as ignoring any form of 'close time' – a rest period during which herring were deemed not yet big enough to be sustainably caught, or were spawning. Any attempt to harvest these stocks would have longer-term negative consequences. There was an unofficial 'close time' on the west coast for herring, which lasted from mid April to mid May. The East Coasters felt under no obligation to recognise this ban; they had their own later 'close time' for North Sea herring, so presumably felt that one was quite enough.

At a time when herring stocks in the west were relatively low, between 1892 and 1895, the island fishermen and the East Coasters came into conflict on the matter. On 23 April 1892, there were reports of 'an indignation meeting' convened by Stornoway fishermen,[50] protesting at the incursion of the East Coast boats into West Coast waters while close time was in operation. On the following day, the police and the Scottish Office were advised that a boatload of Stornoway men had left harbour, intent on sailing to Loch Clash (Kinlochbervie) in order 'to intimidate fishermen who are to begin the early fishing there'. Almost certainly, this level of official attention to ill-defined threats of violence owed much to the very real events on Skye and Lewis in the preceding years: it was not desirable that such violence should be brought over by the boatload to the mainland. The Chief Constable of Ross and Cromarty was hurriedly dispatched to Kinlochbervie and was doubtless relieved to discover that, although the Stornoway men had arrived looking very fierce, no trouble ensued. His laconic telegram to London read: 'No disturbance Lewis men went home.'

But this was far from being the end of the affair. In the following year, in the same season, the Chief Constable kept a beady eye on his west coast, but was able to advise London that 'quietness prevails'. In that year, in any case, the East Coasters actually found no herring to catch in April or May. In early April 1894, despite two years of peace and quiet, the Fishery Board suggested that a gunboat be sent to protect the East Coasters. This nervousness may be explained by a report of events in Stornoway. In the first week of April, the Fishermen's Association of Stornoway 'issued a public notice . . . intimating that the close time would be held, as formerly agreed on, from 15 April to 15 May, and intimating that no herrings would be received in Stornoway between these dates'.[51] Clearly, this statement threw down the gauntlet to the fish-curing trade, which was eager to process any and all herring, big or small. 'The indirect challenge to active hostilities thus thrown out has been promptly taken up . . . by some persons who profess to speak for the other side, as when the towns-folk turned out to their work yesterday they found all the walls in the burgh placarded with large posters.' Stornoway had probably never seen anything like it. The placard was of some length, and the exciting bits read as follows:

> Fishermen, – Your leaders have declared their intention to ruin Stornoway. We do not believe you are all in sympathy with this policy, but you must all be branded with the intention until you repudiate it. We have denied your right to prevent fishing at Stornoway . . . If you think you can prevent us from carrying this out you are welcome to try. We defy you to do it . . . You will be met by equal measures . . . – an eye for an eye, or a tooth for a tooth . . . Stornoway shall not be ruined. This says the Vigilance Committee of the inhabitants of Stornoway.

Startled by the animosities now plastered all over the town, the local magistrates panicked. They contacted the Fishery Board, who in turn telegraphed London. With considerable promptness, on 20 April, sailing orders were issued to the spanking new torpedo-boat HMS *Niger*, which proceeded to Stornoway and remained there for a full month. No disturbances were noted. In the following year, taking no chances, another torpedo-boat was sent north – this time the equally new HMS *Renard*: one might be forgiven for wondering whether the Navy was using the anticipated disturbances simply as an excuse to play with its new boats. Confrontation continued in high season and in low: in December 1893, a frustratingly short news item reported that

> the fishermen of Broadbay, Lewis, yesterday captured a North of England trawler while engaged, the captors allege, working the trawl in Broadbay, within the three mile limit. The fishermen brought their prize to Stornoway, and handed her over to the fishery officer.[52]

It was not as if any of these confrontations should have come as a surprise to anyone. It had been known for some time that the East Coasters were flouting tacitly agreed conservation measures. Roderick Ross, medical officer of Lochs on Lewis, produced a long list of grievances before Napier in 1883: of these, 'The fourth grievance is destructive fishing – fishing herring on this coast when the herring are in an immature condition, and when they are spawning. This has done a great deal of damage to this parish . . . The remedy is a close time.'[53] In February of 1891, Charles Fraser-Mackintosh MP wrote to the Secretary for Scotland, noting that herring was vanishing from the Minch and that the East Coast boats were to blame. Having exhausted North Sea stocks, the East Coasters 'long for "new fields of devastation to carry on their deadly trade"', and were now undertaking trawling which will 'sweep the waters as bare as a billiard table'.[54]

The dip in the herring harvest was, as it happens, only a temporary one, lasting four or five years – but it was an indication of things to come. Wider opinion over the preservation of herring stocks was divided. In 1861, James Methuen of Leith, 'the greatest herring curer in the world', had voiced his concerns – 'The herring fisheries of Scotland have been the greatest and most productive in the world, and are the gift of God to man for food. Genesis 1: "Have dominion over the fish of the sea." Dominion does not mean extermination.' On the other hand, a government-sponsored report into the herring industry in 1877 decided that, since the gannets of Ailsa Craig caught an estimated twenty-one million herring in a season and the local fishing boats only twelve million, then, obviously, 'nothing that man has yet done, and nothing that man is likely to do has diminished, or is likely to diminish, the stock of herrings in the sea'.[55] History proved the Greatest Herring Curer correct and the Government – most surprisingly – wrong.

As we shall see, the animosity between fish-curers and fishermen also spilled over into the debates about railway lines to the west coast. But such high feelings were scarcely new. At the start of June 1883, on the very day that Lord Napier and his team were dropping in on the astonished residents of St Kilda, a 'battle' of sorts took place at Strome Ferry, at that time the western terminus of the railway from Dingwall. Essentially, the matter revolved around the observance of the Sabbath; the Free Church objected to railwaymen being asked to work on Sundays to transfer the herring catches from ship to train.[56] On 1 June 1883, a Friday, the Stornoway fishermen stayed in port, because to do otherwise would have meant either offloading their catch on a Sunday, or seeing it spoil by a delay until Monday; the Stornoway men had in any case spent the day listening to 'incendiary speeches' – even then! This was a 'demonstration of several thousand crofters', stirred up by the Land Law Reform Association to prepare for the Commission's visit:[57] by Saturday morning they were in no fit state to do any fishing. But, of course, the East Coasters had their own priorities. So it was that, just after midnight on Sunday 3 June, three steamers full of both fresh and kippered herring, which had been landed by East Coast boats and processed at Stornoway on Friday and Saturday, arrived at Strome Ferry. Unloading began at one o'clock in the morning, whereupon Sabbath-day protestors suddenly descended like Assyrians out of the surrounding night, put the crane and its driver out of action and prevented the unloading of fish-boxes. Fist-fights broke out; Sabbath-day reinforcements arrived. By daybreak, 150 protestors had taken possession of the pier and the unloading of fish had stopped completely. As the first reporter on the scene put it rather colourfully: 'By last advices, the Sabbatarian garrison were in undisturbed possession of the abandoned station and the decaying fish.'[58]

After several hours, six constables and their long-suffering chief arrived by special train from Dingwall (thereby proving to any doubters that railways had indeed some uses), but were so outnumbered that they could only stand by and look very stern indeed. Members of the Free Church attending Sunday service were encouraged – although it seems they needed little enough – to take up cudgels (literally) and join in. It was only at the stroke of midnight that the protest ceased abruptly, but with a bold warning that the Sabbatarians would all be back a week later. Four men were subsequently arrested, the arrest of one of them being delayed as a result of 'stoning of the police' by the man's neighbours – shades of the crofters' uprisings in Skye. Understandably jittery, the Chief Constable requested seventy soldiers and their officers from Edinburgh. These were placed on standby at Fort George the following weekend, and for the avoidance of mischance, a further sixty-one policemen from Airdrie were dispatched to a 'secret destination' – clearly one not at all far from Strome Ferry. On Sunday the 10th, however, realising that this time the authorities had the upper hand, the protestors simply stood and glowered as the Sabbath was broken by the herring. 'The affair has caused a great sensation in the county.'[59]

Even more of this kind of unpleasantness on Highland Railway territory might conceivably have occurred had the Highland gone ahead with its grandiose plans for transporting entire fishing boats across Scotland.[60] In 1869, the principal engineer on the Dingwall line was asked to prepare plans and a budget for changes to the railway which would permit boats to be loaded onto special wagons at Dingwall in the east or Strome Ferry in the west and transported within hours to the opposite side of Scotland, thereby avoiding a dangerous passage through the Pentland Firth. And although the railway was widened at Garve station specifically to allow 'boat-wagons' to pass each other – and despite preparing a purchase order for £580 to be spent on cranes – the Highland eventually decided to shelve the idea. All of which, from the point of view of a nervous young herring in 'close time', was most likely to the good.

If the 1913 statistics released by the Board of Trade are anything to go by, the good times for Scottish fishing continued right up to the war. A rather languid executive summary of the annual statistics[61] stated that the quantity of fish landed that year was just under 7.3 million hundredweight ('a fairly normal amount', yawned the statistician); the quantity of herring thereof merely 'an average one' of just under 4.5 million hundredweight. Some 90,000 persons found employment in the industry – of whom 38,250 were fishermen, 16,250 were gutters and packers, 14,500 in 'the carrying trade' and the remainder vexingly undefined. (In a minor aside of historical interest, the report also noted: 'The catch of whales has gone down, and the Fishery Board record their view that the supply is becoming depleted.' Indeed.) Across Scotland as a whole, the year of 'peak herring' was 1907, when 2.6 million barrels (455,000 tons) were caught, of which 70 per cent was exported. The figures for Stornoway are, however, slightly different: 1891 and 1898 were peak years, separated by a distinct slump in the intervening years, probably due to the occasional unpredictability of fish. These years tellingly coincided with the outbreak of 'close time' animosity between East and West Coast men. Exports, however, remained on a level in this depressed period, so that in the worst year, 1893, almost all of the herring catch was exported: this is suggestive of long-term fixed contracts with Baltic purchasers. Otherwise, the Stornoway figures averaged around 100,000 barrels per annum between 1877 and 1910, with between 50 and 70 per cent destined for the domestic market.[62]

The domestic market: therein lies much of our tale. As Mr Anderson of Oban pointed out, getting the fish to the UK market was problematic. Time and again, this conundrum was the main argument underpinning the promotion and construction of railways to the west coast of Scotland. The Napier Report put it succinctly: 'We are, however, of opinion that the fishing industry of the Outer Hebrides can never be fully developed until the railway is extended to the sea at some central point on the west of Inverness-shire.'[63]

4

'The Railway Would Be the Making of the Place'

Agitation for Railways and Better Communications

The Napier Commission was appointed under a Liberal government led by Gladstone; the Crofters' Act was passed under a Liberal government led by Gladstone. Also under Gladstone, in August 1885, the post of Secretary for Scotland was resurrected after a hiatus of 140 years. Now, at least, some attention was being paid to matters in the far north. In August 1886, largely as a result of the Irish Home Rule policy, the Liberal administration was replaced by a Conservative one under Lord Salisbury; but matters Scottish did not thereby vanish from the governmental agenda. The Highlands and Islands had been ushered onto centre stage by the events on Skye and the ensuing Napier Report, and could not easily be shooed off again; the recently formed Highland Land League succeeded in having five MPs elected at the start of 1886, and these MPs formed themselves into the short-lived Crofters' Party. They took their seats too late to have any influence on the drafting of the Crofters' Act; but who can say if the Act would have been any different had it been drafted slightly later? With their presence in Parliament alongside other members of the Liberal Party proper, and with the encouragement of newspapers, interest in the north-west and the islands continued and grew.

VISITATIONS BY POLITICIANS

'A Gardener Reading Livy and a Keeper Solving Calculus'

Thus it was that our indefatigable Liberal MP, James Caldwell, decided on a trip to Stornoway. In May 1889, *The Scotsman* printed the text of letters between Caldwell and his prominent party colleague Joseph Chamberlain – letters explicitly intended for publication.[1] Caldwell, as we have noted already, was a man sympathetic to the cause of improving the lot of West Highlanders. In his letter to Chamberlain, he reported on his fact-finding mission. 'I proceeded on 15th *ult.* to visit the island of Lewis, travelling over the route of the proposed railway from Garve to Ullapool, thence by steamboat to Stornoway, returning by steamboat via Strome Ferry. On the journey from Inverness to Ullapool, I was accompanied by Mr Paterson, engineer, Highland Railway Company.'

Caldwell reported to Chamberlain on the poverty on Lewis – which he stressed was 'not altogether' due to laziness; he explained that crofting alone would never provide a decent living, despite every effort being made to cultivate the appalling soil. He suggested optimistically that, under the new Crofters' Act, it should be possible for crofters to extend their holdings and so provide a standard of decent living. He then went on to describe major obstacles to a decent fishing industry: poverty forced some fishermen to sell off boats and gear; access to the markets was very limited; even access to the sea to launch boats was fraught with physical difficulty. Narrow-gauge railways were being proposed from Stornoway to Ness via Barvas and from Stornoway to Carloway, and to these he gave his full support. And, somewhat in the Irish tradition, he proposed State funding for any and all improvements. Caldwell took the opportunity to report that he was very impressed with the case for a railway line from Ullapool eastwards which, because of the problems in getting fish to the domestic market, was as much in the interests of the people of Lewis as it was of the people of the mainland. 'The expectation, therefore, is that both Stornoway and Ullapool will immensely benefit by the opening up of the proposed communications, each developing the fishing industry under its more immediate sphere.'

And then, when he returned to the mainland, the MP was greatly inspired by the progress of the pupils in the Ullapool board school, several of whom were learning Latin and Greek. Even more impressed was he by the report of a 'gardener who was reading Livy, and a keeper on an estate who was engaged in solving the differential calculus. These facts', he argued, 'tell of the progress which may be expected from such a population if opportunities of communication were within their reach.'

Railways, by now, were firmly on the agenda. Napier had recommended them. They constituted the solution for the transportation of fish, and thereby the salvation of the crofters and fishermen. Perhaps also they delivered the means by which learning, in all its many forms, could be nurtured amongst the common people.

Chamberlain replied in like form to Caldwell, agreeing that something ought to be done. He himself had been on a tour of Scotland and the Hebrides in 1887, so he was fully aware of conditions there. But now, making a slightly nervous comparison with the rebellious population of Ireland, he suggested that the condition of the crofters of Lewis 'is a permanent source of danger to the whole of the community, and their disaffection . . . may be a nucleus of widespreading and serious agitation'.[2] Chamberlain was a man greatly set against Irish Home Rule, a matter which had recently split the Liberal Party; he now feared the contagion would spread to Scotland. But his preferred solution to the immediate problem in Scotland was migration and emigration, rather than State assistance:

> it may be feared that the rapid increase of the resident population will quickly overtake the opportunities afforded them . . . and that even larger numbers than at present will be tempted to prefer a precarious subsistence in these ill-starved districts to the prospect of successful industry under more favourable conditions elsewhere in the United Kingdom or in the colonies.

Chamberlain's position, at least, was clear: one could avoid an Irish debacle by shunting the impoverished and disaffected Scots to industrial hell-holes, or the colonies.

Not to be outdone by the Liberal Party, the Conservative Secretary for Scotland – Schomberg Henry Kerr, 9th Marquess of Lothian – also made a trip to the farthest extremities of Scotland 'to investigate the condition of the people of Skye and Lewis', again with specific reference to the fisheries and transportation.[3] His was really not unlike a Royal visit: Lord Lothian travelled in some style aboard the Admiralty yacht *Enchantress,* accompanied by the naval fisheries protection vessel *Jackal.* (We remember that the *Jackal's* namesake and predecessor, a gunboat, had been in these waters several times in the preceding decade, specifically during the suppression of the 'Glendale Revolt', and again in 1886 when both crofters and landlords on Skye refused to pay their rates; but the new incarnation of the boat came in peace.)[4]

For two weeks in June 1889 – His Lordship sacrificed his Whitsun holiday – Lord Lothian took in Oban, Portree, Lochmaddy, Stornoway, Lochinver, Ullapool, Poolewe, Barra and Lochboisdale, before returning to Oban. Wherever he went, he was met by large delegations of local dignitaries, speeches on both sides were applauded and everyone was wined and dined. After all, as Lothian himself boasted in Stornoway, 'I am the first Secretary for Scotland who has come here' – not necessarily the best advertisement for governmental care of the people, but almost certainly true. Only half-jokingly did the welcoming party in Stornoway suggest that Lothian's visit was the most important since that of King James V, some 350 years previously.

The post of Secretary for Scotland had only recently been resurrected. There had been several such Secretaries between 1707 and 1746, before the office fell victim to the Jacobite Rebellion. After 1746, there was to be no more pandering to the Scots: that part of North Britain became just another responsibility of the Lord Advocate and then the Home Secretary. The post to manage 'Scotch affairs' was revived under Gladstone in August 1885, when an Act which had been toyed with for three years finally passed through both houses in Westminster. The responsibilities of the new Secretary covered many things, from roads to lunatics, fisheries to public parks, public health to turnpikes; and he had one finger in the education pie. As such, the post was not welcomed by everyone – the MP for Edinburgh and St Andrews Universities was heard to prophesy that it was

> intended to accentuate the differences between England and Scotland for the future, and, in my opinion, it will tend to convert Scotland into a Province, with the narrower peculiarities of Provincial existence. No country can less afford than Scotland to narrow the ambition of its educated classes or to parochialize its institutions. If it

separates itself from England in administration and education it need not be surprised if in time England becomes less of an outlet for Scotch enterprize.[5]

He had evidently not noticed that Scotland had already functioned as a 'province' for some considerable time. It is significant that the post was proposed, and filled, just at the time when the crofters' issue was hitting the headlines; there had been an equivalent position in Ireland for several centuries, so doubtless it was thought that a stripped-down version of this would do the job of calming tempers in Scotland and particularly of strangling in infancy any idea of Home Rule. But Lord Lothian found himself as the fifth occupant of the revived post, the previous four – all come and gone in the space of nineteen months – barely finding time to get their feet under the desk in Whitehall before being replaced.

And here the eminent Secretary for Scotland now was, like King James V before him, in Ultima Thule; he listened urbanely to all the reports and arguments presented to him. He spent some time on Lewis and Skye, and the construction of railways on both islands was discussed. He spent rather less time at Ullapool, where it was also the first time anyone so important had visited. Arriving there from Lochinver at 1 p.m., he was piped up to the Royal Hotel for lunch, which he enjoyed in the company of the Ullapool minister Angus J. Macdonald, Arthur Fowler of Braemore and other local notables. He made a short speech; whenever he mentioned the railway to Garve, he received much applause, but he took care to give no opinion in the matter. This did not discourage a deputation from bending his ear on the subject for quite some time, arguing that 'no other undertaking would be so well calculated to stop the rapid descent of the entire district into the state of abject poverty which had overtaken the Lews and some parts of the mainland'. After lunch he sailed up the loch with Fowler in the *Jackal* to view the precipitous slope of the hill at Braemore, then departed by sea for a brief inspection of Poolewe. And then he retired to a well-earned dinner on board ship.

As Lord Lothian discovered, wherever he went, he could not avoid talk of railways.[6] In Roshven (where it was wet and misty) and Mallaig, he sought the views of crofters and fishermen on matters related to fish, and was told quite bluntly that a railway from Fort William was required; when he processed in state to Broadford on Skye, he spoke briefly of this and that, and then made the mistake of mentioning railways to Ullapool, to Kyleakin and to Roshven, only to be sharply reminded of proposed railways on Skye itself – from Uig and Dunvegan to Portree and from Portree to Kyleakin. The Reverend Alexander Cameron of Sleat took the opportunity to challenge His Lordship on the imminent Light Railways (Ireland) Act, under which the Government would be spending 'not only thousands but, he thought, millions on the making of railways [in Ireland]. He thought the Highlands of Scotland were entitled to some consideration. (Applause).' Lord Lothian's self-satisfied reply to this ill-concealed jab met with applause, too, although it is rather difficult to see why: 'the position of the Government was like that of a lady with a great many lovers – and the claims of each would have to be considered before they bestowed their favours'. On abandoning Broadford for his supposed wooers in Portree, he was assailed by those who wished to construct a railway from the west coast of Skye to Portree and beyond. Myles McInnes, a local blacksmith, stated with endearing optimism that 'if there was a railway from Dunvegan to Portree, and a line to Mallaig [from Fort William], he had no doubt at all the people in Skye would become very prosperous'.

In the middle of Lord Lothian's grand tour among his great many lovers, the Skye agitators struck a jarring note. Prior to the Secretary for Scotland's departure from Portree, John Mackay of the Skye Land League – probably the same veteran land-rebel who had been a rebellious crofter at Glendale – sought an interview with him on the matter of 'the land question', which was 'at the bottom of much of the unhappy condition of the people'. Mackay argued in a letter to Lothian that 'the land was unequally distributed', and that the Crofters' Act and the Crofters' Commission had fallen well short of meeting the people's demands. The Land League 'took the liberty of pressing upon His Lordship that the Crofters Act should be amended so as to empower the Commissioners to divide all large farms into suitable holdings for smaller tenants, and so relieve the congestion' – clearly, contumacious crofters on Skye had not retired gracefully back to the soil. Finally, Mackay 'urged that the question of paramount importance was the placing of the people on equitable terms on the land, as the fishing was precarious on their coasts'.

This was certainly an alternative view to that of the pro-fishing, pro-railway lobby; and not at all one that Lord Lothian wished to engage with. As far as both Tories and Liberals were concerned, the Scottish land question had been resolved in 1886, and it was no longer mannerly to debate it. Lothian chose not to meet with Mackay, contenting himself with a letter dictated to his secretary on board the *Enchantress* stating in no uncertain terms that 'the general aspect of the land question, and any modification of the existing law on the subject, are matters entirely foreign to the object of Lord Lothian's visit to the West Highlands'.[7]

And with that, the Admiralty's yacht upped anchor and put Skye behind it, heading for Lochmaddy on Uist. Even here the Mallaig line was being politely promoted. Stornoway, the next stop, was worse again: a visit to Carloway on the west coast to inspect fishing infrastructure was immediately followed by an uncomfortable trip in a 'conveyance' back to Stornoway along the route of the proposed light railway. At one place, Lothian was 'memorialised' by the local people: if *The Scotsman* is to be believed, the content of the 'memorial' was apparently a matter of considerable debate beforehand on how to present the state of the fisheries – one faction 'holding that a good fishing would assist them in their claim for a railway, while another supported the representation of a bad fishing as being likely to enlist more sympathy for their condition'.[8] In the end, the 'good fishing' faction won the day – probably for the best: bad luck was unlikely to find much sympathy with a Victorian government.

In the various meetings and back-slapping receptions which followed in Stornoway, Lothian was urged to support the Carloway railway, while the Garve to Ullapool proposal was also mentioned in positive terms by fishermen. New harbours and piers and subsidies for bigger boats were sought, but Lord Lothian replied to each and every request with a patronising smile and the statement that 'it would be his duty to consider all the proposals laid before him'. At this point, he returned to his yacht, wined and dined the local bigwigs, and then sailed the following day to Lochinver. There he was met with a deputation who wished to have the Ullapool Railway 'Plus' scheme – i.e., to extend a Garve to Ullapool railway as far as Lochinver. In short order thereafter he had the claims of Ullapool itself pressed upon him, and then those of Aultbea and Poolewe. If he had not got the message by then, he was never going to. But, as he had told the people of Lewis: 'with reference to a railway on the mainland, he could not give an opinion as to where the terminus should be . . . How that could best be done was a matter for future consideration.'

'Future consideration': how those words would mock the ever-hopeful fishermen and crofters of the West Highlands and Islands.

ROADS AND RAILWAYS AND STEAMERS

'A Bold, Thorough-Going, Well-Planned
and Comprehensive Scheme'

Transportation was always a problem around the incredibly complex and varied landscape of the western Highlands and the islands. It still is. Certainly, no other part of the British Isles poses so many challenges in such a vast area; the topography is perhaps unique to all of Europe. Even today, the task of getting persons or goods to certain points of north-west Scotland is fraught with danger and excitement, not least of the problems being regular landslips on main trunk roads – possibly one consequence of a devastated and denuded landscape. The modern ferry network, too, is at the mercy of strong seas and stronger winds. Three hundred years of struggle have made a dent in the problems, but not fully resolved them.

The first real attempt to open up the Highlands (if we discount certain desultory attempts by the Romans) was made by General George Wade, under instruction from a London government that had been shaken by the first abortive Jacobite rising and was fearful of a second one. Between 1726 and 1732, General Wade oversaw the building of four major roads which sliced open the Highlands: from Crieff to Dalnacardoch; from Dunkeld to Inverness; from Inverness to Fort William; and from Fort Augustus to Dalwhinnie – a total of around 300 miles. The traces of the roads and their bridges are easily visible today, even though most of the roads are returning to the soil. Wade's efforts were supplemented by those of his successor, Major William Caulfeild, who added a further 800 miles of road before 1767. Some of Caulfeild's roads still do service today, as emergency backup for more modern roads (for example, the A82 at the 'Rest and Be Thankful').

The purpose of these roads was clearly to facilitate troop movements and discourage independently minded natives; amusingly, the 1745 rebels also made good use of them to speed across country.

At the very start of the nineteenth century, the multi-talented Thomas Telford turned his attention to the transportation problems of his native land. Under his guidance over a period of some twenty years, almost 1,000 miles of new road were built, along with countless bridges, harbour improvements, canals and not a few churches. And the village of Ullapool. Many of these structures and roads still do good service. But most effectively for transportation, he oversaw the improvement of the Crinan Canal and the construction of the Caledonian Canal, both still functional today, both capable in their heyday of greatly easing the transportation of goods between the four corners of Scotland. Telford had the good fortune to find patrons in William Pulteney, purportedly Britain's richest man and promoter of the fishing stations of Wick, Kinlochbervie and Ullapool, and Nicholas Vansittart, later to become Chancellor of the Exchequer. In short, he had government support and – far more importantly – government funding for his extra-ordinary plans and achievements. At a later date, as the post-Napoleonic depression began to set in, the Government continued to provide finance through the Public Works Loans Act of 1817, which aimed to fund the relief of the 'Poor of Great Britain' by employing them usefully in public works and fisheries. Under Telford, some of the major roads to the west coast were also opened up: Fort William to Arisaig, Glengarry to Loch Hourn, Glenmoriston to Kyle of Lochalsh.

Wade and Caulfeild opened up the main cross-country routes; Telford opened up some of the lesser glens; and so, in the second half of the nineteenth century, it fell to the railways to deploy technological advances and improve the speed at which people and goods could travel across these routes. The major difference here, however, was that Wade and Telford had the purse of the British government yawning open for them: money was produced, things happened. The railways, by contrast, were funded largely by private capital seeking high returns, which introduced an element of danger and excitement; or, for the avoidance thereof, the heavy hand of caution. Railway investors were not at all anxious to venture to the very edges of the ocean just because it seemed like a good idea, or lay down unprofitable lines up glens to ease the lives of a small and impoverished population. 'Public good' had come face to face with capitalism. Where it was possible to sniff out a profit, railways were duly constructed. Where profit appeared elusive, then no railways were built – unless, due to some governmental oversight, finance became available. There was no Wade or Telford of the railways.

That the problems were not fully addressed until very late in the nineteenth century is not necessarily a surprise; after all, the resident population had almost no money and not much of a voice. The easiest way to move goods or people was by sea, and it was the shipping company of David Hutcheson & Co. that first began to run regular services up and down the west coast from around 1850 onwards; in 1879, the company was taken over by David Macbrayne. Smaller cargoes could be moved by, for example, the Clyde Puffers, but it was the larger steamers which took up the strain. The steamer routes were many and varied, and in theory they offered relatively swift and painless travel options to and from these more inaccessible parts of Britain. Macbrayne's full timetable included practically every harbour and village you've ever heard of, and some you may not; in all, around 120 places large and small were visited by Macbrayne's boats. These stretched all the way from Thurso in the north to Islay in the south. Many of the smaller places would have been visited as part of longer routes to the main ports such as Castlebay, Loch Ephort (near Lochmaddy), Stornoway, Portree and Oban.

As a quaint reminder of glory days, the 1890 Macbrayne's 'Summer Tours' brochure alerted travellers to the company's steamer service between Fort William and Inverness; this was undertaken by a very small boat along the Caledonian Canal, and the 55-mile journey lasted about four and a half hours. (When the Napier Commission ended its summer tour at Lismore, in August 1883, it was by this very route that they returned to civilisation and caught the train south.)[9] But in the face of competition from the railways, the Inverness service – in its final days a weekly freight service only – did not last much longer. Although Macbrayne ruled the seas and continued to do so for many decades, he had no control over land-based transport. In one rearguard action in 1887, he challenged the promotion of the Clyde, Ardrishaig and Crinan Railway, which threatened his virtual monopoly of the western seaboard. Despite being approved, the plan for this railway – a little network of lines linking Dunoon to Furnace, via an intervening ferry over Loch Fyne, to Lochgilphead and the Crinan Canal – was finally abandoned in 1892. The abandonment was something of a pyrrhic victory for Macbrayne, since the attentions of the investors were then concentrated on a railway to Fort William and Mallaig. Macbrayne fought that one, too. And lost.

When Macbrayne had taken over Hutcheson's shipping company, there were about twenty steamers in operation; by 1890, there were thirty-three – sixteen of them for passengers only, the remainder for both freight and passengers. In an effort to keep down costs, about half of the fleet was acquired second-hand and kept as long as possible; in 1914, seventeen of the company's 'major' ships had been in service for at least twenty-five years. One, the *Glencoe*, was then a sixty-eight-year-old veteran (we shall come across this ship again later).[10] The fleet was not only deployed on regular timetabled sailings, but was also made available for special summer cruises and – as occasion demanded – for the swift transportation of policemen and soldiers to the trouble spots of Skye and Tiree. In April 1882, for example, it was the steamship *Clansman* that brought fifty of Glasgow's finest to Portree to assist in delivering eviction orders at Braes;[11] and in November 1884, the MV *Lochiel* was chartered to the Government for three months as a floating barracks for the policemen keeping the peace in northern Skye. Laudably, on that occasion, the captain and most of the crew of the *Lochiel* resigned in protest.[12] This same *Lochiel*, incidentally, had been one of the two ships involved in the Sabbatarian stramash at Strome Ferry the previous year: Sail Macbrayne's and See Some Action.[13]

Macbrayne's fares were not necessarily cheap: a typical steerage fare from Stornoway to Oban might set you back either 17 shillings single or £1 5s 6d return, and from Oban to Glasgow another 17 shillings (single) – so, around £2 10s for a one-way trip from Stornoway to Glasgow; something to think twice about. Nor were the journeys particularly fast, the Stornoway–Oban trip taking around ten or twelve hours, and the voyage from Oban to Glasgow another seven and a half hours.[14] Other steamship services were, of course, available – the Western Isles Steam Packet Co., the Islay Steam Packet Co. and even those operated by the Highland Railway. But these were no match for Macbrayne, and soon folded.

Much like today, steamer services were subject to the vagaries of Atlantic weather and sundry acts of a malevolent god. Not only would

services be cancelled altogether in bad weather, but delays – occasionally stretching into days – were a common feature, and the cause of bitter
complaint. While the steamers were sometimes scheduled to connect
conveniently with such trains as serviced the west coast, frequently – and
inconveniently – they did not. A typical situation would be that some
accident or breakdown had incapacitated one steamer, leaving gaps in
the timetable, mails not delivered and fish at the dockside.[15]

Not much has changed, the stoical CalMac customer today might
think.

In early 1891, a deputation from the Ross and Cromarty Liberal
Unionist Association, largely composed of gentlemen from Stornoway,
had an audience with George Goschen, the Tory Chancellor of the
Exchequer; they were there to 'call the attention of the Government
to the dissatisfaction that had been expressed by the islanders at the
unpunctuality of Mr Macbrayne's steamers'.[16] The deputation was not
in London to seek improvements to the steamer service, but to ask for
its partial replacement by railways on Lewis and on the mainland
(Ullapool or Aultbea). To be fair, such chronic problems were not all
the fault of the steamer company; but this was clearly a situation which
could be vastly improved by some intelligent and forward-looking
central planning.

No such thing existed.

Railways in the nineteenth century had the potential to bring many
benefits to a population: raw materials and manufactured goods, food-
stuffs and people could be transported more swiftly and cheaply;
remote districts could be connected to larger communities in which
there were better medical facilities and institutions of learning; mail
and newspapers could be delivered to the farthest corners of the land
within hours, rather than days; offices of government and justice could
be reached without delay; transport would be swifter and more reliable – barring leaves on the line – than by road or sea. As the Reverend
Duncan Finlayson stated to the Napier Commission, apropos of the
Kinlochbervie area, 'the railway would be the making of the place.
The means of communication are very bad.'[17]

There were downsides to railways, admittedly: the movement of
goods on the Sabbath, the ease with which policemen and soldiers
could be whisked to trouble spots, dreadful accidents with loss of life

and limb, noise and smoke. Several crofters lamented to Napier that the railways had taken away their other livelihoods (as cattle-drovers and lime manufacturers) and others that the railway companies had taken the most fertile parts of their meagre allotment of land to put down their tracks.[18] But these negatives were far outweighed by the positives. In 1889, a Scottish Liberal newspaper had declared: 'It is not the making of one or two short branch lines that will suffice, but a bold, thorough-going, well-planned and comprehensive scheme' of railways up and down the entire west coast, as well as on Skye and Lewis. 'Government', it proclaimed, 'must not grudge a little outlay in the beneficent work of ameliorating the hard lot of a large and deserving section of the population.'[19]

London politicians had looked at Ireland and decided that the subsidising of railways was a Good Thing, considering all the social and economic benefits they brought to distressed areas. That the Government and its representatives, apparently so sure of the railway solution, found it difficult to contemplate subsidies for Scottish railways is curious; arguably the disconnect between lofty ideal and sad actuality is partly due to the iron grip that the private companies had on Scottish (and British) railways. In other parts of Europe, things were done differently. In France, the planning of railways was effectively centralised from the 1840s onwards, and the State itself constructed the lines; in Russia, the railway was purely and simply a State institution; in Germany, after the unification of its component states in 1871, the railway companies were nationalised; similar policies were pursued in Belgium, Italy and Austro-Hungary; and the Swedes judged that it was perfectly satisfactory for the main-line railways to be constructed by the State. But Britain, the foremost industrialised country and the place where railways began, disdained such policies as arrant nonsense, only fit for Europeans or the simple Irish.

Why was so much hot air expended on encouraging railways, by politicians – from the Secretary for Scotland upwards and downwards – and by newspapers of every respectable shade? The answer is that this was something of a diversionary tactic. Not a conscious one, however – that would be paying too much of a compliment to the British establishment. The underlying problem, admitted by Lord Napier as much as by land-agitators, was the inequity of landownership. For the agitators, and for many crofters and cottars, the solution lay in the redistribution of land amongst those from whom it had been taken. For the legislators and the landowners, the solution lay in switching attention from land to sea: the land was restricted, but the seas were boundless. Exploitation of the sea meant promoting the fisheries. If the fisheries could be made successful, thereby improving the income and standard of living of crofters, then the social and political problems would surely go away. To make the fisheries work profitably and effectively, better transportation options were needed. And better transportation options meant investing in more and improved railways. As a strategy, it made complete sense.

And so we now turn our attention to the complete foul-up, by government and private enterprise alike, of this laudable endeavour.

5

'Encumbering Rocks and Great Hilliness'

The Garve to Ullapool Railway Proposal

Transportation to and from the north-west was not in a good state. Roads were poorly maintained, steamer services were frequently random and persistently late, railways were many miles away. All very twenty-first-century, one might argue. In September 1888 there was a terrible accident at Braemore: it was reported that

> the mail coach left Garve for Ullapool on Wednesday afternoon with a large complement of passengers. When driving down Corrie Halloch, a dangerous and very steep decline, the pole gave way, and the horses, feeling the pressure of the vehicle, became quite unmanageable, and bolted down the brae at a great rate, throwing the conveyance violently on its side and smashing it to pieces. All the passengers were thrown out, but with the exception of two, who were seriously hurt, they all escaped with a few bruises . . . Had the accident happened a few yards further down, the results would have been dreadful, as the road at that particular spot runs almost on the edge of a precipice at least 150 feet in depth.[1]

This incident, whilst exciting for those involved, was not unusual; as in much of the rest of the Highlands, the roads and the methods of transportation in the county of Ross and Cromarty were primitive. To be in a coach, even one that tipped over, was sheer luxury. For the average traveller, almost all of the west coast of Scotland north of the Clyde was inaccessible except by steamer, until the Dingwall to Strome Ferry railway was completed in 1870, and then the Oban railway in 1880. And, as we have seen, even the steamers were notoriously unreliable. Encouraged, perhaps, by the hints given out by the Napier Report, a campaign for improved communications began.

THE ULLAPOOL RAILWAY PROJECT

'Quite Impossible that Any Such Proposal
Could Be Entertained'

We have a precise date for when a proposal to build a railway between Garve and Ullapool first appeared: during Lord Lothian's visit to Ullapool in 1889, he was advised that 'four years ago the people of Lochbroom were moving for the construction of an Ullapool railway'.[2] And indeed, according to a letter later written by one of the promoters, Major Houston, there had been 'an influential meeting' in Ullapool on 4 May 1885, at which 'resolutions were passed declaring the necessity of railway communication from Ullapool to the south'.[3] Later in the same month, there was a flurry of articles in, and readers' letters to, the *Ross-Shire Journal* of Dingwall, which drew attention to the new proposal. On 15 May, for example, Lady Matheson of Lewis was reported as having inspected that fine body of men, the 'Ullapool Volunteers', and in the attendant hours of patriotic speeches and flag-waving, a railway from Garve to Ullapool was being talked up. On the 18th, a letter was written to the newspaper, urging government to spend money on the Garve to Ullapool railway rather 'than spend uselessly their millions on railways on the sandy desert of the Soudan or on the ungrateful fallehs of Egypt'. (Foreign aid? Pah! Is it not gratifying to encounter that familiar angry tone of letters to British newspapers down the ages? This letter was penned by one 'Seth-Bhraonich'. The practice of using amusing pseudonyms when writing to newspapers was all the rage in Victorian times: this cod-Gaelic one means literally 'also drizzly', or possibly 'also of Loch Broom'). On the 29th, 'A Native of Lochbroom' wrote, congratulating 'Seth-Bhraonich', and making particular mention of the contribution of Mr Macleod, 'the admirable, spirited teacher of the Lochbroom (Inverlael) Public School at the meeting held in connection with the proposal'.[4] In the spring of 1885, then, the idea had surfaced, was making the rounds, and was finding popular local support.

There was evidently a lull of a couple of years before things began to happen. The Honorary Secretary of the Garve and Ullapool Railway, Mr P. Campbell Ross of Ullapool, gave a brief history of events thus far in a letter to *The Scotsman* in March 1890 (and more of this letter later). According to him, the line was first proposed in 1885, and there had been no objections to the proposal. 'When we revived the movement in October 1888', again no one objected. Only in May 1889, when it looked likely that there would be governmental assistance, was there any opposing party (he meant, as we shall see, the bitter rivals in Aultbea, down the coast). But there was no self-interest here: 'My committee, and the friends who support us . . . were guided entirely by considerations of the importance to the public at large of having destitution banished – not by means of eleemosynary aid . . . but by giving them an opportunity of earning an honest livelihood . . .'[5]

Mr Ross had a way with words.

Propelled by self-interest or not, in early 1889 things began to move; the proposers had organised themselves into a 'committee', complete with Ross as secretary. It was not all plain sailing. On the occasion of Caldwell's brief trip to the north-west, which we noted earlier, local landowner and famed railway engineer Sir John Fowler not only turned down an invitation to chair a welcoming supper, but proceeded to pour a bucket of cold water over the whole idea of a railway to Ullapool: 'until more information has been obtained respecting the proposed Ullapool and Garve Railway, I should not feel justified in allowing my name to be associated with it'. He wanted to acquire 'reliable data' on the cost and the route of the railway; he wanted a proper survey done. Sir John had not become one of the richest and most famous railway engineers of his time by pursuing pipe-dreams. He signed off his letter by insisting that Ross read it out both to his committee and to Caldwell, so that no one could be left in any doubt.[6] This was probably not the reply the Ullapool committee really wanted.

Mr Ross carried out his duties as secretary to the committee both frequently and conscientiously; over the course of 1889 and the following years, he fired off letters, memoranda, copies of petitions and other supporting documentation to the Secretary for Scotland, and almost any MP who made the mistake of sounding interested. The reaction was not always what he hoped for: when he wrote to Whitehall in early January of 1889, sending on a copy of a resolution passed at a public meeting in the Loch Broom area, an under-secretary (R. W. Cochran-Patrick – until 1885 Conservative MP for Ayrshire North) in the Scottish Office in Dover House scribbled dismissively on the file: 'Yes, but quite impossible that any such proposal cd. be entertained.'[7] In the early summer of 1889, Ross put together a three-page foolscap document for handing to the Secretary for Scotland at lunch.[8] It lauded the waters of the Lochbroom area as sheltered places teeming with fish. It would also be an excellent location for a Royal Naval Reserve station, not to mention a terminus for ferrying passengers, livestock, fish and mail to and from Stornoway. All of this was backed up with detailed estimated revenues from steamer, mail and passenger traffic.

While Ross was assailing London, he and others were also laying siege to the Inverness offices of the Highland Railway, which jealously guarded a monopoly of the railways north and west of Inverness. In early February 1889, the Highland had been sent letters from 'inhabitants of Loch Broom' (i.e. Mr Ross), asking that the company give its support to the Ullapool Railway. In reply, Andrew Dougall, General Manager of the Highland Railway, indicated that the Highland was prepared to work a Garve to Ullapool railway on what he was pleased to call 'reasonable terms'; he also wished to know how much 'substantial support' there was from local landowners.[9] In April, despite – or because of – his stated concerns about 'reliable data', Sir John Fowler wrote to the Highland, asking that their engineer should conduct a 'flying survey', which Murdoch Paterson duly did for the princely sum of £80. He did this in the temporary company of James Caldwell MP, when the latter was on his way to Ullapool and Lewis. A year later, Sir John sent a telegram to Dougall, suggesting his own 'reasonable terms' for working the new railway.[10] 'Reasonable' is never actually defined by anyone.

As a result of letters, telegrams and relentless ear-bending, the Ullapool line was being mentioned in debates in the House of Commons in early March 1889,[11] and was in the same year the subject of investigations by the renowned 'radical' Liberal Joseph Chamberlain, as well as being elegantly evaded by Lord Lothian (as we have seen above). Progress in Britain in the late nineteenth century, however, required the intervention of persons of more exalted rank, financial clout and social significance than Members of Parliament. In short, it required the Matheson clan and the Fowler family.

THE PROMOTERS OF THE ULLAPOOL RAILWAY

'These Lands are Mine'

Quite who was on the Garve to Ullapool 'Executive Committee' apart from P. Campbell Ross is a little uncertain. There was certainly the Rev. Angus J. Macdonald; probably one or two local businessmen; doubtless also Arthur Fowler, eldest son of John and frequent resident of Braemore House, the 'big house' on the estate purchased by John Fowler in 1865. Sir John himself was almost certainly on the Committee, but very much in a consultative capacity: he made himself useful when technical discussions required it, but otherwise took little active part in the work of promotion. Indeed, there was a move at an early stage to have him removed, due to persistent lack of attendance at meetings. His son Arthur was subsequently one of the legal 'promoters' of the railway, and his fellow promoters were the Mathesons.

As well as Lewis, the mainland village of Ullapool was at this period owned by Lady Mary Jane Matheson, the widow of the 1st Baronet of the Lews, Sir James Matheson. James (1796–1878) was a founder of the firm Jardine & Matheson, a trading and banking firm in the Far East, still flourishing today (head office: Bermuda), but best remembered for its utterly disreputable role in the so-called Opium Wars with China (Chinese authorities objected to opium being imported by European traders, European traders imposed their will; just the usual *modus operandi* of imperialism) A satisfyingly fawning 'History of the Mathesons' of 1882 glossed over this disgraceful episode as follows:

> In 1839, when serious differences arose between the British and Chinese Governments, Mr Matheson rendered most important services to the Civil authorities of his native country, as well as to the officers of the army and navy.[12]

James returned to Britain in the 1840s, loaded down with a very large fortune indeed, and proceeded to snap up the Isle of Lewis (in 1844, for £190,000), the village of Ullapool (in 1847, for £5,250, from the Countess of Cromartie) and various other parcels of land on the main-land. In 1843, he had married Mary Jane Perceval, a daughter of the illegitimate son of Spencer Perceval, the only British prime minister (so far) to have been assassinated. They had no children: on James's demise, the estate passed to his widow and, on her death in 1896, to their nephew Donald Matheson.

The Matheson family as a whole proved itself quite adept at making a mint of money. A nephew of Sir James had followed him into the family business in the Far East and also returned with unimaginable wealth: Sir Alexander Matheson (1805–86), 1st Baronet of Lochalsh (and Attadale and Ardross) was the son of Margaret Matheson, sister of Sir James, who had married John Matheson (a confusion of identical surnames) of Attadale. Alexander became a director of the Highland Railway after 1880. Like his uncle James, Alexander married (as his third wife) a granddaughter of the hapless Spencer Perceval, who thereby at least proved himself of some use to posterity. Alexander was not short of ready cash either: on his return to Scotland in 1840, he purchased estates to the value of around £800,000 (in nineteenth-century money: around £80 million today);[13] these were concentrated mostly around Loch Duich and Lochalsh, but were also spread over Ross-shire (it was partly on these estates that the objectionable Walter Winans had rented some of his vast shooting playground). In total, he had an annual income from his estates of £23,000. Some three or four decades after his purchases, the Napier Commission was informed by his factor that Alexander had 'spent every penny derived both from the east and west coast estates somewhere on the estates'. When ques-tioned more closely, it emerged that £205,000 in total had been spent; arithmetically speaking, the expenditure does not come anywhere close to the income.[14]

Alexander Matheson had clear views about farms and crofts: in his own submission to Napier, he made the bold statement that 'I have made up my mind on no account to break up a farm to make crofts . . . At the same time I won't evict a single tenant I have so long as they pay their rents.' A list of the 359 farms and crofts on his west coast estates showed that 154 of them gave him an annual rent of less than £4 – indicative of tiny acreage; in contrast, twenty-eight farms yielded between £30 and £900 per annum. Not surprisingly, then, he expressed a fond hope for his crofters: 'I would be glad if one half of them would go to America or somewhere.'[15]

Despite protestations to the contrary, the Mathesons uncle and nephew were by no means averse to evicting crofters from their vast land holdings. In the 1870s, Alexander was busy evicting tenants from his more fertile Easter Ross estate. In the aftermath of the Strome Ferry Riots of June 1883, when locals prevented the trans-shipment of fish on the Sabbath, he identified some arrested men who worked on his estate, and sacked them (but strenuously denied this to the Napier Commission).[16]

Sir James, for his part, acted to remove tenants from his Lewis estate over 1,300 times between 1847 and 1851, as well as encouraging emigration, by the simple means of subsidising it.[17] In 1871, he stated that any crofters owing more than two years' rent and refusing his offer of free passage to Canada would be evicted. Forty-eight crofters were evicted in 1851, many being moved into overcrowded townships around Uig. He spent vast amounts on improving his estate, but nothing on improving crofts or housing. But because he paid for emigration (of 2,715 people between 1848 and 1851), he retained something of a good reputation.[18] In a memorandum submitted on behalf of his Lewis estate to the Napier Commission, it was claimed he had spent £11,000 on 'emigration'. Doubtless a worthwhile investment.[19] He had bought himself a large steam-yacht (the *Mary Jane*) in 1846, and in February of the following year the yacht took some 200 young seasonal migrants to Glasgow, free of charge, so that they could earn money to send home. (The steam-yacht was in 1851 sold on to Hutcheson & Co., was later renamed the *Glencoe,* and steamed up and down the west coast under Macbrayne's colours until 1931. When it retired it was one of the oldest operating steamships in the world.)

Not everything that James Matheson did was either selfless or welcome. The story of the Stornoway foreshore is of some interest.[20] In July 1862, Sir James applied to the Treasury to be granted full possession rights to the foreshore which lay in front of his beautiful new castle overlooking the upper reaches of Stornoway Bay. The foreshore in question stretched for more than six miles between Arnish lighthouse in the west round to Holm Point in the east, and included all the sea frontage of Stornoway. He had a strong objection to fishermen using the foreshore for 'purposes which are offensive in themselves' (fires, tarring, repairing nets) and which were immediately adjacent to his 'private pleasure grounds'. The land included the 'Big Quay', a pier located on the opposite shore to the castle. There was an implication in his request that he would improve and manage the pier, although no actual commitment was given. In November of the same year, the Treasury granted Matheson's application, on receipt of £400; the entire foreshore was deemed to be part of the Crown Estate, and the Treasury was quite at liberty to sell it on as it saw fit.

It was only in the following February that the people of Stornoway realised what had happened, and they were not best pleased. Not only was the foreshore traditionally considered in the western Highlands and islands as a community resource; but worse, the Big Quay had been built largely by public subscription in 1816 – £311 had come from local contributions, the balance of £115 from the landowner who had preceded Matheson; locals unable to pay had donated their labour towards the construction. For almost fifty years the pier had been managed by a small committee, and pier-dues were collected for maintenance. In short, the pier was under community ownership, something Matheson had chosen to ignore and the Treasury had not bothered to check. To make matters worse, sixty or so Stornoway townsmen had been induced in 1860, by Matheson, to request that he should arrange an Act of Parliament to bring the harbour under proper management, to which end, the community would hand over their accumulated pier dues of £259 9s 5d.

When it was discovered that no such Act had been applied for, and that Matheson had now bought the foreshore from under their feet (at a net cost to him of £140 10s 7d), they were incensed. Letters and petitions were written by fishermen and traders, the local MP was collared and goaded into action. Finally, after two years of stonewalling by Matheson's lawyers, the two parties came to an agreement that the pier would be owned and managed by a Board of Trustees – three members from the town and three nominated by Matheson, with Matheson or his factor as chairman. (Matheson's Edinburgh solicitors wrote to the town confirming this, but sowed some confusion by referring to the disputed construction as 'the Big Quay at Stromness'. Lawyers, eh?) It is probable that Matheson had the best of intentions when trying to take over the quays and foreshore, but he did so in a manner which typified even the most benign of landowners – by utterly ignoring local feelings and tradition.

It was John Murdoch the land reformer who pointed out to the Napier Commission that James Matheson's huge outlay on his estate (£134,000) did not, in fact, much benefit the crofters or cottars. The improvement of land – trenching, draining and levelling – was restricted to about 2,000 acres, including the 600-acre grounds of Stornoway Castle, the Mathesons' large house overlooking the foreshore. 'Not much', said Murdoch, quoting from an official document of 1881, 'has been done with the crofters.' But the writer of that official document was at pains to produce an excuse: 'When it is remembered that there are about 3500 crofters' houses on the island, including squatters, and that wood, lime, and slates have all to be imported, it can well be imagined what a large and expensive task the thorough improving of the crofters' holdings really is.'[21] Indeed.

After James Matheson's death in 1878, his wife took over the administration of the estate. Although inheriting the estate at a time when land agitation was beginning to flourish, she was no pushover for those who were keen on reform. When, in January 1888, cottars on the west coast of Lewis approached Lady Matheson, asking her to divide up a newly vacant farm for crofting land, she replied loftily: 'These lands are mine, and you have nothing to do with them.' She was playing a rather risky game: in 1888 and 1889, Lewis was afire with acts of civil disobedience – land raids, destruction of cattle and sheep, illegal deer-hunts; the Lewismen were imitating the Skyemen, it seemed. The cottars who had been turned away by her Ladyship took to tearing down fences and walls on the vacant farm, which led to violent confrontations with the police. Land League meetings took place in every township, where a later enquiry encountered 'half-clad and half-starved people living in squalor within wretched and overcrowded houses'; 'lawlessness' manifested itself everywhere. As on Skye, reinforcements of police and soldiers had to be dispatched from the mainland. Extraordinary events took place at Aignish, a large sheep-farm on the peninsula just north of Stornoway: here, it was decided by around a thousand land-raiders that the cattle and sheep occupying the land should be driven away and set to graze on the lush green pastures that constituted the gardens of Stornoway Castle.[22]

Lady Matheson attracted some attention in her own right, and not for the best reasons. In 1889, in a parliamentary debate about providing money to relieve the worst affected island communities, Mr Anderson, the member for Elgin and Nairn, put it exquisitely bluntly: the Government's

> chief proposal as to land is to give £10,000 to emigration. Now, the Hon. Gentleman who introduced the Amendment has said, and I think very truly – if he did not say it, at any rate I will say it – that the payment of that £10,000 is simply putting so much money into the pocket of Lady Matheson – and here I would tell the Government that we intend, or at least I, certainly, intend, to oppose that grant altogether, for the reason that the Government has selected certain parts of Scotland that they intend to benefit. Why is the estate of Lady Matheson only to be benefited by this grant? If you are to introduce a scheme of State-aided emigration – as to the policy of which I have grave doubts – I cannot understand why one estate should be mainly benefited . . . Their attempt is a small patch-work attempt, which will do no good to anyone but the landlord.[23]

Lady Mary Matheson was one of the promoters of the Garve and Ullapool Railway. From what we now know of her and her late husband, we might be justified in asking why she should have bothered. The answer would probably be that it was to promote a project which supported fishing and not crofting. Additionally, society would find it easier to reach her island kingdom for summer visits. And, in any case, she owned Ullapool: a railway might prove profitable to the village, and therefore herself. A later newspaper report suggested that she had dipped into her purse to the tune of £2,000 to promote the scheme; that would all have been swallowed up by the deposit for the Act. But she could afford it.[24]

Several of her relatives were also promoters. Donald Matheson was her nephew, the son of Sir James's brother; on Mary's death in 1896, Donald inherited her estate. Donald's son Duncan was an army man by trade, and sometime Governor of H.M. Prison in Ipswich; he inherited Lewis from his father in 1901, but sold up to Lord Leverhulme in 1918. With the inherited estate came inherited attitudes – in 1913, Duncan was implacably opposed to the (Scottish) Congested District Board's plans to create new crofts on Lewis.[25] Another promoter of the railway was Major James Flower Houston, a nephew of Lady Mary through her sister Anne; Houston was also the brother-in-law of

Sir Alexander Matheson's daughter (by his second wife – Alexander's third, you will recall, being a granddaughter of Spencer Perceval); Major James's mother was, if you hadn't already spotted it, yet another granddaughter of Mr Perceval.

Somewhat spoiling the effect of a tight family business was the fifth promoter, John Arthur Fowler, commonly known as 'Arthur' to distinguish him from his more famous father, Sir John. Fowler the elder (1817–98) had been, along with Benjamin Baker, the chief engineer for the Forth Bridge. He had made his money in railway engineering since the 1840s, principally in London, where he engineered the Metropolitan underground railway (he had a short life-sized mock-up of a Metropolitan Railway tunnel built in the garden of Braemore House – the nearest Braemore ever came to a railway). He was at the top of his profession, still much in demand throughout the Empire in the 1880s. Even as late as August 1895, aged seventy-eight, he charged the Highland Railway a £500 fee for his work as consulting engineer on the Inverness to Aviemore line. This was a man who appeared to have boundless energy. In photographs from the 1890s, he appears keen-eyed, sporting a white 'neck-beard' – one of those Victorian styles which made it appear as if your false beard had slipped badly under your chin. He looks combative and ready to argue a professional case with all comers. Arguing with other professionals was what had got him to the top, and he never left off. He was knighted in 1890 after the success of the Forth Bridge.

Back in 1865, he had purchased the Braemore estate, which began a few miles east of Ullapool and covered 43,000 acres. Summer visitors to Braemore in the 1860s and 1870s included painters such as Edwin Landseer and John Everett Millais. From the evidence presented to the Napier Commission by John Fowler himself and several local people, it seems that he was a better landlord than most, but not above criticism; he conceded that more than half of his estate was deer forest which had previously been a single large sheep-farm. He was of the strong opinion that his estate, like much of the Highlands, was too 'thickly populated'; this provoked the astonished response from Fraser-Mackintosh – 'Two hundred people upon upwards of 40,000 acres – can you call that thickly populated?' Fowler replied: 'I should say it is the utmost number upon that property,' pointing out that only a tenth of the land was arable.[26]

Arthur Fowler, to return to the five promoters of the Garve to Ullapool railway, was not a railway engineer, nor yet a landowner, but he had a close interest in the affairs of the Loch Broom district. He was the principal tenant of his father's estate, with sub-tenants on the more arable land at the head of Loch Broom. Photographs from the 1890s depict a family man with a serious expression, and a hairstyle and beard reminiscent of Edward VII. After P. Campbell Ross, Arthur was the most energetic of all those involved in agitating for the railway. By contrast, the Matheson clan usually found better things to do when it came to letters, petitions and the necessary stirring up of legislators and financiers.

SUPPORT FROM ORDINARY RESIDENTS

'The Shillings and Sixpences of Poor Fishermen'

Cast in the role of secretary to the Garve and Ullapool Railway Committee was an unsung local hero. This was Patrick Campbell Ross, who described himself as a 'political agent', resident of Ullapool. He was born in 1831, the second-last of thirteen children of the Rev. Thomas Ross, who for thirty-five years was Church of Scotland minister of Lochbroom parish (this rural parish, just to be clear, was separated from Ullapool itself after 1829). The Rev. Ross went over to the Free Church in the Disruption of May 1843 and died very shortly afterwards; his immediate successor in the Church of Scotland, John Macleod, arrived to preach his first sermon 'but was so disappointed with the congregation' that he left again.[27] Little is known of young Patrick before he emerged at the forefront of the campaign for the Garve and Ullapool Railway in 1889, but by the 1880s he was clearly a man on a mission. He signed himself with the resonant 'P. Campbell', and was, as we shall see, a man of strong opinions who paid little attention to social niceties – as happy to insult the Secretary for Scotland as he was to malign some rival of equal social status. He had inherited his father's ability to write stirring letters and pamphlets, and without him it is doubtful whether the Ullapool railway campaign would have got as far as it did. In later years, he was celebrated as 'the doughty champion' of the railway project.[28]

Also unsung were the massed fishermen, crofters, tradesmen and middle-class professionals of the area around Loch Broom. Rarely do their names appear in any of the correspondence and documentation thrown up during the campaign. Very few of the petitions they signed have come down to us intact, but the Scottish Office, to whom most were addressed, assiduously counted the signatures, then summarised the totals for the filing system. The names which have survived are those of church ministers (Angus Macdonald of Ullapool and William Cameron of Lochbroom) or local entrepreneurs. It was Macdonald, for example, who greeted Lord Lothian at Ullapool and subsequently took to print in order to challenge certain claims from the Aultbea rivals. Both Macdonald and Cameron were Church of Scotland ministers; their Free Church colleague, John MacMillan, albeit based in Ullapool, is not mentioned in dispatches. But, by and large, the Free Church was far more engaged with social campaigns across the north-west Highlands and Islands. On Lewis, vociferous support for the Ullapool Railway came from the Free Church minister of the parish of Back. That the names of the professional class should be recorded rather than those of ordinary people is no surprise: it was ever so. Nonetheless, the campaign for a railway to Ullapool did find strong support amongst ordinary fishermen and crofting men – and doubtless their wives as well, although not once do we get to hear from the women.

And it was the ordinary people who turned up regularly to public meetings, voted on resolutions read out by the middle-class agitators and put their names to countless petitions. In 1891 there were, in truth, not many of the ordinary people in the area around Ullapool, and almost none at all along the 33 miles of the railway line. According to the population census of April 1891, Ullapool itself was home to 934 people, with 500 more living in the immediate area north and west. Among the small settlements that bordered Loch Broom eastwards of the village as far as Braemore, there were 706. And in Coigach and as far as north as Inverpolly, a further 1,071 men, women and children; southwards, in the Little Loch Broom area, another 754. A total, therefore, of around 3,881 souls. (The School Board Census of August in the same year determined that 3,858 people lived in the Loch Broom area, 922 of them in Ullapool. A satisfying statistical match of which everyone could be proud – some movement of people probably occurred in the intervening months.)[29] According to the Napier Commission Report of 1883, there were around sixty-seven crofts in and around Loch Broom. Those who did not define themselves simply as crofters eked out a living as fishermen, servants, labourers, gamekeepers; or at various trades such as carpenters, shoemakers, 'wirefencers', weavers and shepherds. And not a few followed the popular profession of paupers and tramps.[30]

The Napier Commission, in its relentless pursuit of knowledge, asked about wages in the Ullapool area. Sir John Fowler estimated the summer wage of a crofter, when employed at manual labour, working for the summer visitors, or in fishing, to be between 15 shillings and 18 shillings per week. A crofter from Leckmelm near Ullapool agreed that farm-labourers could earn about this same figure. And a local land-owner named Alexander Pirie (of whom more shortly), not a man much plagued by generosity, reckoned that 17 shillings was a good wage.[31] In short, an average annual income of £44.

The average wage in the UK in the 1890s was somewhere in the region of £50 to £60 per annum. This ranges from people such as farm-servants at the lower end of the scale (£26 + board and lodging) to the seaman on a steamer at the higher end (£86 per annum), with miners and railway workers somewhere in the middle. In 1889, the Great North of Scotland Railway Company was proposing to adjust engine drivers' pay to start at 27 shillings a week, rising to 39 shillings after twenty-five years, and goods clerks were on £55 a year.[32] Even a qualified teacher could not hope to earn much more than £135 per annum (if you had the good sense to be a man – a woman was quite reasonably paid half of that).[33] Almost unbelievably, doctors in the north-west in the last years of the nineteenth century might not earn much more than £120 per annum (some were on £45), which they would have to supplement in creative ways.[34] In the Ullapool area, there were not many urban labourers, apart from some weavers and mill-workers. The majority of lower-class residents were fishermen and their families, or estate workers. And quite how crofters and cottars fitted in to this scheme of things is doubtful: the phrases 'scratching a living' and 'abject poverty' come to mind. For both groups, a weekly wage was a thoroughly alien concept. Despite the brief optimism of the Napier Report and the Crofters' Act, very little had changed for the rural inhabitants.

But even if they could never afford to travel on it, the people of the area around Ullapool clearly felt that a railway would be a good thing for the development of the fisheries. In June 1889, the Reverend Macdonald suggested to Lord Lothian that the proposers of the line 'had not a single landed proprietor or man of wealth among their number, the preliminary expenses so far having been met by the shillings and sixpences of poor fishermen'.[35] While this claim seems a little economical with the truth, we must know that a minister of the Kirk would not tell outright fibs. And it is certainly quite plausible that the men of wealth had not yet emulated their inferiors by putting their hands in their pockets; Scottish railway projects of the time massaged the egos of many wealthy people who failed to follow up investment promises with actual money. But poor fishermen with cash to spare were almost certainly in a tiny minority; for most, the best expression of support was attendance at meetings and voting for resolutions. In June 1890, the fishermen of Ullapool signed a petition supporting the railway, to be presented to the latest commission of inquiry; three months later, 300 voted to express disappointment at the conduct of the very same commission. From November 1892 the Scottish Office retained one of the very rare documents naming an ordinary person: a petition sent in by the fisherman John Cameron of Pulteney Street. In 1893, there were further petitions from the people of Little Loch Broom, from Ullapool and from the fishermen of Tanera (on the Summer Isles), all expressing 'regret and disappointment' at the latest abandonment of responsibility by the Government.[36]

If the people of Loch Broom and Coigach were becoming adept at drawing up petitions, the people of the Isle of Lewis were past masters. At the very end of 1889, a meeting of crofters and fishers on the east coast of Lewis held a mass meeting to support the Ullapool project and 'denounce' the alternative railway to Aultbea; a week later, they were at it again, this time condemning the 'dissentients supporting Aultbea'. On the third day of January, the Reverend Hector Cameron of the Free Church at Back wrote proudly of 500 families in his parish who were 'dead against Aultbea as the railway terminus for this island'; and at the end of that same month, crofters and others from Carloway convened on a dark winter evening to support Ullapool and pour scorn upon Aultbea. Not everyone on Lewis was pro-Ullapool, however: in these same weeks, crofters at Barvas came out strongly for Aultbea, and the secretary for the Aultbea project responded to the Reverend Cameron with a letter in which he asserted that 'not only do the great majority of the Lews fishermen prefer Aultbea, but so do the fishcurers, merchants, traders, and all business men throughout the island'.[37]

Eighteen months later, Lewisian enthusiasm had not let up: when the Great North of Scotland company was seeking signatures in support of their proposed takeover of the Ullapool Railway, a good half-dozen petitions were immediately forthcoming, signed by at least 200 fishermen from townships all over Lewis (some signatories were East Coasters).[38] Quite why there should be animosity on Lewis between the Ullapool and Aultbea factions is not clear: one would have thought that either mainland railway terminus would be perfectly acceptable. It may be that the controversy simply offered a convenient excuse to air underlying grievances which had been long festering in the darkness – perhaps between fish-curers and fishermen, or between the citizens of Stornoway and the residents of outlying townships.

In any event, most of these petitions were politely ignored in London. If they did any good at all, they served to give credibility to the letters written by Campbell Ross and Arthur Fowler. But no politician, Conservative or Liberal, paid much attention to them. Least attentive of all was the Highland Railway. In March 1894, a newspaper reported that, a couple of days earlier, in the presence of Sir John Fowler and Andrew Dougall (the General Manager of the Highland), an extraordinary bounty of herring (5,000 crans) was fished around Isle Martin and landed on the shores of Loch Broom. 'It was curious', noted the newspaper a little acidly, 'to see the good-natured expression on his [Dougall's] countenance when he heard the regrets constantly expressed as he passed along that the railway to Garve was not already in operation.' Possibly the presence of Sir John put a lid on more robust expressions of regret against the Highland.[39] But it is hard to imagine a more apt demonstration of the thwarting of the ambitions of local fishermen than this enormous harvest and the resulting problem of getting it to market.

THE ROUTE OF THE RAILWAY

'There is a Great Fall Down to the Sea'

With local support and some money promised from the wealthy, but with little heed to the likelihood of success or failure, the promoters

moved ahead. The *Edinburgh Gazette* of 26 November 1889 printed a
verbose notice informing the public of the intention to apply for an Act

> for the purpose of making and maintaining, within the Counties of
> Ross and Cromarty, the railway and works hereinafter mentioned,
> or some part thereof respectively, together with all necessary sidings,
> stations, approaches, works and conveniences connected therewith
> respectively [for] a railway commencing at or near the Garve
> Station . . . and terminating at or near the north end of the steam-
> boat pier at . . . Ullapool.[40]

A 'deposit' copy of the proposed Act was published on 20 December
1889. The relevant plans, sections and books of reference would be
available for viewing.

As a legal necessity prior to the submission of the Private Bill which
led to the 1890 Act, a full survey of the route of the proposed line was
carried out. The promoters contracted the Highland Railway to
undertake this, probably with some misgivings from the latter. The
two engineers who carried out the survey were Murdoch Paterson and
C. R. Manners, both of Inverness (the latter had been personally
recommended by Sir John Fowler). Paterson had been the senior engineer with the Highland Railway since 1867.

The 'Plans and Sections' document which the two men produced is
a masterly piece of work. It divides the proposed railway into nine
sections, starting at Garve and ending at Ullapool; each of the first
eight sections covers exactly four miles, the ninth the remaining
1½-odd miles. For each section, there is a detailed map indicating the
line to be followed by the railway; a 'lateral deviation' is marked for a
hundred yards on either side of the line, which would allow the builders of the railway some leeway in the event of unforeseen obstacles
such as deceptive bogs, rocky outcrops, sudden torrents, uncooperative
cattle and so on; on each page, underneath the mapping was drawn a
vertical section of the same stretch with relevant gradients. Where it
proved necessary, enlarged sections and maps were shown. A separate
Ordnance Survey one-inch map was also attached, with the proposed
line marked in bold red pencil.[41]

Accompanying the plans was a separate 'Book of Reference',
containing details of the ownership of all land traversed by the line. A

No. on Plan.	Description of Property.	Owners or Reputed Owners.	Lessees or Reputed Lessees.	Occupiers.
480	Burn (Ghamhainn)	Lady Mary Jane Matheson	Alexander Macrae, John Cameron and Alexander White	Alexander Macrae, John Cameron, and Alexander White
481	Rocks, bushes, and rough pasture	Lady Mary Jane Matheson	Alexander White	Alexander White
482	Arable land	Lady Mary Jane Matheson	Alexander White	Alexander White
483	Arable land	Lady Mary Jane Matheson	Alexander White	Alexander White
484	Arable land and ruin	Lady Mary Jane Matheson	Alexander White	Alexander White
486	Sea-beach, sand and rocks, etc., below high water-mark	The Crown, The Board of Admiralty, and The Board of Trade		The Crown, The Board of Admiralty, and The Board of Trade
488	Public road	The Road Trustees of The County of Ross and Cromarty, *per* William John Duncan, Clerk		The public
490	Boat slip	Lady Mary Jane Matheson		Lady Mary Jane Matheson
491	Strip of pasture (above high water-mark)	Lady Mary Jane Matheson		Lady Mary Jane Matheson
492	Shore Street, Ullapool	Lady Mary Jane Matheson and the public		Lady Mary Jane Matheson and the public
493	Pier	Lady Mary Jane Matheson	David Macbrayne	David Macbrayne
494	Stores	Lady Mary Jane Matheson	Kenneth Cameron	Kenneth Cameron
495	The sea	The Crown, The Board of Admiralty, and The Board of Trade		The Crown, The Board of Admiralty, and The Board of Trade

Figure 5.1 Sample page from the Book of Reference which accompanied the 1890 railway plans. This page shows the items of interest at the Ullapool end of the line. (National Records of Scotland RHP916)

total of 495 items are listed here – fields, pastures (these were more plausibly just bog, although sometimes described with the oxymoron 'pasture (deer forest)' . . .), streams, rivers, roads, tracks, houses; also, towards the end, 'The Sea' which we are pleased to note was owned by 'The Crown, the Board of Admiralty and the Board of Trade'. Apart from the sea, a couple of public roads and a manse, almost all of these items were on private estates. The estate-owners constitute an interesting mixture of the rich and aristocratic (though not necessarily of ancient lineage) and the simply rich. Almost all, the attentive reader will notice, had some connection to the Mackenzie clan.

Since we do not have the benefit of an actual railway carriage in which to sit back and enjoy the passing scenery, let us travel the nine planned sections on paper, observing the route taken and the gradients involved. For those blissfully ignorant of gradients on what are termed 'adhesion' railways – in that word 'adhesion' lies a hope and a prayer – for comparison: the steepest gradients on the Dingwall to Strome line were 1:50 – i.e. a one-foot vertical rise for every 50 feet of horizontal progress; the steepest mainline one in Britain was 1:38, and one of the steepest standard-gauge gradients in the world is in Norway, at 1:18; but rest assured that in a Scottish winter in the 1890s, even 1:50 was due some respect. (In the notes below, British Ordnance Survey grid-references are provided in the format 'NH111999' to assist the sedulous reader in more exact identification on modern maps.)

Section 1: Garve Station to Achnaclerach

Our virtual train leaves the safety of the Dingwall to Strome Ferry line at a point about 220 yards (10 chains) east of the present station buildings. Doubtless there would have been a special platform built to accommodate the new route. The railway to Ullapool then runs parallel with the Dingwall line as far as a bend in Blackwater river, at which point it follows the right bank of the river and crosses the road just before the bridge (NH403640, beside Torr Breac). At the bridge, the road would require a slight diversion to the north to permit a level crossing at 90° to the railway. After crossing the road, the line proceeds along the right (west) bank of river. The gradients are mostly 1:116, but there were two short sections of 1:40.

Some of the land here was owned by Charles Hanbury, son of a founder of Truman, Hanbury and Buxton brewers of London (now

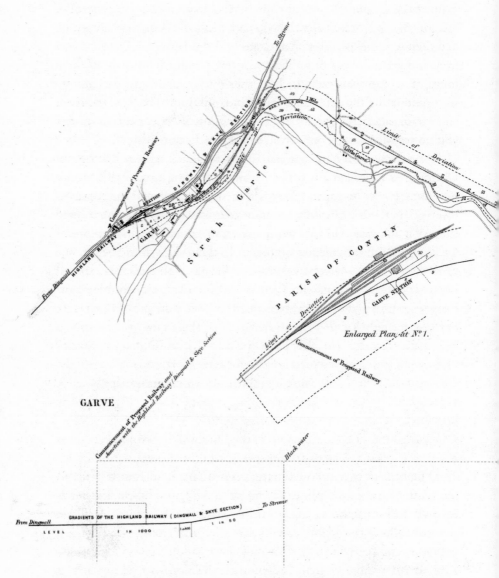

Figure 5.2 Plan showing how the Ullapool railway would branch off the Strome Ferry line at Garve station. (National Records of Scotland RHP916)

Truman's Brewery); his main lessee was Harry Panmure Gordon, stockbroker and founder of a still-extant financial firm of that name. Further up the line, we venture across the estate of Captain Alexander Watson Mackenzie, distillery owner of Muir of Ord, near Dingwall; and then stray into the Inchbae estate.

Section 2: Achnaclerach to Black Bridge

Our train rattles on, following the right (west/south) bank of the river. The strath is largely level, with a couple of small 1:50 gradients for our engine to wheeze up. We have now crossed into the Inchbae estate (21,000 acres), owned by (late) Lt-Col Duncan Henry Caithness Reay Davidson (also owner of Tulloch Castle and inheritor of the Mount Gay sugar plantation in the West Indies; not a Mackenzie, but married to one). In 1890, this estate was managed by a group of trustees, and some of it was sub-let to Mr Panmure Gordon and to Walter Shoolbread, scion of a family owning a successful London department-store. We also traverse land owned by William Dalziel Mackenzie, the son of Edward Mackenzie of Fawley Court, banker and railway entrepreneur; Fawley Court is said to be the inspiration for Toad Hall in *The Wind in the Willows*. Finally we reach the southern edge of the Strathvaich estate; a road leads off northwards from Black Bridge to Strathvaich Lodge, still today a hunting lodge. The Strathvaich estate was owned by Sir Arthur George Ramsay Mackenzie, 11th Baronet of Coul, son of a premier of Queensland. So far, we have seen very little in the way of houses or people.

Section 3: Black Bridge to Glascarnoch

The line continues to follow the right (south) bank of river. It passes to the south of Aultguish Inn, to the north of Aultguish house (missing it by only 20 yards) and to the north of Glascarnoch house. The latter two houses have now disappeared below the surface of the Glascarnoch reservoir (completed in 1957), making an occasional ghostly reappearance in times of drought. The house at Glascarnoch is situated at NH312725, about halfway along the present loch. The hills rising up to Beinn Dearg loom above us to the north. The route of the railway is still fairly level, with one small stretch of 1:48.

We are now travelling through the northern part of the estate of Kinlochluichart, owned by the Lady Ashburton. Her Ladyship was

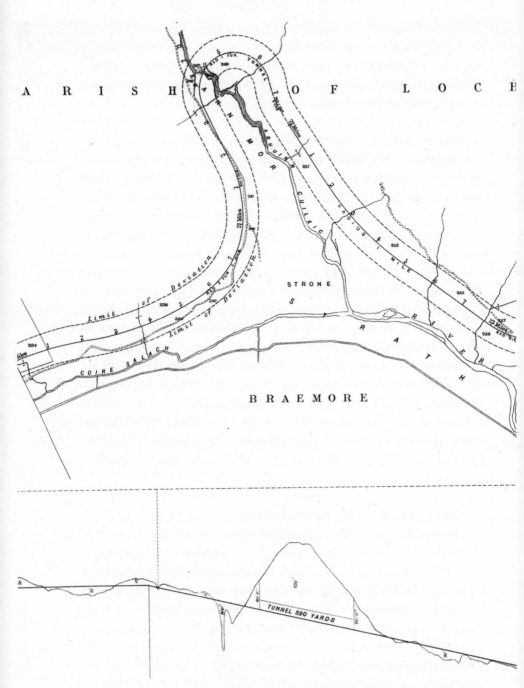

Figure 5.3 Detail from Paterson's plans, showing the proposed tunnel at Braemore –
top as a map, bottom as a cross-section (National Records of Scotland RHP916)

Louisa Caroline Baring, née Stewart-Mackenzie, daughter of a governor of Ceylon (the man who sold Lewis to James Matheson). She lived for a time at Brahan Castle, but subsequently, with her husband, owned castles up and down the land. Her 20,000-acre estate at Kinlochluichart was one across which the Dingwall to Strome Ferry railway now ran – she would have hit the jackpot with this proposed second railway. She led an interesting life as an art collector and philanthropist, her name being linked with, among others, John Ruskin, Thomas Carlyle, Edwin Landseer and even Florence Nightingale. After the death of her husband she seems to have had an affair with the American sculptress Harriet Hosmer, and simultaneously with the poet Robert Browning. After her own death in 1903, she was buried at Kinlochluichart Church.

Section 4: Glascarnoch to Loch Droma

Remaining in Lady Ashburton's territory, the line continues up the strath as far as a point about halfway along little Loch Droma. At the nearest (east) end of that loch, we cross the border between Contin parish and Lochbroom parish. The railway line continues to follow the right (south) bank of river and south bank of loch. It is arguably the dullest section of the entire route; the gradients here are perfectly reasonable, although the end of this section is also the highest point on the line, at around 900 feet.

Section 5: Loch Droma to Braemore Lodge

We now reach the Braemore estate, owned by Sir John Fowler KCMG. It should be observed in passing that Fowler owned around ten miles of the proposed 33-mile branch line: like the Matheson clan, the Fowler family had a vested interest in the construction of a railway. The train puffs along the south bank of Loch Droma, then crosses the burn named Allt a Mhadaidh and follows the south (left) bank of Abhainn Droma river. It becomes a little more hilly as we approach Braemore, with a couple of lengths at 1:50.

Section 6: Braemore Lodge to Auchindrean

If the journey has so far been quotidian, it now abruptly changes to something of a white-knuckle ride. The railway has to descend the precipitous slope cut through by the Corrieshalloch Gorge. Engineer

Murdoch Paterson was faced with two choices: either follow the route of the road to Ullapool (now the A835), which would have involved an almost impossible gradient of 1:22 over two miles, or find another way down. Paterson elected to turn westwards, span a 100-foot gorge, thrust the line inside the hill and build a curving 590-yard tunnel, 130 feet below the surface, which would pop out further down the hill. It was a master-stroke.

In detail, then: the line follows the route of present-day A832 (to Dundonnell) westwards as far as NH187778; it then crosses the road (the road would need to be dropped by a foot to permit a level crossing), leaps over the Cuileag river (a hundred feet below), then clings to the hillside, about 220 yards from the road. At NH185780, the railway enters a long tunnel which curves to the right to follow the line of the river and glen. The curve of the tunnel is marked as having a radius of '1 Furlong' – 220 yards, which is quite tight on a railway. On exiting from the tunnel, there is a descent to sea level at a gradient of 1:40 for two miles – a very respectable slalom – shooting over a number of gorges and mountainside streams. It is breathtakingly simple. Doubtless, the builders of the line would have referred to that bible of a railway engineer, *Practical Tunnelling* by Frederick Simms, which was then in its third edition of 1877; over 350 pages it provided detailed guidance on how to dig tunnels for railways. On the long descent to Auchindrean, several significant gorges have to be crossed – one 56 feet deep, and two others 100 feet deep. The line passes to the west of Auchindrean and the section ends, with a sigh of relief, at the stream named Allt Cuil an Droghinn (at NH188811)

Alas! – our tunnel was never to be. Six years later, Sir John Fowler wrote to his son Arthur: 'Respecting the tunnel for which £14,750 was estimated, and to which Mr Paterson thinks £2,000 should be added, the answer is that there will be no tunnel at all, as was ascertained immediately after the plans were deposited. I was under the impression that this important fact was communicated to Mr Paterson at the time, or very soon afterwards.'[42] One supposes that it was Sir John himself who vetoed the proposal: he was, after all, the pre-eminent railway engineer of his time. But it is all rather murky: in April of 1889, Paterson had written to John Fowler, apropos of the flying survey, specifically asking him to sketch on a one-inch Ordnance Survey map how he thought the line should be carried beyond Braemore Lodge, 'where there is a great fall down to the sea . . . Your suggestion as to where the line should be would be of the utmost importance.'[43] It is unlikely that Fowler failed to reply, and this would suggest that a tunnel – or some descent down the western slopes – was under consideration by the great engineer himself. It is frustrating that we no longer have his response, for we know neither what he had in mind for the western slope, nor – equally significant – why he did not favour the eastern side. However, to the unpractised eye, the eastern slopes seem even more precipitous than the western ones, and that is likely to have been the deciding factor.

Ultimately Sir John decided firmly against the tunnel, and it seems likely that someone forgot to inform Paterson; which was lucky, as it might have broken his heart. What we do not have any more is Fowler's alternative plan for descending the hill at Braemore. While we can be assured the finished line would have been both robust and safe, we must also allow for the construction being difficult and expensive. All Fowler would say later was that, from Braemore to Ullapool, 'a greater amount of earthwork and masonry would be necessary, in consequence of the more irregular nature of the ground'.[44]

Section 7: Auchindrean to Inverlael

Between Auchindrean and Garvan, several significant gullies were still to be crossed, one of which was 30 feet deep. Our train careers on downhill at gradients of up to 1:40, passing to the west of Garvan, Auchlunachan and Croftown, before crossing the River Broom next to the church at NH177848. This church and its manse were the buildings around which Lochbroom parish was centred, and the surrounding land was therefore owned by the Church of Scotland. The railway crosses both the road and the River Lael at NH182855, then runs parallel with, and to the east of, the public road. Having passed behind Inverlael farm, this section ends one mile north of it. The land as far as the crossing of the River Broom was part of the Braemore estate, but managed by Arthur Fowler as tenant. On the east side of the river, the Inverlael estate (14,000 acres), was owned by Sir Arthur G. R. Mackenzie (also the owner of Strathvaich – see above), with lessees Walter Mundell and his two sons; another lessee was the 9th Earl of Cavan, a Liberal politician and MP for South Somerset.

Section 8: Inverlael to Corry Point

We can now sit back and enjoy views over Loch Broom and the hilly peninsula to the west. The train, if it has survived the helter-skelter down Braemore, will jounce bravely onwards to Ullapool. The railway runs on the east side of road, passing behind Ardcharnich and Leckmelm. It crosses the road at NH148923 – the road would need to be raised by three feet to permit a level crossing. Just north of Braes, the line runs almost on the foreshore and has to cross several deep gullies, but the gradients are a mere 1:62 or so.

At the start of this section, we enter the Leckmelm estate. Leckmelm had been owned since 1879 by Alexander George Pirie, paper manufacturer of Aberdeen (Stoneywood Mill, on the River Don near Dyce). He had purchased the land from Lt-Col Davidson (see Inchbae, above), and immediately began to deliver eviction notices to twenty-three of the tenant families, an action which brought down much condemnation on his head – not least from the Lochbroom Free Church minister, the Rev. John Macmillan. It was Macmillan who spearheaded a campaign to denounce Pirie's actions. According to a contemporary:

> The noble conduct of the Rev. Mr. MacMillan, in connection with those evictions, deserves commemoration . . . At the urgent request of many friends of the Highland crofters, resident in Inverness, Mr. MacMillan agreed to lay the case of his evicted parishioners before the public. Early in December, 1880, he delivered an address in Inverness to one of the largest and most enthusiastic meetings which has ever been held in that town . . . Though his remarks do not seem to have influenced Mr. Pirie's conduct, or to have benefited his unfortunate subjects, the Inverness meeting was the real beginning in earnest of the subsequent movement throughout the Highlands in favour of Land Reform, and the curtailment of landlord power over their unfortunate tenants. Mr. Pirie can thus claim to have done our poorer countrymen no small amount of good, though probably, quite contrary to his intentions, by his cruel and high-handed conduct in dealing with the ancient tenants of Leckmelm.[45]

Public condemnation did little to prevent Pirie from going ahead with the evictions and removing the roofs from the affected cottages. Three years later, now a little calmer but no less opposed to evictions, Rev.

Macmillan laconically observed to the Napier Commission that 'the Leckmelm case [was] a world-wide business'.⁴⁶ He now even went so far as to say that Pirie treated those few tenants who remained very kindly; but the only one of these who gave evidence to Napier, agreeing that Pirie had built 'a great many' new houses, pointed out that 'none of them [is] occupied by the tenants' – they had been given to 'incomers'.⁴⁷ Pirie himself gave lengthy evidence to Napier, and was quite unabashed about the eviction incident ('it caused a great outcry among outside agitators', he scolded). He had this to say in reply to a question concerning his changes to the tenancies:

> Do you think the reducing of the crofters from the status of crofters to labourers dependent upon you is for their benefit?
>
> —Certainly, because I think a man who is able to work and make his own livelihood is in a far nobler position than a crofter who every five or six years has to go and cry out 'I am destitute and want help.'⁴⁸

On further questioning, it emerged that Pirie was still intent on knocking down cottages and moving his tenants into what was attractively called a 'barrack', largely because he wanted to build his own residence on the land occupied by the old cottages.

Before we reach the end of this section on the plans, we enter another estate which is owned – not unnaturally – by a Mackenzie: to be exact, the 2nd Earl of Cromartie, Francis Mackenzie, son of the third Duchess of Sutherland, who was also the 1st Countess of Cromartie. This Earl of Cromartie was named as a director of the Garve and Ullapool Railway in a civil action raised by the Highland Railway in 1892: he may have come to regret his earlier enthusiasm for becoming involved in the whole thing.

Section 9: Corry Point to Ullapool Pier
(1 mile, 5 furlongs, 4 chains and 50 links)
The railway line continues between coastline and road, before joining (or running parallel to) Shore Street. It terminates at the junction of Shore Street and Quay Street, at the landward end of the pier. There are some interesting physical features to be overcome, since the immediate approach to Ullapool is a bit hilly: within the 1.5 miles of this

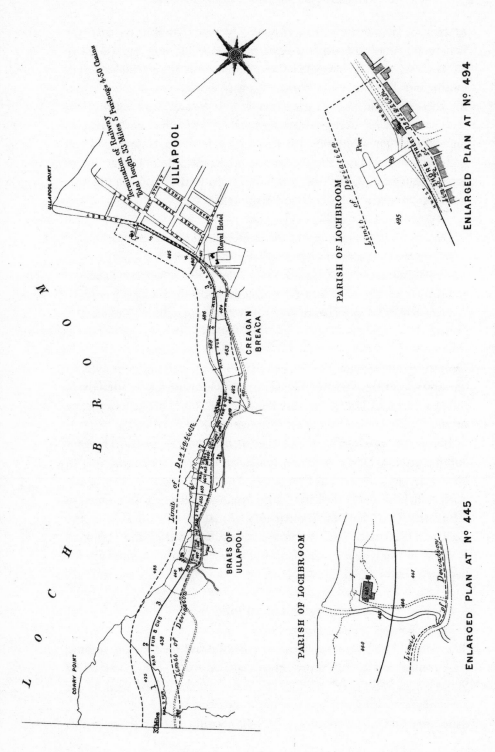

Figure 5.4 Plan showing the terminus of the railway from Garve at Ullapool pier (National Records of Scotland RHP916)

section, one mile was at 1:40. The land was owned partly by Cromartie, as above, but mostly by Lady Mary Jane Matheson. In and about Ullapool itself, her land was leased to a variety of people and bodies: this included Shore Street (along with 'The Public'), the Pier (lessee: David Macbrayne, the steamship magnate) and the Stores (lessee: local mill-owner Kenneth Cameron)

We have arrived safely in Ullapool. It probably took us about ninety minutes to get here from Garve (we travelled first class, and it cost us 8s 9d; our manservant went third class for 2s 9d). As we have seen, for much of its 33 miles, 5 furlongs, 4 chains and 50 links, the railway travels across fairly easy ground. It rises from around 230 feet above sea level at Garve, to around 900 feet at Loch Droma, then drops back to sea level at Inverlael. Apart from the area around Braemore, there are only a couple of steep gradients to be overcome, but nothing that Victorian ingenuity in construction, and some careful engine-driving in operation, could not handle. Only the descent from Braemore was a problem – a problem but, very briefly until Sir John Fowler got to hear of it, the jewel in the crown of the line. No stations are defined, but it was envisaged that there should be 'about six' along the line, of which three would require platforms and short sidings.[49] With one exception, we can only guess at their locations. Since the number of residents between Garve and Braemore was negligible, any stations built in that stretch would have been for the convenience of the estate owners alone.

But such things as stations and gradients are mere details. The big thing was the concept itself, a Garve to Ullapool Railway.

6

'Bodies of Distinguished Strangers'

The Campaign and the Commissions

The campaign for the Garve to Ullapool Railway really kicked off at the start of 1889. There was almost certainly a guiding hand behind it, and that hand belonged to P. Campbell Ross: it was his name at the foot of almost every single letter sent out. He frequently wrote in the name of the 'Executive Committee of the Ullapool and Garve Railway', describing himself as its 'Honorary Secretary'. The Committee's campaign consisted of public meetings to discuss the proposed railway and collect names on petitions; letters with and without accompanying memoranda, sent to politicians – usually the Secretary for Scotland; letters to newspapers; and meetings with sundry eminences and itinerant commissions.

The first public meeting of note took place in Ullapool on the final day of 1888, and three days later Ross had copied the resulting Resolution down to the Scottish Office.[1] In the following three months, he fired off letter after letter, some to London, others to the Inverness offices of the Highland Railway, and by the end of April was able to report to the Secretary for Scotland that there would be a 'flying survey' of the proposed line; the Highland Railway probably felt it had to do something, since in the space of a few weeks, its board received urgent requests from 'the inhabitants of Loch Broom', the local MP Dr Macdonald, and Sir John Fowler himself.[2] In February, Andrew Dougall of the Highland was already indicating that his company was prepared to work the railway 'on reasonable terms'.[3] A minor coup was achieved in May of that year, when the crofters and fishermen of the district of Little Loch Broom, who actually lived closer to the rival village of Aultbea than to Ullapool, were persuaded to come out in support of the Ullapool railway.[4]

And in April a golden opportunity arose when, as we have seen, the Liberal MP James Caldwell passed through Ullapool on his way to investigate what was happening with railways and fisheries and the reading of Livy. Campbell Ross wrote to Sir John Fowler, asking him to honour everyone with his presence and preside over the dinner. (The tone of the letter is a model for how invitations ought to be composed: 'It would be in accord with the eternal fitness of things, that the most eminent engineer living – the most generously liberal proprietor of the Highlands should be in the chair on the occasion, to adorn it by his occupancy of it, while he would be rejoicing the hearts of those whose famous co-parishioner he is – distinguished as a philanthropist as he is notable in science . . .') Sir John, however, rather snippily regretted etc. – he was otherwise occupied in bridging the Forth; and although the welcoming supper was not quite what Ross had hoped for, it would have left Caldwell in no doubt as to the best possible mainland railway route.[5]

The correspondence between Caldwell and Joseph Chamberlain which was published in *The Scotsman* in May 1889 spawned a flurry of enthusiastic and opinionated letters from the residents of Loch Broom. One was signed by 'A Highlander', another by 'Truth' and another by 'Pro Bono Publico', all extolling the virtues of the railway line to Ullapool, and taking merciless digs at anyone supporting the rival Gairloch and Aultbea railway: 'The Gairloch people', wrote 'Truth', 'make much capital out of their crofting population, local fishing, and tourist traffic. They might add another traffic – the traffic in smuggled whisky.' 'Where', wrote 'Pro Bono Publico' boldly, 'is there a safer anchorage, better harbour accommodation, or easier modes of access than Lochbroom? . . . A day of success will crown our efforts.' A letter signed by 'Ross-Shire' was even more sanguine in its hopes for the 'much-needed railway':

In course of time Ullapool would become another Oban, and a famous sea-bathing place. There is some beautiful beach all the way to Ardmair, and also on the south side of Loch Broom . . . All honour is due to Sir John Fowler, Mr Caldwell and Mr Chamberlain for their efforts to get this scheme set in motion.[6]

It was clear that the supporters of the Ullapool line saw their main rivals in the contemptible supporters of the Aultbea line. No love was lost between the two camps – more of the frequently ludicrous details on this are provided in Chapter 8. To the people of Ullapool, the Aultbea railway scheme was nothing more than an *arriviste* spoiler, an attempt to ruin Ullapool's chances; in early letters, reference was made to messages of support for the Ullapool scheme which had come out of Gairloch and Poolewe not so very long before.[7] Things came to such a pass that, on 11 June 1889, the Committee Promoting the Garve and Ullapool Railway saw fit to issue a printed refutation of the Aultbea claims, whose rival Gairloch Committee had dared to rubbish the Ullapool proposal. The Reverend Macdonald prepared this document, and we summarise it below – the 'Gairloch Claim' followed by the *'Ullapool Refutation'* in italics.[8]

1. Ullapool is fifteen miles from the Minch and more than fifty from Stornoway.

   Ullapool is 43 miles from Stornoway, and even shorter if passing through the Summer Isles.

2. The approach to Ullapool via the Summer Isles is beset by rocks and reefs, and requires a pilot.

   The entrance is two miles wide, with no reefs or rocks, and never in living memory has a pilot been required.

3. The entrance to Loch Broom is narrow and subject to sudden squalls and calms.

   Loch Broom is six miles wide at its mouth, and utterly devoid of squalls and calms.

4. Vessels have to contend with the tide for fourteen miles out of Ullapool.

   'This objection is extremely silly' – does not the tide flow everywhere at sea?

5. Ullapool was only used for mails while Sir James Matheson was alive.

   Ullapool was for twelve years the preferred mail packet station for Lewis, and was used by the people of Lewis as the shortest crossing to the mainland.

6. Ullapool has been condemned as a fishing station. When herring in the loch failed, fishing languished and the town is in decay.

Ullapool has never been condemned by anyone, and is in any case flourishing.

(NB this assertion by Aultbea repeats almost verbatim a claim made by the Napier Commission.)[9]

Bullishly, Macdonald went on to point out that: Aultbea is 64 miles from Garve; a railway line from Achnasheen via Gairloch to Aultbea would be 11 miles longer than from Garve to Ullapool; and Aultbea is much exposed to gales. *Touché!* Battle lines had been drawn between Ullapool and Aultbea, and considerable local venom was expended in trading fruitless mutual insults.

The Ullapool campaign's next great opportunity came when Lord Lothian was touring his demesne. He made a stop at Ullapool on 18 June 1889, where his party disembarked and made their way to the Royal Hotel, only to be held back from luncheon by Macdonald stopping him at the door and delivering an interminable address. His lordship replied in the usual vague terms and finally sat down to his soup; he was immediately 'waited on by a deputation from the committee promoting the Ullapool and Garve Railway' – in the person once more of Mr Macdonald. 'No other undertaking', stated the minister, 'would be so well calculated to stop the rapid descent of the entire district into the state of abject poverty which had overtaken the Lews and some parts of the mainland. It would not only open up the country, give speedy access to southern markets, and relieve the distress, but it would work a social revolution by enabling the people to profit by the fishing industry.' Macdonald was at pains to point out that the campaign was strictly non-political, and that their local support came largely from 'poor fishermen'; additionally, 'The fishermen of the Lews, West Sutherland, and the East Coast were in favour of the proposed line; the inhabitants of Upper Assynt petitioned in support of it, and it had been commended as far south as Fort-William'.[10]

His Lordship's ear was further bent by the factor for Lord Cromartie and by P. Campbell Ross, who was 'glad to be able to inform his

Lordship that at the present time there was a large quantity of herrings in Lochbroom'. A further contribution was made by Mr Cameron, who thought that a curing station could be established at Ullapool, in competition with Stornoway, and that fishing boats would then much prefer to bring their catches directly to a railhead at Ullapool. How would the fish-curers of Lewis feel about that? asked Lord Lothian. They would not like that at all, replied Mr Cameron, and that was the secret of their opposition to the scheme. The Highland Railway was said to be 'in sympathy'. 'The deputation then withdrew,' allowing the Secretary for Scotland to enjoy his dessert in peace.

No sooner had Lord Lothian sailed away from Ullapool than P. Campbell Ross felt that some memory-jogging was required. Within the next fortnight, he wrote three times to Lothian, firstly to complain that his lordship's entourage was already advising the *Glasgow Herald* reporters that they favoured the Aultbea line; then to remind him that there were plenty of herring in Loch Broom; and finally to forward an affidavit from a steam-yacht captain that the loch was entirely safe and navigable. As if that was not enough, a letter from the Executive Committee of the Ullapool and Garve Railway, addressed to the Secretary for Scotland and dated 18 June – it had perhaps been handed to Lothian over lunch – provided a little background history: 'after approaching landed proprietors and other gentlemen of influence' in 1885, 'agitation was allowed to drop, as the opening up of the country by means of railways had not then commended itself to those in power'. This had now changed because of newspaper reports and MPs taking up the cause against poverty – 'taking prompt action in order to avert what would be a national disgrace, and might become a national danger'. In a slightly distracting postscript to the serious tone of the letter, it was also stated that 'the scenery of Loch Broom is almost without rival'.[11]

The Secretary for Scotland could not, by the time he returned to London, have any possible excuse for ignoring the Ullapool claim.

Meanwhile, the Highland Railway Company was also being approached. The company had a vested interest in (a) extending its line from Strome Ferry to Kyle, and (b) not supporting any other line that would take West Coast traffic away from that route. And yet, despite this, in April 1890 the Highland signed a 'Heads of Agreement' document[12] with Arthur Fowler, which stated that:

The Garve and Ullapool Railway would pay the Highland Railway (HR) 2s 2d per train mile for every train run.

No fewer than two trains each way would run every day (Sunday excepted).

The HR would allow a rebate of 10% of the gross earnings over the HR's system of all traffic to and from the Garve and Ullapool line.

The Garve and Ullapool would maintain its railway and works for a period of 12 months from the date of opening of the line for passenger traffic.

This agreement would endure for 10 years from the date of opening of the Garve and Ullapool line.

So far, so promising. Quite why the Highland would agree to have anything at all to do with the Ullapool railway remains obscure; but evidently they felt that momentum for the rival line was gaining, and that it was better to be working with the promoters than against them. Machiavelli might have learned much from the Highland Railway.

By now, the Mathesons and Fowlers felt that things were going their way; accordingly, they made arrangements for a Private Bill to be debated in Westminster, which would in turn lead to an Act of Parliament to construct the Garve and Ullapool railway. The promoters were so convinced of success that they even put their hands in their pockets: apart from the lawyers' bills for the parliamentary process, a deposit just short of £10,000 was required. A Bill was duly prepared by lawyers in London and Inverness, and published in the *Edinburgh Gazette* on 26 November 1889.

In due course, the Board of Trade was invited to scrutinise the survey; this was required before the Bill could become an Act. The Board was not immediately inclined to accept the level crossings. So in April 1890, they dispatched Major-General Hutchinson, their tireless Inspector of Railways, to cast an expert eye over the proposed crossings. He reported on all four crossings that were mentioned in the plans, but objected only to the one at Torr Breac, where he recommended building a road bridge over the railway instead. This was due to the fact that Garve-bound trains would cross the road immediately on exiting from a cutting and a curve – not a good mix with stray sheep or luckless horses and carts. His report concluded rather drily that road traffic in the area was very light, and he did not envisage any problems whatsoever.[13]

And so, having fulfilled all the pre-conditions and been voted through Parliament, on 14 August 1890 the Garve and Ullapool Railway Company came into legal existence: the main promoters were named as 'proprietors of the undertaking', and four of these (only the gentlemen, of course) as directors of the new incorporated company. It would have a capital of £240,000 to be sold in shares of £10, with borrowing rights for a further £80,000. Crucially, a time limit for compulsory purchase of lands was set at three years from the date of passing the Act; a further stipulation was that if the railway was not substantially constructed within five years, the powers of the Act would lapse. As with all such Acts for the construction of railways, upper limits were set on the ticket and freight charges, the carriage of small and large parcels and the fees payable to other railway companies. The Highland Railway Company was named in the Act as the operating company.

An interesting light is shed on the class divisions in one (legally standard) paragraph, which prohibited the acquisition of more than ten houses – presumably for the purpose of knocking them down – which were inhabited by 'persons belonging to the labouring class [which] includes mechanics artizans labourers and others working for wages hawkers costermongers persons not working for wages but working at some trade or handicraft without employing others except members of their own family and persons other than domestic servants whose income does not exceed an average of thirty shillings a week'.[14] But there was no provision for knocking down the houses of the better off.

More bizarrely, an entire and lengthy stipulation was included in the Act (Section 23) 'for the protection of the estate of Alexander George Pirie': that the line would only and exactly follow the line on the plans, unless otherwise agreed between Arthur Fowler and Pirie's agent; that fences would be erected where appropriate; that trees, dykes and quarries would only be 'interfered with' by strict agreement; and that

> the Company shall not construct any public station on any part of
> the said estate but they shall construct on some part of the estate in

such position as may be reasonably required . . . a platform on the railway and siding therefrom for the exclusive use and accommodation of the owner at which no train shall be stopped otherwise than with the consent of the owner and if and when reasonably required for the purposes of the estate any train shall be stopped at the said platform by a signal.

Here at least, one of John Fowler's six stations. Pirie's condition was entirely absent from the draft version of the Act; so no one had thought to ask him – but he was not a man to be ignored. He demanded that the railway be run though his Leckmelm estate entirely at his convenience. Would that the general public could arrange things in similar manner in these, our dissolute modern times![15] Twenty-five years earlier, Lady Ashburton had engaged in similar tactics when the Dingwall to Strome Ferry line was being pushed through her estate at Kinlochluichart: her original demand for a payment of £4,000 for the use of the land and the construction of a private station was later amended to shared use of her 'private' platform with the great unwashed, plus a contribution of £100 towards it.[16]

The Ullapool Railway Act now being passed, things should have begun to look rosy. But instead they took a rapid turn for the worse.

THE WESTERN HIGHLANDS AND ISLANDS COMMISSION, 1890

'Drivel'

While campaigners had been hard at work, the Government, for once, was not idle. Faced by proposals and suggestions and arguments and counter-arguments, an entire commission of experts was appointed by Lord Lothian in December of 1889 'to inquire into Certain Matters Affecting the Interests of the Population of the Western Highlands and Islands of Scotland'. Stripping out the rather coy 'Certain Matters', this body of gentlemen was more commonly known as the Western Highlands and Islands Commission. Its brief was specifically to determine (a) if there was a sufficient quantity of fish in the sea to justify a fishing industry, and (b) whether there were sufficient boats, harbours, piers, and road and rail transport to bring the fish to market.

The six-member commission was led by Spencer Walpole, a grandson of Spencer Perceval (so the deceased prime minister proved his worth yet again), and included the designer of the Tower Bridge in London; for a list of all members, see Appendix 4. In April of 1890, they duly arrived in the north of Scotland to examine and report on the claims of these rival schemes. Lord Lothian did not make it easy for them. Just before they set off on their travels, he wrote to them asking them to include in their itinerary both the entire north coast of Scotland, and the Orkney and Shetland Islands. Then, when they were already en route, he asked them also to call in at Islay in the south. They visited Ullapool in early April, where 'we conferred personally with the inhabitants on the subject of their requirements'[17] – this claim was seriously doubted, as we shall see; they examined the proposed route of the Garve to Ullapool railway, then proceeded to Poolewe to look at the route of the Achnasheen to Aultbea railway. Then they sailed off to Lewis, and subsequently to as many other Hebridean islands as they could fit in – the *Jackal* had naturally been put at the disposal of the party, to be replaced at a later stage by the *Enchantress*. And no, Islay was not forgotten.

For all of April, May and half of June, they criss-crossed the west coast and the islands, landing here, asking there, making notes everywhere. After a few weeks of hurried reflection, they presented a 25-page report to Parliament in August 1890; it covered not just the railway lines, but also steamer access, piers and harbours, lighthouses and buoys and everything else they could think of. In the less balmy months of September and October, three heroic members of the Commission – possibly selected by short straw – manfully battled their way through wind and rain to visit the north coast and northern isles, but because of appalling weather failing to see anything of Shetland outside of Lerwick. They produced a supplementary 13-page report in December.

Overall, the Commission was deeply unimpressed by the West Coast natives. They discovered a 'reluctance of the people to help themselves'. The work of a croft, or at the fishing, only kept them occupied for a few weeks a year, so 'they pass much of their time in idleness'. Neither was the combination of crofting and fishing good for any one man, as either occupation distracted from the other. By some means of measurement known only to themselves, the Commissioners had established that West Coast fishermen were barely half as energetic and productive as their East Coast equivalents. And the term 'overpopulation' made its appearance, not least in their report's conclusions, where they opined – despite the matter not being in their original brief – that emigration from the islands should be strongly encouraged. A second, more imaginative, solution to the perceived overpopulation crisis was offered: the stationing of a naval training vessel at Stornoway, so that all the under-employed young men could be trained up for the Royal Navy, sail off and die at sea for the Empire.

Tellingly, while the Secretary for Scotland was dispatching commissions to investigate 'certain matters' affecting the economy, other parliamentary committees were at the very same time evaluating the emigration of crofters and cottars from Lewis and Skye to Canada. Their conclusions were, broadly, that emigration – specifically colonisation of places like Manitoba and British Columbia – by the people of the Isles was a Good Thing. Nodding approvingly, they reported that 'The Settlers are in a satisfactory condition . . . Colonisation on a much larger scale . . . is practicable.'[18] Support, should it have proved necessary, came from a 'British Farmers' delegate' who stated that: 'Many other instances may be given of what men with a moderate amount of brains and energy can do when settled in Canada.' The parliamentary reports also mentioned other far-off lands which could benefit from being colonised at a modest price (calculated at £150 per family) – New Zealand, South Africa, even Brazil and Argentina.

Leaving aside their preferred option of emigration, the Commissioners' evaluation of the Ullapool railway proposal was not very positive:

> Ullapool is situated some miles from the sea . . . and thus, to render it fairly comparable with the line to Aultbea, the projected line ought certainly to be extended for about 6 or 7 miles to some place on the coast easy of access and provided with proper sea protection.[19]

For this reason, it was quite unsuitable for the fishing fleet, which was mostly still powered by sail. This was a curious conclusion, to say the least: even a cursory glance at the map will show that Aultbea is just as far from (or as near to) 'the sea' as Ullapool. But from this, the Commission concluded that it would be necessary to plan an extension of the line westwards to a place not defined, but possibly Isle Martin or even Achiltibuie; this, however, would incur additional construction costs of some £50,000 over the £195,000 already envisaged.

And there must be some suspicion that the Commission had been a little less than careful in their survey. Accompanying each copy of the report were two maps: the first showed the routes of all the existing and proposed railway lines; the second showed the present and proposed routes of steamer services. In both maps, 'Ullapool' is clearly marked as being somewhere in the region of Leckmelm – i.e., around four miles further up the loch, away from the open sea. One wonders whether this was shoddy cartography, or whether the Commission had no idea at all of geography; or whether indeed there was a conspiracy, possibly initiated in Gairloch (more of which later). All other towns and villages appear on the maps in their correct location. (Civil servants in the Scottish Office did not appear to have good cartographical skills: an internal memo, dated May 1889, described the various railway schemes and marked them out, for easy executive comprehension, on a map torn out of *Bradshaw's Guide*. On this map, Ullapool was carefully positioned at Braemore, Loch Gairloch bore the handwritten legend 'Loch Ewe' and Roshven had been relocated to Kinlochailort. Still, they were at least within hailing distance of salt water.)[20] But regardless of its position, the perceived ill-suitedness of Ullapool as a fishing station meant that, despite the Garve to Ullapool railway having lower projected costs than all the other lines save the one to Kyle of Lochalsh, it was effectively a non-starter.

Their other conclusions were a fudge; the members of the Commission really were quite indecisive. They recommended that the railway to Mallaig should be built, with guaranteed returns on capital and a government grant to build a proper pier at Mallaig. But because this would make Mallaig 'a formidable competitor' to the extension to Kyle, then the Treasury should also give these exact same financial terms to the Highland Railway – which had refused to construct the extension without government support. As for the other contenders, the Lochinver line was deemed to be better than the Ullapool one, since it had a safer fishing harbour. They thought that the Aultbea line should also be positively considered, just as long as there was some kind of station in the village of Gairloch along the way. Recoiling from the very idea of actually making a definitive choice, the Commission merely suggested a grant of £40,000 each for 'two other railways on the mainland'. They recommended support (not financial) for the building of lines on Lewis and Skye, which would cost someone £450,000. And then there were subsidised steamer services, grants for new harbours on Lewis, and piers and boat-slips elsewhere (but specifically not at Ullapool), and buoys and lighthouses. All in all, the Government could be expected to cough up £250,000 for myriad improvements.

The Commission was unimpressed by the natives, and the feeling was entirely mutual. The Commission's report did not go down well in Ullapool. In September, Arthur Fowler wrote a long letter to Lord Lothian relaying the 'extreme disappointment' of a public meeting of 300 fishermen and crofters in Ullapool. He pointed out that the Commission had not held a public meeting in Ullapool, merely some informal conversations with persons unnamed. This was in contrast to the public consultations which had taken place in Aultbea, Lochinver and even Applecross and Glenelg. Ullapool had been treated on a par with such unimportant spots as Scoraig, Elgol on Skye, and Eigg. He also pointed out, rather bitterly, the discrepancy of Ullapool's curious location on the map: 'Of course it is not suggested the mistake is intentional.' As a non-suggestion, this lacked conviction, for he also wrote that 'the mistake is calculated to mislead'.[21]

P. Campbell Ross was less circumspect: he advised the Secretary for Scotland that the report was 'drivel', written by 'a Commission of so-called experts'.[22]

Ullapool was not alone in being upset. Questions were asked in Parliament about this report, and they were not at all supportive. Dr MacDonald, MP for Ross and Cromarty, declared that

> nothing has approached the slovenly way in which this Commission did its work. The Commissioners scuttled from place to place; they went to Ullapool; they saw nobody, they went away, and express an opinion as to what should be done, and so on in other districts. I should go beyond the terms of the Motion were I to say much upon this, but I may say that great dissatisfaction exists in the Highlands as

to the way in which the Commissioners performed their duties. There are some wise recommendations in the Report, but there are some that are very unwise.[23]

THE CONCERNS OF RIVAL RAILWAY COMPANIES

'A Hostile Company in Their District'

No sooner had Walpole's commission hit the road, than the railway companies themselves started agitating to have their opinions heard. The Highland Railway in particular was still not keen on anything except its own scheme for Kyle of Lochalsh, and even then it wanted a government subsidy. Despite being named in the Act of 1890, the Highland was in no mood to appear in the least enthusiastic about a railway to Ullapool. After considerable delays – time enough for one commission to come back and report, and just before a second one set out – and little progress, Arthur Fowler and Major Houston asked for a meeting with the Highland, which took place in London on 13 April 1891. But the two parties could reach no agreement on how to proceed with funding and construction. Andrew Dougall for the Highland agreed to work the Garve and Ullapool railway in perpetuity, but only if all the capital for its construction 'was found for them'. This was unhelpful. The meeting adjourned and reconvened the following day at the offices of the Treasury, where they met W. L. Jackson, Tory MP for Leeds and Financial Secretary to the Treasury. Who was also unhelpful. The day ended with no agreement reached.[24] Perhaps, had Sir Alexander Matheson still been alive and still been Director of the Highland, family ties to the Garve and Ullapool promoters (his aunt Lady Matheson and his cousin Donald Matheson) would have counted for something. But, there again, perhaps not.

At this point, Fowler and his fellow directors threw up their hands in despair and declared they had had enough. They turned their attentions to the rival Great North of Scotland Railway (GNSR). This was the company which built and operated lines in the north-east of Scotland, an area stretching from Aberdeen as far as (but not west of) Elgin. The GNSR had for many years been itching to get to Inverness and beyond, into territory north and west of the town. So an invitation from the Garve and Ullapool, a few days after the abortive April meeting, was a dream come true: the GNSR could potentially run trains on the Highland line between Inverness and Garve. According to the company's parliamentary agent, the GNSR board fully understood that, even with state subsidy, the Ullapool line would make an annual loss 'for many years'. But they had no problem with this. The Highland Railway would not have been at all pleased with such an outcome: an observer noted that the Highland 'would be at once prepared to accept almost any terms rather than that a contingency which might interfere with their present monopoly should occur'.[25]

The GNSR duly rubbed its hands and approached the Treasury man Jackson to ensure the proposal ran smoothly. Jackson had by now perfected the art of being unhelpful. He immediately wrote to the Highland, warning them of the new plan and pointing out that a GNSR operation on the Garve and Ullapool line would mean 'a hostile company in their [Highland Railway] district'.[26] He further poured oil on the fires by reminding the Highland of the 'Heads of Agreement' reached a year previously; his unstated implication was that the Garve and Ullapool board was now acting illegally. The Highland reacted with energy. First of all it offered to re-open negotiations with the Garve and Ullapool. The latter remained thoroughly unmoved. Then the Highland resorted to legal counsel, who in quite unsatisfactory manner advised that, since the agreement pre-dated the Act, there was nothing to be done. Letters and telegrams flowed back and forth between all interested parties in May and June 1891, to no avail: the Garve and Ullapool had got into bed with the Great North of Scotland.

Now, this move was a little curious. Barely a year earlier, in late February of 1890, there had been reports of the GNSR objecting to the Ullapool line:

> An announcement, it is stated, has obtained currency in the North to the effect that the Great North of Scotland Railway Company are seeking to oppose the bill for the construction of a line of railway from Garve to Ullapool. A question as to their *locus standi* has, it appears, arisen, and will shortly be heard.[27]

Locus standi, simply put, is the legal right to poke one's nose in. At this time, the GNSR was flexing its muscles, and making strenuous attempts to break westwards out of Elgin, where they had so far been hemmed in by the Highland Railway. The Highland was adept at blocking its rivals – a common tactic was to get permission for railway lines which were subsequently never built, solely to prevent any rival from building their own lines in the same district (a tactic also used by certain large supermarket chains in the UK in the early twenty-first century).[28] Despite some half-hearted discussions with the Highland in the winter of 1889–90 on a possible amalgamation, the GNSR was itself full of cunning plans to stab their neighbour and rival in the back. A list of the Private Bills to be submitted to Parliament in the winter of 1889 – a disparate collection, mostly of railway extensions and electric lighting schemes – included several proposals by the GNSR: firstly, to extend from Elgin to Inverness; secondly, to build a line within Inverness itself to link to the Highland; thirdly and most preposterously, a line from Fortrose on the Cromarty peninsula to Urray (halfway between Beauly and Dingwall and very clearly in sacred Highland Railway territory). Did the GNSR somehow think it had the right to object to a railway from Garve to Ullapool, deep in the heart of the Highland?

P. Campbell Ross very definitely did not think so. In a letter to *The Scotsman* in March (written from the rather grand-sounding 'Garve and Ullapool Railway Committee Rooms' in Ullapool), he railed bitterly at the opposition from the GNSR. 'We have worked hard,' he lectured, 'we have given expression to nothing that we are unable to prove to the utmost; and, therefore, we protest against such an uncalled for interference on the part of a company which has no earthly connection with this part of the country.' The Ullapool committee 'hope that the North-West Highlands are not to be governed by a deputation in Aberdeen'. Rather over-stretching his argument, he attempted to tug at the heartstrings with a disingenuous appeal to democracy: 'We are poor people, and cannot afford a contest with wealthy men who assail us through a company, whose career has been a comparative failure.'[29]

Fortunately, the arbiters at the Court of Referees, meeting in late April 1890 to consider a number of petitions of *locus standi* in respect of Private Bills, agreed with Ross. The GNSR had characterised the Garve and Ullapool as 'practically part of the Highland [Railway] system'. But their petition was refused on the grounds that, if the Garve and Ullapool was an independent concern, then the GNSR had no *locus*; and if it was indeed part of the Highland Railway, then the interests of the GNSR were already protected in law by agreements between the two companies dating from 1884.[30] So that was that. No matter: for now, only a year later, the GNSR had hit upon a new way of both annoying the Highland and getting a toehold in the west. And the Garve and Ullapool directors really had no choice but to go along with the GNSR's astute scheme. (In a curious embellishment, the GNSR now wondered about extending the Ullapool to Garve line eastwards to join the Highland line at Muir of Ord. There seems no particular logic to this, except perhaps as a means of penetrating ever deeper into the Highland fiefdom.)[31]

The GNSR proposed to 'construct, complete, maintain and work [the line] in perpetuity' just as long as they could receive a guaranteed grant from the Treasury of £6,000 per annum, for twenty-five years after the opening of the line. This suggestion doubtless provoked much hilarity in the Whitehall clubs. The Highland Railway immediately countered by proposing exactly the same terms. The Garve and Ullapool board was unmoved, and stuck with the GNSR. Accordingly, the GNSR started collecting signatures for a petition supporting their takeover, in both Lewis and the mainland. One hundred people of Stornoway duly obliged.[32]

Nothing, however, was simple. In order to formalise this new arrangement, a further Bill had to be passed by Parliament. At the end of May 1892 – over a year later; nothing was swift either – the House of Commons discussed a Bill which 'proposes to transfer to the Great North of Scotland Railway certain powers which were obtained by the Garve and Ullapool people from this Parliament by the Bill of 1890'.[33] Put simply, the GNSR was applying to take over the Garve and Ullapool company. Included in the Bill was a clause which basically stated that, if the Highland did not provide 'adequate facilities' to the GNSR between Elgin and Garve, then the GNSR would have the right to run their own rolling stock on the Highland rails: cause for apoplexy in Inverness. With the support of local MPs, the Bill reached a second reading. Mr Cameron, the liberal MP for Wick Burghs, arguing in its favour, wondered why the Government was inclined to take the side of the Highland: 'It is the interest of the country they ought to have at heart, and not the interest of the Highland Railway.' He knew 'that the directors of the Highland Railway are very influential gentlemen and in favour with the present Government'. In the same session,

Dr MacDonald (Ross and Cromarty) thought 'the Secretary to the Treasury ought to be the first to help the Garve and Ullapool people, because they have been considerably at the mercy of the Highland Railway in the past'.[34]

At that time, the Directors of the Highland Railway included: the Marquis of Breadalbane; the Duke of Atholl; the Duke of Sutherland; the Marquis of Tweeddale; the Earl of March; Lord Colville; Sir Kenneth Matheson; and a clutch of minor landowners – not necessarily a group of people we would expect to uphold the interest of the country.

A strong reek of desperation leaks out of the wording of yet another petition which turned up in Whitehall. This one came from Stornoway on 11 June 1891, pleading with Lord Lothian to do something – anything:

> Your petitioners strenuously deprecate existing controvercies [*sic*] as to the special advantages of the several rival routes projected, as having the tendency to retard the interests which Her Majesty's Government have in view, and humbly submit that the Garve and Ullapool Line, being without barrier and having the means of construction and management at disposal, should be proceeded with.[35]

Even more heartfelt was the strong letter sent by P. Campbell Ross to the Scottish Office in October 1891. Impatient that nothing appeared to be happening, he was unable to contain his wrath: 'The temper of the people of this district is becoming a matter of grave concern to me.' The people were irritated at being kept in suspense – so many broken promises! Lochbroom was at that very moment teeming with herring, but the fishermen had no access to market. Ross summoned up the Spirit of Fenianism: 'People who are not without advisers who would not be sorry to see them resorting to Irish methods which have been so highly satisfactory to the Irish . . . Politically, the conduct of the Government is suicidal in so far as the Highland constituencies are concerned . . . The administration has done nothing but make promises and spend public money on Commissions and on whose reports action was not taken.'[36] Strong words indeed. But water off a duck's back in Whitehall: the file is annotated: 'I don't think it necessary to do any thing further at present.'

Some of the notes written on the Scottish Office file copies of these items of correspondence are revealing. On Arthur Fowler's letter of September 1890, for example, someone had the response off pat: 'The acknowledgement seems to have been quite simple. It would be well therefore to say that the Memorial and letter will receive due consideration.' In a rather more acid tone was the comment regarding one of P. Campbell Ross's letters of June 1890, in which he enclosed yet another petition from Ullapool: 'This resolution', wrote the official rather tartly, 'takes a great deal for granted.'[37] It was clear that the staff at the Scottish Office were becoming weary in the face of letters, petitions and more letters.

THE NORTH-WEST COAST OF SCOTLAND RAILWAYS COMMITTEE, 1891

'Interesting Recommendations'

Despite all these criticisms, Whitehall had in fact done something, although it was not necessarily a useful something. In the spring of 1891, Scottish MPs voiced their frustration that almost nine months had gone by since the Walpole report and nothing had been done about any of the recommendations. Others criticised the fact that vast amounts of money were being spent on improving the lot of the people of Ireland, and very little at all on the people of Scotland. And so, in the best tradition of government inquiries, a new commission was appointed in May 1891. It comprised Major-General Charles Hutchinson, Rear-Admiral Sir George Nares and Henry Tennant. Hutchinson was the Board of Trade Inspector of Railways (the same man who had inspected the proposed level crossings between Garve and Ullapool); Nares had made a name for himself in Arctic and South Atlantic exploration, but was now in the Board of Trade, and was included to cast an expert eye over The Sea; Tennant had just retired after two decades as the Chairman of the North Eastern Railway – 'north-east', that is, of England. (For more details on these gentlemen, see Appendix 5.) Their very specific brief was to look at the various railway schemes also examined by the first commission, and inquire

I. Which of the projected schemes is best calculated to promote the interests of the crofting and fishing population in the districts in question

II. What amount of assistance would be required from public funds . . . to secure the construction of the line

III. Which of the schemes, if any, you would recommend the Government to assist.[38]

The Scottish Office and Treasury proved, as always, most helpful: the new inquiry was instructed to seek out and talk to the main promoters of the various schemes, but warned strenuously that 'there are no papers connected with Lord Lothian's visits to the Hebrides, nor any others at this Office which his Lordship thinks would be of service to the Committee'.[39] And so once more, in July and August, some southern gentlemen ventured blindly to the north of Scotland to examine each of the original six contenders. Before setting off, they re-branded themselves as the North-West Coast of Scotland Railways Committee.

They started at the top: Lairg, Kinlochbervie, Lochinver. They paused to amuse themselves with a weekend in Inverness. They stayed there another day (27 July) to meet with the Highland Railway board; and since that meeting was not minuted, we can only guess what deals may have been struck regarding the Kyle line and its near neighbours. The later official report suggests they only talked about possible 'arrangements' on the Culrain to Lochinver route. Thereafter, the Committee moved rapidly on to Ullapool, Poolewe, Kyle of Lochalsh and Mallaig, interviewing relevant persons and listening impatiently to the advantages and disadvantages of each proposal put to them. Then they claim to have revisited Ullapool, Lochinver and 'certain parts of Ross and Sutherland' before retreating south to spend several months sucking their pens and considering what to write in their report.

The report, when it finally appeared, had a title not much shorter than its content: 'Report of a Special Committee appointed to Inquire into Certain Schemes for the Improvement of Railway Communication on the Western Coast of Scotland'. We note that 'Certain Matters' of the earlier report have now become 'Certain Schemes'. Whitehall files show that the report was actually received there on 28 November 1891, but proofs were sent to the Treasury for revision of 12 March 1892, and the document was not actually published until 24 March: Whitehall had sat on it for four months. And no wonder. On 1 April the full text appeared in one of the Dingwall newspapers (under the dry headline 'Interesting Recommendations');[40] and by mid April there was public outrage bordering on riot in the Loch Broom area.

The report ran to all of three and a half pages.[41]

The task of this committee had been to look at the railway proposals for: Lairg to Laxford; Culrain to Lochinver; Garve to Ullapool; Achnasheen to Aultbea; Strome Ferry to Kyle; and Banavie to Mallaig. It was, in other words, a virtual re-run of one of the main tasks of the Commission of 1890, this time undertaken by two seasoned railway experts and one hoary coastal navigation expert. What could possibly go wrong?

According to their own report, Hutchinson, Nares and Tennant had toured the north of Scotland in July and August 1891. They had visited Ullapool on 29 July, where they participated in a public meeting with influential inhabitants – Hutchinson had clearly taken note of the criticisms levelled at the previous commission, since he adopted the precaution of naming twenty-four of the Ullapool inhabitants including Major Houston, William Gunn, Campbell Ross, an assortment of hoteliers, fish-curers, merchants and teachers, '+ others including fishermen';[42] and paid another visit to the village at a later unspecified date. They received correspondence from all and sundry. One letter was from Mr Gunn, the factor of the Earl of Cromartie, who lived at Badentarbet, near Achiltibuie. In a minor diversion to the main thrust of the investigations, Gunn advocated that the Ullapool railway should 'follow the shore to Ardmair bay – with a station – then following the valley of the Runie to the north of the Big Rock or Ben More – by a chain of lochs – Lurgan, Bad a'Ghaill and Osgaig and on to Badentarbet . . . Such a line is absolutely clear of any <u>costly</u> or difficult work of construction.'[43] Or so he thought.

The Committee duly noted that there were 'considerable difficulties from an engineering point of view' for all the proposed railway lines. They estimated construction costs of £8,000 to £10,000 per mile, and suggested that two lines be built: one to the north of Strome Ferry and one to the south. In the end, they seemed inclined towards a line to Mallaig, another to Lochinver, and the extension of the Dingwall to Strome line as far as Kyle of Lochalsh. One might raise the objection that this meant two lines south of Strome – but that would be sheer geographic pedantry.

They had obviously done some homework in respect of Ullapool, and had been advised of continued and extraordinarily enthusiastic support:

> As regards the local support towards the construction of the Garve and Ullapool Line, the cost of the preliminary expenses has been found by landowners, who are also prepared to give their land in exchange for shares. In addition to this, there has been a share subscription to the amount of about £2500, and about 400 labourers have agreed to co-operate by contribution to the purchase of shares one-sixth of the money they would earn if employed upon the construction of the Line.

Assuming this report to be accurate, it does demonstrate that ordinary local people felt strongly enough about the proposal to sacrifice considerably more, in relation to their wealth and income, than the actual promoters of the railway. The 'labourers' in question were doubtless crofters and cottars.

However, the authors of the report rather blotted their copybook with their patchy geographical knowledge. 'Ullapool,' they stated,

> is situate [*sic*] 16 statute miles up an arm of the sea, having an approach emcumbered [*sic*] with islets and rocks, and narrowing for the last three miles to a channel two-thirds of a mile in width . . . The locality is unsuited for a fisheries centre.

These words simply repeated what the 1890 Commission had wrongly determined; and, as we shall see, they rather closely echoed the arguments of the misguided supporters of a railway to Aultbea. Given that Rear-Admiral Nares had, in his previous career, carefully charted a considerable portion of the terrestrial globe, it is a matter of astonishment that scant attention was paid to the coastline at Ullapool. As a picture of the sea-approach their description was scarcely accurate; and, where accurate, scarcely worrying. But it was a description that came back to haunt all concerned over the next few months; and it was a determining factor in the final decision. Their view on the navigational problems was all the more surprising given that Major Houston had written to this same committee in late June of 1891, specifically to point out that the geographical knowledge of the first commission was faulty.[44]

Even less convincing was their bright idea of a north-westwards extension of the Ullapool railway, arguing that a better harbour was located at Lochinver, which would be more suited for the fishing boats, leaving Ullapool as a steamer port. All that would be required would be a longer railway line. They conceded that the countryside between the two places was 'very hilly' (something of an understatement) and would probably increase the cost to £420,000. For which perfectly valid reasons, they ended up with a different solution: the building of a line between Culrain and Lochinver, and none at all to Ullapool. Which left potential steamer passengers disembarking at Ullapool a little inconvenienced.

The report noted that none of the proposals examined seemed to be commercially viable, and it highlighted that the Braemore gradients rendered the Ullapool project particularly difficult. The report recommended, however, that the Mallaig extension be seriously considered, and be given a government subsidy of £100,000; and that a further £45,000 be given as a subsidy for the extension of the Dingwall line to Kyle. In the event, the Mallaig line was offered the generous terms of a guaranteed return of 3 per cent over thirty years on a capital outlay of £260,000, plus £30,000 as a grant for the new pier.[45] This was something of a death-blow to the aspirations of the Garve and Ullapool Railway. Finally, the Committee strongly favoured the Lochinver line as the northern route to the coast, and indicated that the Highland Railway had stated it was prepared to construct and work this line, with government support. It was later revealed that the construction cost for the Lochinver line would be £250,000, but the Government was prepared to offer the same financial incentives as for Mallaig.[46]

Understandably, Ullapool was once more greatly displeased. At a meeting of 'the inhabitants of Lochbroom' on 7 April, the report was described by Arthur Fowler as 'stupid, irritating and mischievous'.[47] A letter 'condemnatory of the report was authorised to be immediately forwarded to Lord Lothian' in which the inhabitants 'desired to express their indignation and astonishment'. On the 20th of April, *The Scotsman* ran a short report (sandwiched neatly between a court report concerning a brothel in Aberdeen, and the news of a gunboat being dispatched to the Shetland island of Whalsay, where fishermen were on strike against the fish-curers – all very nineteenth century):

> A large meeting of fishermen of the extensive district of Coigach was held last night to consider the report of the Special Committee on railway communication in the north-west. Resolutions were unanimously passed condemnatory of the recommendation for a line of railway to Lochbroom [*sic*: this can only be an unfortunate misprint for 'Lochinver'], which would be of no benefit to the important fishing interest of the north-west Highlands. The meeting strongly supported the proposed Garve and Ullapool railway.[48]

At this same meeting in Achiltibuie, 'the oldest inhabitant', being roused to pass comment on the dangers posed by the Summer Islands in the approach to Ullapool, shook his head and stated that he had 'never seen or heard of any casualty happening to any shipping at these islands'.[49] Further afield, on 23 May, a meeting of 'the merchant traders and townspeople of Dingwall and district' was reported to have carried unanimously a resolution which stated 'that this meeting is of opinion that the line of railway which would confer the greatest boon upon the greatest number is the proposed Garve and Ullapool railway'. The town clerk of Dingwall followed this a week later with another petition from his fellow citizens.[50]

In October 1892, welcoming a new Secretary for Scotland to the maelstrom of controversy, P. Campbell Ross was less than complimentary. He wrote two letters on the same day to George Trevelyan. 'Our people are weary of Commissions, Committees and those sorts of things . . . I hope we shall have no more bodies of distinguished strangers making enquiries in our midst.' The report 'might as well have been drawn up in London without putting the country to great and unnecessary – useless – expense'. It was 'even more astonishing than that of the previous year . . . It appears to have been chiefly drawn up in the interest of the Highland Railway Company.'[51] The report of the first commission, declared Ross, 'will speak for itself in all its drivel'.

Of course, the report did not please the Highland Railway either, despite the company being the greatest beneficiary. Andrew Dougall wrote to the Chancellor of the Exchequer at the start of June, stating that the Highland was prepared to extend from Strome to Kyle only 'on condition that the Government does not subsidise any other Line to the West Coast'.[52] An exception was made for the Lochinver line, which they were prepared to build and work 'in perpetuity', just as long as the Government subsidised it heavily – Lochinver was presumably far enough north to be no competitor, or easily forgotten afterwards.

In a letter to his son Arthur four years later, Sir John Fowler reflected on how 'the Commissioners went so completely and curiously wrong as to Ullapool being a convenient and safe harbour, by strangely ignoring the opinions of the fishermen and of every one using it'.[53] His son clearly agreed: he and Kenneth Cameron (Chairman of Ullapool Parish Council) had sent a memorandum to London, 'disposing of the objections' raised in the report.[54] And on 20 May, Lord Lothian, the Secretary for Scotland, received a high-level deputation of Ullapudlians at his office in Dover House. The deputation comprised Sir John Fowler, his son Arthur, no fewer than three MPs (those of Inverness-shire, Wick and West Aberdeenshire) and Major Houston. Amongst the many things said at this meeting, Sir John Fowler, 'speaking as an engineer', begged to differ from the report's view that Ullapool was unsuitable for 'a water terminus', and Houston, representing Lady Matheson, considered that 'all of Lewis' much preferred Ullapool to Lochinver. By now, of course, the whole affair was firmly entangled in the controversy between the Highland Railway and the Great North of Scotland Railway. At the end of the meeting, Lord Lothian muttered some platitudes and Fraser Mackintosh (MP for Inverness-shire) 'conveyed to Lord Lothian the thanks of the deputation, who then withdrew'.[55] All very stately.

And of course none of it did any good.

MPs were strangely slow to react to the Hutchinson report. Although questions were asked in the House by a Crofters' Party MP in June 1892, these were limited to the Lochinver proposal and did not address the strange assessment of Ullapool.[56] It was not for a full year that any others attempted an intervention – by which time it was far too late for anything to be done. In July 1893, in an entertaining exchange concerning the report of the second commission, Mr Whitelaw, MP for Perth, asked the Chancellor of the Exchequer (Harcourt) if he was

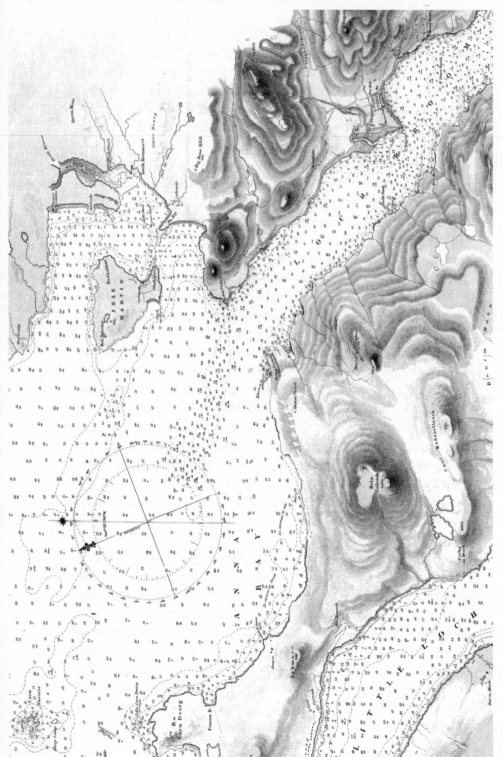

Figure 6.1 Section of Admiralty chart for Loch Broom, showing the area (remarkably rock-free) between Ullapool and the Summer Isles (Crown Copyright)

aware that the members of the Committee which condemned Loch Broom as unnavigable never went near either Ullapool or Loch Broom in order to take evidence from those accustomed to navigate the loch, which large steam and sailing vessels do navigate by day and by night with perfect ease?

Harcourt, something of a yachtsman himself, blustered that 'I have myself navigated Loch Broom, and can speak personally of the loch, but I believe the Report was founded on a very careful examination of the matter by a Commission.' A few days later, James Weir, Crofters' Party MP for Ross and Cromarty, put the question to the Admiralty Secretary (the splendidly named Sir Ughtred Kay-Shuttleworth): 'whether the Admiralty charts show that there are islets and rocks in Loch Broom preventing the safe navigation of the loch from its entrance to Ullapool?', to which Kay-Shuttleworth could only reply: 'There is nothing to prevent the safe navigation of Loch Broom from its entrance to Ullapool. The Sailing Directions state that it is remarkable for being perfectly free from rocks and dangers of any sort, excepting the squalls natural to narrow seas encompassed with mountainous land.' So much for accuracy, then. Returning to the fray in September, Mr Weir asked innocently whether 'the Secretary to the Admiralty is incompetent to give an accurate opinion, and that the Admiralty charts are inaccurate?'[57] Even the Conservative MP for Perth, Mr Whitelaw, had been reliably informed that 'of the Committee who reported on this harbour not a single man went near it, or took any local evidence upon it'.[58] Significantly, there is no report that anyone in Whitehall denied these allegations against the Committee.

Several years later, P. Campbell Ross, still functioning as the Honorary Secretary of the Ullapool Railway, wrote a snippy letter to the Secretary for Scotland – by now, this was the Conservative Lord Balfour of Burleigh – highlighting several failures to communicate decisions and proposals back to the relevant people. In some cases, letters and memos issued from the Treasury and the Scottish Office had only reached Ullapool weeks, months – and in one case years – afterwards.[59]

The selfless attempts by the GNSR to acquire rights to the Garve and Ullapool Railway were by now going nowhere. In March 1892, questions were being asked in Parliament about the negotiations and why they were not yet completed; the Lord Advocate replied smoothly that the whole thing 'was attended with difficulties for which a solution could not be found'.[60] In April 1892, fake news – initiated, possibly in error, by the hapless local MP Dr MacDonald – that the GNSR was abandoning its attempt to take over the railway project was denied by the GNSR in an expensive telegram to Ullapool. Dr MacDonald thereby found himself pilloried as 'ignorant and untrustworthy' in the local papers, and thereafter kept very quiet throughout the parliamentary debates on the matter.[61] But by November of 1892, the GNSR was indeed beginning to think of a gracious exit: they agreed to sponsor the Bill of Transfer only if the Government stumped up 3 per cent of the requisite capital, which was never going to happen.

7

'The Day for Promises, Evasion and Trifling is Past'

Costs, Revenues and Government Prevarication

It will be obvious by now that money was always a problem when it came to building a railway. A lot of money was required, and the Government was never likely to give you any. To give some idea of the costs involved, they are summarised in Table 2.

TABLE 2 ESTIMATES AND COSTS FOR VARIOUS
HIGHLAND RAILWAYS

Route	Length (miles)	1890 estimates		1892 estimate	Cost to govt	Actual total cost
		total	per mile			
Fort William to Mallaig	40	£285,000	£7,120	£330,000	£206,000	£540,000
Strome to Kyle	10.5	£115,000	£10,952	£180,000	£45,000	£270,000
Achnasheen to Aultbea	39.5	£293,000	£7,417	£300,000	£176,400	–
Garve to Ullapool	33.5	£195,000	£5,820	£200,000	£104,800 or £117,600	–
Culrain to Lochinver	42	£260,000	£6,190	£250,000	£147,000	–
Lairg to Laxford	37	£220,000	£5,945	–	–	–
Lines on Lewis	101	£310,000	£3,069	–	–	–
Lines on Skye	45	£140,000	£3,111	–	–	–

Columns headed '1890' represent the estimates provided by the 1890 West Highlands and Island Commission, and the column headed 'Length' is the Commission's estimate of the mileage; '1892' the estimates provided by a reliable under-secretary at the Scottish Office, W. C. Dunbar; the 'Cost to govt' column shows Dunbar's calculation of nett governmental liability through grants and guaranteed interest payments.[1] 'Actual total cost' means exactly what it says.

Two things stand out: firstly, that estimates were wildly inaccurate when compared to actual costs. Secondly, the cost per mile varies quite considerably. The estimates provided in documents, letters and memoranda range from about £5,000 to upwards of £10,000 – these are figures for standard-gauge lines; for 'light railways' as envisaged for Skye and Lewis, the costs are lower at around £3,000, although some optimists were inclined to put them as low as £2,000. When hard-headed railway engineers were involved, things were conceivably more accurate. In 1896, Sir John Fowler put an estimate on the Ullapool railway of £5,000 per mile for a standard-gauge line, although he thought it could be done for £4,400 with a light railway;[2] Charles Forman, the engineer on the West Highland Railway, put the cost of a railway from Spean Bridge to Fort Augustus at £8,000 per mile, and a light railway on Skye at £5,700 per mile.[3] Naturally, the cost per mile was completely dependent on the terrain to be covered, but it also took into account the number of bridges and culverts, the number of stations and halts, and any requirements for short lengths of double-track ('crossing loops') to allow trains to pass each other.

Because the Government was so extremely tight-fisted with loans and subsidies to Scottish railway projects, it was obvious that any railway would have to have some serious capital investment behind it. The Highland Railway came rather badly unstuck with its estimates for the Kyle extension, and was only saved from grave difficulties by virtue of having a large operational network to provide constant revenues. Legislation recognised the dangers, not least because of the countless bankruptcies caused by 'railway mania' in the middle of the century. Applying to build a railway necessitated a Private Bill, which would be closely examined before it became an Act of Parliament. The Act for the Garve and Ullapool Railway in 1890 is a good example of the financial terms and conditions involved: the capital for the company was set at £240,000 – more than enough to cover construction and start-up costs; the Company was not permitted to borrow from the banks more than one-third of their share capital – i.e. £80,000 to begin with; a sum of 5 per cent (£9,780) of the estimated costs of construction (£195,600) had been lodged as deposit with the Treasury – this was a prerequisite for getting the Act passed. The deposit was deemed non-refundable unless the railway was open for business within the set timescale. In Ullapool's case, presumably, the money was lost; who had contributed is not known, but one supposes it was the Mathesons. They could afford it. But this would be another enormous obstacle to railway promoters with little financial backing. And it was also the reason why almost every single application for a railway also begged the Government for a guaranteed annual return on investment for a lengthy period – typically, 3 per cent per annum for thirty years, with any actual profit percentages deducted.

HOW TO FINANCE A RAILWAY

'Dung Compost, Manure – Per Ton Per Mile One Penny Halfpenny'

Construction costs were one thing; operating costs another. Once again, these would be dependent on the physical nature of the countryside and the weather, as well as on the type and volume of traffic. The Highland Railway had been around for a while: when a small company came asking for contracts to 'work and maintain' their little branch lines, the Highland would frequently quote costs of 2s 2d (£0.11) per train mile. Some found these costs too high, but never did such people later find themselves running a railway. The Highland would doubtless have built in to that 2s 2d some profit margin for themselves. It was down to the railway companies to set charges by which they could recoup running costs; but the charges had upper limits defined. In the case of Ullapool, the possible charges were contained within the paragraphs of the Act.

- 'Persons' could be carried at 2d per mile (or 3d, 'if carried in or upon a carriage belonging to or provided by the Company' – an interesting, if confusing, distinction). The maximum fare was to be 3d per mile for first class, 2d for second class and 1d for third class. There would be a minimum charge-distance of three miles.

- Animals:
  - Horses, mules, asses or 'other beasts of burden' – 2d per mile
  - Oxen, cows, bulls or 'head of neat cattle' – 2d per mile
  - Calves, pigs – 1½d per mile
  - Sheep or 'other small animal' – 1d per mile
- Goods
  - Dung, compost, manure (except guano and artificial manures), lime etc – 1½d per ton per mile
  - Coal, coke, 'culm', charcoal, cinders, stones, bricks etc. – 2d per ton per mile
  - Sugar, grain, corn, flour, timber, guano, nails, anvils etc. – 3d per ton per mile
  - Cotton, wools, manufactured goods and fish – 4d per ton per mile

(Fish would therefore cost 11 shillings per ton for the full distance; we have the word of a newspaper that in 1894, 'the carriage from Ullapool to Garve for fish is 40s per ton, a rate that is simply prohibitive'.[4] We also remember that Mr Anderson of Oban spoke of fish-carriage costing 3s 10d per cwt all the way to London – slightly less than 2d per ton per mile.)

- Carriages – 6d per mile for those weighing up to a ton, 1½d per each additional quarter-ton
- Parcels
  - up to 7lb in weight, 3d; 7 to 14lb, 5d; 14 to 28lb, 7d; 28 to 56lb, 9d;
  - 'any parcel exceeding fifty-six pounds in weight such sum as the Company think fit'

Finally, luggage accompanying paying passengers was not permitted to exceed 120 lb (first class passenger), 100 lb (second class) or 60 lb (third class). Everything, in short, had been thought of and regulated.

It should be clear from this that recouping costs in a sparsely populated area was going to be heavily dependent on goods traffic. Let us, like Caldwell's admirable gamekeeper, do some calculus.

Above. Francis, Lord Napier, who chaired the wide-ranging inquiry into crofting and economic conditions in 1883. (Image public domain, Scottish National Portrait Gallery)

Right. John Murdoch, journalist and relentless campaigner for land reform in the Highlands and Islands. (Image public domain)

The HMS *Lively* served as transportation for the Napier Commission until it was wrecked off Stornoway in June 1883. (*Illustrated London News*, June 1883)

Sir John Fowler, railway engineer and co-designer of the Forth Bridge, seen here c. 1895 with his grandson Alan. (Courtesy of Peter Newling, Ullapool)

Arthur Fowler, eldest son of Sir John Fowler, seen here c. 1892 with three of his children. Promoter of the Ullapool Railway in 1890 and 1896. (Courtesy of Peter Newling, Ullapool)

Above. The rear of Braemore House, near Ullapool – built for Sir John Fowler, who had purchased the Braemore Estate in 1865. The house no longer stands. (Courtesy of Peter Newling, Ullapool)

Right. Sir John Fowler designed London's Metropolitan Railway. In the grounds of Braemore House, there was a full-sized mock-up of one of the London tunnels to test ventilation. This was the closest Ullapool came to having a railway. (Ullapool Museum / ULMPH-2000-0128)

Murdoch Paterson, chief engineer of the Highland Railway, was commissioned to draw up the Ullapool Railway plans in 1890. (Courtesy of the Highland Railway Society)

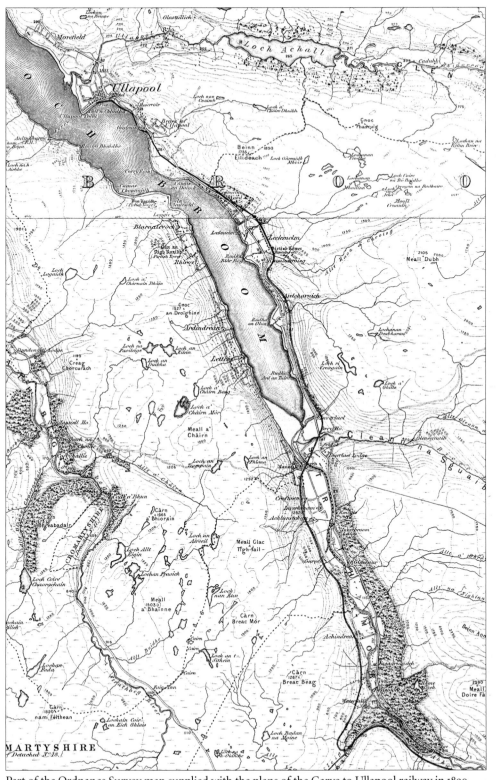

Part of the Ordnance Survey map supplied with the plans of the Garve to Ullapool railway in 1890. The route of the railway was marked in red ink. (National Records of Scotland / RHP916)

John Henry Dixon co-ordinated the Aultbea railway campaign from his residence at Inveran, near Poolewe. (Gairloch Museum / GARHM IMG357)

View across the western end of Loch Maree from Inveran House. The proposed railway to Aultbea would have traversed the far hillside, by means of two tunnels and some terrifying descents. (Gairloch Museum / GARHM IMG365)

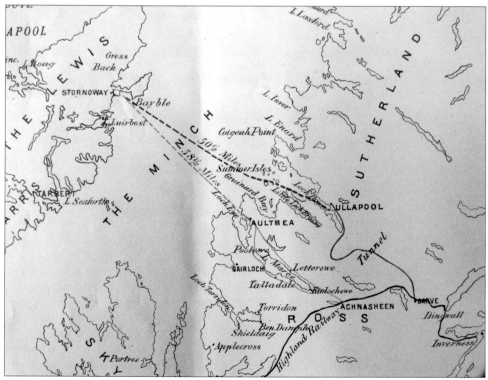

Part of John Dixon's map of the proposed Aultbea railway and its rival to Ullapool. Note the wildly exaggerated deviation in the Ullapool line, and the offset position of Ullapool itself. (National Records of Scotland / AF67/203)

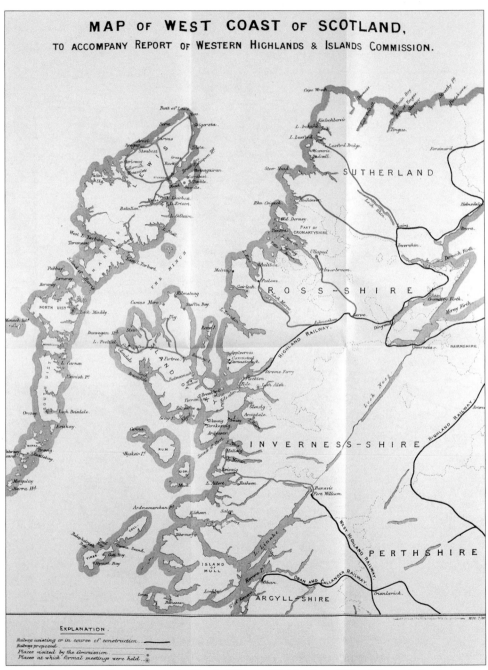

A map of north-west Scotland, prepared by the Western Highlands and Island Commission in 1891, showing all the proposed lines to the west coast. Ullapool is neatly out of position.
(National Records of Scotland / AF67/201)

Stornoway Harbour c. 1906, bristling with the masts of fishing boats. All the proposed railways were to transport fish landed at Stornoway. (University of Aberdeen / GB 0231 MS 3792/C1127)

A modern photo of the western end of the Pentland Road, at Carloway, running alongside the river. Plans were drafted for a light railway to run over this road to Stornoway. (Courtesy of Jack Kernahan)

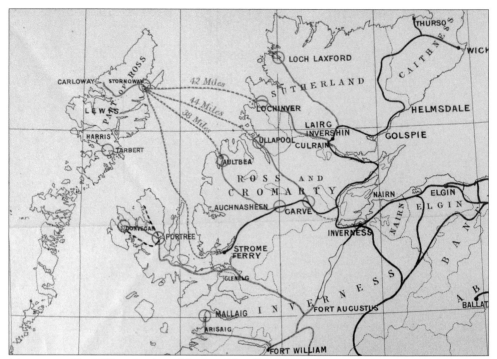

Map prepared by William Dunbar of the Scottish Office in 1892, showing most of the proposed railways. (National Records of Scotland / AF67/201)

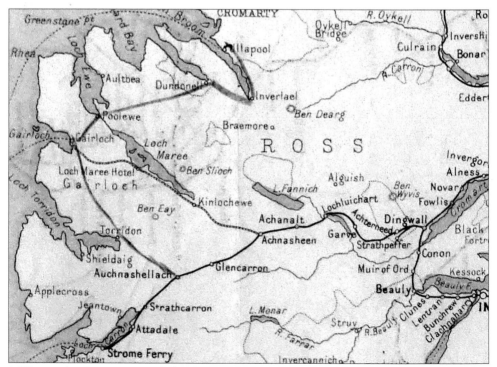

William Munro in 1889 proposed a 'compromise' railway which would link Achnashellach, Gairloch and Loch Broom. His imaginative proposal was sketched out on a Bartholomew's Map of the 'Caledonian Railway and its Connections'. (National Records of Scotland / AF67/201)

Above. Present-day view south-eastwards up the strath at the head of Loch Broom. Murdoch Paterson planned for the railway to tunnel under and then descend the hillside on the right. (Photograph by author)

Left. Rev. Montague Fowler, third son of Sir John. Photograph taken c. 1900. Montague inherited the Braemore Estate in 1915 and chaired the Lochbroom Executive Committee of 1918. (From Charles Dant, *Distinguished Churchmen*, London, 1902)

Enjoying the sunshine, D.S. Ross (right), Inspector of the Poor, and secretary of the Lochbroom Executive Committee of 1918, and Dr Wallace (left), local physician and committee member. (Courtesy of Joan Michael, Ullapool)

Commander Clare Vyner (standing beside the Queen Mother), owner of Keanchulish estate near Ullapool. Local philanthropist, proposer of an Ullapool railway in 1945. (Ullapool Museum / ULMPH-2000-0340)

The Garve to Ullapool railway was to run for just over 33 miles; this would be a nominal operating cost per journey (at 2s 2d per mile) of £3 11s 6d. Assuming most people would travel the full distance, because there was not much reason to stop en route, then to break even on passengers alone would require the sale of a dozen second class tickets (or nine of the better sort). Let us be more realistic and suppose just five people travelled on an average journey – around £1 7s 6d revenue: another £2 4s had to be found. To break even, you would need to fill your goods wagons regularly with the equivalent of two tons of fish (that would be 16 barrels of the 'English wine' variety), a ton of coal, a ton of assorted building materials and guano, a cow, a couple of sheep and maybe some nice big parcels. If this kind of usage could be sustained and exceeded, then the line would begin to pay; but to recoup the capital investment would require more passengers and more freight on a regular basis over many years.

There were other sources of income: the Highland Railway was known to offer a 10 per cent share of revenues for passengers and goods whose end-to-end journey was undertaken on both a Highland line and a branch line – for example Ullapool to Garve and then onward to Dingwall and Inverness. And it might be possible to secure a contract to carry mail for the General Post Office. Indeed, with a sensible long-term contract with the fishing industry, and with passengers joining a steamer service to and from Stornoway, a train service between Ullapool and Garve could conceivably pay its way. But it would have to do so in fierce competition with the Dingwall to Strome Ferry line. The operation of a small branch railway was essentially a social service, not one for making investors rich quickly; and unless it was given some kind of leg-up by the Government, it could not even start.

(The operating cost of 2s 2d per mile in 1890 equates to around £11.00 in the second decade of the twenty-first century. In 2012, Scotrail reported operating costs of £9.60 per train kilometre – £15.36 per train mile. The figures are, over time, remarkably similar.)[5]

As we might expect, P. Campbell Ross had his own take on the costs and revenues of running the Ullapool railway. These he set out in a number of 'statements' which were submitted to the 1890 Western Highlands and Island Commission.[6] From the fisheries, he coolly expected two-thirds of all herring cured in Stornoway to pass through

Ullapool – in an average year just under 68,000 barrels, which would bring in £3,000. Estimating fifteen passengers on each of four train journeys daily (so 18,780 journeys, with a fifth of passengers luxuriating in first class and the rest rattling along in third), the revenues would be £3,100 annually, exclusive of hordes of tourists. From livestock and goods a further £1,800, and from a GPO contract to carry mails, £1,000. His livestock calculation is a model of hopefulness: estimating 45,000 sheep resident in the area, he expected two-thirds of them to be shifted by rail annually; similarly with the cows and horses. For the mails, he produced a table which proved that letters would reach Stornoway three hours earlier than via Strome Ferry. As for operating costs, based on the 'Heads of Agreement' with the Highland, these would come in at just over £4,000. A tidy nett profit, therefore, of around £5,000 per annum. No mention is made of maintenance, repairs or replacements – it is unlikely that the Highland would think of paying for those under its contract. But Ross could perhaps be forgiven for pipe-dreaming.

Operating costs would also include track maintenance, repair and refurbishment; staff costs; and maintenance of rolling stock. There would be capital outlay on engines, carriages, wagons, sheds and so on. These items were not cheap. In 1892, John Anderson of the Callander and Oban Railway was asked to estimate costs for a light railway on Lewis.[7] He reckoned £81,000 to construct 18 miles of railway, then two trains, each with one engine, one carriage for passengers and four wagons for goods at a total expenditure of £2,620, and finally £3,000 for sheds and workshops. Anderson does not tell us the route of the railway, but it was probably the one from Stornoway to Carloway, and the train would come back to Stornoway laden with fish. Because this was a light railway, all of the rolling stock would have been lighter and cheaper than the equivalents for standard-gauge.

Another item of both capital and operating cost was a level crossing. There were originally to be four level crossings on the Ullapool line – at Torr Breac near Garve (this was the one deprecated by Hutchinson's inspection); then just west of Braemore where the railway crossed the Dundonnell road; one near Inverlael; and another between Leckmelm and Braes. It should not be forgotten that in those days a level crossing always required a man or a woman to look after it, along with a small cottage for the crossing-keeper to live in. In practical terms, the three approved crossings could scarcely be managed by a local resident from somewhere just along the road – least of all on the bleak and windswept road up at Braemore junction. They would all have to be installed in a specially built residence adjacent to the crossing. (It would be a peculiar existence, one perhaps best combined with tending a patch of ground. Or solving the differential calculus. The more romantic reader may be irresistibly reminded of *La Bête Humaine*, Émile Zola's classic lust-fuelled novel in which the level crossing and its keepers played such a fateful role.) According to an estimate for a railway line on Lewis, one could expect a gatekeeper's house to cost the princely sum of £150, with all the paraphernalia for the crossing a further £100. However, given the costs and trouble of additional staff, as well as the potential for unforeseen accidents, the railway company might well have decided to eschew crossings in favour of initially more expensive road bridges.

We can get a better idea of the costs and revenues of a proper railway by looking at the half-yearly statements of accounts issued by the Highland Railway.[8] The average cost of a new engine came in at about £2,500, carriages at about £350 and goods wagons at £100. Across its 400-plus miles of track, with between 80 and 115 engines, trains travelled around a million miles in six months. In that accountancy period, the company calculated revenues that averaged: mails £28,000; passengers anything between £72,000 and £118,000; parcels £20,000–25,000; goods £50,000–60,000; livestock £10,000–15,000. The wages bill across all departments amounted to around £60,000. What is interesting is that the revenues from mail and parcels did not vary much across the years, suggestive of longer-term fixed-price contracts. It should be observed in passing that in the years 1890–99 the Highland was posting annual operating profits of around £200,000 – testimony, one might suppose, to saying 'no' to every small-time rival. But it is not irrelevant that the Highland railways were all of the main-line variety – not a single branch railway to be seen. There was no pandering to the public good in Highland's realm.

And what, exactly, did the travelling public get for their money in those days? By modern standards, journey times were not fast. Ignoring the occasional PR stunts, a train could travel from Edinburgh to London in eight and a half hours, at around 47 mph (in the 1890s a locomotive in America attained 65 mph, but that's the kind of thing those Americans would do). But further north, on the Highland line from Perth to Inverness (this was in 1885, the line at that time running via Forres), the fastest mail train covered the 144-mile distance in four and a half hours – an average speed of 32 mph; the slowest train could take well over seven hours, and the average was between six and seven – around 22 mph. Between Inverness and Wick, 167 miles, the journey took between six and eight hours.[9] On the Dingwall to Kyle of Lochalsh railway, 63 miles in total, a journey in 1897 might take around three hours; it was not a huge improvement on a similar journey on the same line twenty years earlier – Dingwall to Strome in 1876, two and three-quarters hours; and in 1897, two and a quarter hours.[10] On a branch line such as the one to Ullapool, you could never hope for anything going faster than that.

But speed is, as we now know, relative. If a decent road existed, your horse-drawn coach would be travelling at a fast walking pace – say, 5 mph; a homeward-bound and unencumbered horse might do it with a bit more enthusiasm. On foot, a journey from Ullapool to Garve would take you a long day. Getting from Ullapool to Inverness (62 miles) in perhaps three hours was not far short of incredible.

THE LIBERAL GOVERNMENT DECIDES

'The Benefit to the Districts Would Be Greatly Appreciated'

All the hopeful railway schemes were thwarted in their search for finance; no one was prepared to back them. And then, as if things were not tangled enough in the sticky webs of railway company intrigue, incompetent commissions and exasperated civil servants, there was a general election in the summer of 1892. The Conservative government of Lord Salisbury was ejected, and a Liberal/Irish Nationalist coalition came to power under Gladstone. In August, Lord Lothian packed up his personal effects and yielded his desk to Sir George Trevelyan. Part of the population turned briefly optimistic. The people of Uig on Lewis wrote a letter declaring that their public meeting 'hails with delight the return of a Liberal Government'.[11] But this changeover came at a most inconvenient moment for the smaller railway promoters in north-west Scotland. Having expended much energy in telling the

Conservative Secretary for Scotland about their plans, they now realised the necessity of restating everything all over again to a new Liberal
Secretary for Scotland. Another tide of letters, petitions and memoranda rolled southwards in the autumn of the year. Unable to stand any
more, Mr Cochran-Patrick, Permanent Under-Secretary at the Scottish
Office, bowed out to devote himself to numismatics, leaving his deputy
in charge. The deputy was W. Cospatrick Dunbar. Rather than plough
through a mountain of paperwork himself, Trevelyan asked Dunbar to
summarise. He did so.

Dunbar typed up three pages of a memorandum entitled succinctly
'Highlands and Islands (Railways)'. His summary was accurate; he
attached various important documents – the Ullapool Railway Act,
the reports of the two commissions – noting with a slight trace of
subjectivity: 'The advent of the first Report gave rise to the most
interminable correspondence with the Promoters of the various
proposed lines.' In reply to Trevelyan's rather naïve question: which line
does the public prefer? – he replied astutely that Skye was in favour of
Mallaig, 'but the majority in the Lews I think favour Garve and
Ullapool'. He signed off stating that 'I have written this rather under
pressure, and it is a long story. But, if required, can give any further
information S for S may require.'[12]

It is possible he came to regret that generous offer, because by mid
September he was catching boats and trains and carriages across the
wild expanses of north-west Scotland. But he did not complain, and
neither should we. Dunbar, on his own, found out more, and more
accurate, information during his three-week excursion than two fully
manned commissions had managed in the preceding two years. On his
return to London, he had his report printed up and handed over to
Trevelyan.

It is a thorough document – ten times longer than Hutchinson's
and longer even than Walpole's.[13] Between 19 September and 9
October, Dunbar visited the routes of five of the six of proposed lines
(he did not bother with the Laxford route), including, of course, the
villages of Aultbea, Ullapool and Lochinver. He then went on to
Stornoway to consider the Lewis railway requirements (a new era had
opened up in state-funded transportation: he travelled by scheduled
Macbrayne's steamers, rather than gunboat). In Ullapool, he conversed
with locals unnamed, and satisfied himself beyond any doubt that

there was not a single rock, reef or squall at the entrance to Loch Broom. He praised the Aultbea proposal as best for tourists, and the Ullapool one as best for the fisheries; but did not think much of Lochinver. He recommended a railway on Lewis and, having also visited Skye, supported a light railway there. He was in Inverness on 7 October to meet Andrew Dougall of the Highland Railway; and in Aberdeen on the 20th to meet the Great North of Scotland Railway. (Dunbar had a home in Bridge of Earn, and was a keen golfer – he could be forgiven if he engaged in a few holes between these meetings.) He stated that he had been in the north-west several times between 1886 and 1891, and so was no stranger to the area. It is hard to fault him. Indeed, William Cospatrick Dunbar was a man of some talent; born in 1844, the son of the 7th Baronet Dunbar of Mochrum (in Wigtownshire) – whose title he inherited in 1904 – he left the Scottish Office in 1902 and went straight to the post of Registrar General for England and Wales (1902 to 1909): cleverly, he avoided being in charge of an actual census; both the appointment and his term of office gave some indication of his skills.

In his conclusions to Trevelyan, Dunbar recommended that:

- the Loch Maree and Aultbea line should be built if it was necessary to set up a fishery in direct competition with Stornoway;
- neither the Lochinver nor the Laxford lines should be built;
- the Garve and Ullapool should be built if it was *not* desirable to pose any competition with Stornoway;
- a subsidy should be granted to the Strome Ferry to Kyle extension;
- a railway should be constructed from Portree to Dunvegan.

The suggestion that Aultbea might somehow be set up in competition with Stornoway is a novelty. This supposed that Aultbea itself could become not merely a railhead receiving processed fish from Stornoway, but in fact constitute a complete alternative: fishing boats would bring their catches straight to Aultbea ('excellent anchorage'), the fish would be cured and processed there, and then immediately sent onwards by rail. The idea made economic and practical sense. Although not, we imagine, to the fish-curers of Stornoway.

Dunbar was also at some pains to point out that Ireland had benefited greatly from government subsidies for light railways, 'and I am disposed to think that, whilst the expenditure of capital in the construction of such railways would not be directly remunerative, the benefit to the districts served would be greatly appreciated . . . It would afford, amongst other things, the kind of employment which is at present so much needed in the poorer districts.'[14] He attached copies of all the correspondence he had received from companies and individuals during his tour – twenty-two items in all. Dunbar brought a welcome air of thoroughness, clarity and determination to the whole sorry tale. He included in his report a handy map showing the various proposed railway lines and relevant distances to Stornoway by sea. The map was completely accurate and Ullapool was in the right place. Well, almost completely accurate: curiously, the proposed railway extension from Strome Ferry to Kyle of Lochalsh was not marked. This does not seem to be a minor oversight, since he did mark the steamer route to Stornoway from Strome Ferry. Had the Highland Railway executives in some way annoyed Dunbar? Also missing from the map was any indication of the steamer distance between Stornoway and Laxford.

Alas, for all his under-secretary's heroic efforts, the new Secretary for Scotland proved to be much the same as the old one. Nothing was done. The reports of previous commissions were defended in a desultory fashion; renewed letters and petitions were wearily batted to one side. The dreams of crofters, fishermen and railway promoters soon withered. The people of Uig on Lewis who had hailed the new Liberal government may have raised their hopes a little high when they sent in a shopping-list comprising: a railway to Ullapool, a railway from Stornoway to Callanish, improved postal facilities and – best of all – 'Compulsory Powers being given to any Commission, to grant land suitable for cultivation, but now under sheep farms or deer forests, to congested crofter townships.'[15] One can imagine the rolling of eyes in Whitehall.

A year later, P. Campbell Ross, the Hon. Secretary of Ullapool, had lost patience; he sent Trevelyan yet another petition, and accused the Government of leaving its supporters 'in the hands of monopolists'. By this, he meant the Highland Railway. 'You are very much mistaken if you deem Ross and Cromarty "a safe seat" . . . The day for promises, evasion and trifling is past, and the sooner the Government realizes this fact the better for them.'[16]

THE GARVE AND ULLAPOOL RAILWAY (ABANDONMENT) ACT 1893

'Indignant Protests'

Things now moved inexorably towards a conclusion that could have been foreseen in 1889. In November 1892, the GNSR was smoothly stepping away from a workable agreement on the Ullapool line. And in mid December, it was revealed that the Government was about to grant the Highland Railway £45,000 to aid with the construction of their line to Kyle.[17] No one should have been astonished; but reaction from the supporters and promoters of every other conceivable railway line was immediate. J. G. Weir MP summed it all up nicely in a telegram sent to Trevelyan on the 21st of the month: 'Garve Ullapool Railway has Government abandoned scheme indignant protests received from Ullapool Liberals can I see you tomorrow.'[18] Happily, Trevelyan was at his country pile in Northumberland, so could not be seen tomorrow. It would have ruined his Christmas. On the same day, the London agents for the Aultbea line also wrote a strong letter. It did not one whit of good.

In a last-gasp effort to breathe life into the Ullapool project, a new pile of petitions was collected in Ullapool and parcelled up for London. On the archived file containing all these pieces of paper, one member of the Scottish Office staff scribbled: 'If you do not care to pass these on to S for S – or to trouble the Treasury with them – I can consign them to the pigeon-holes as they come in.' Reply: 'Yes, agreed.'[19] Rather disappointingly, the person who made the suggestion was none other than William Cospatrick Dunbar. He had evidently lost any enthusiasm he ever had.

The Highland Railway had been promised enough public money to enable it to proceed with the extension of the line to Kyle; and at the end of June 1893, the relevant Act was passed to permit the work to go ahead. The fact that the Highland was being offered almost the exact same terms and conditions for subsidies and loans as those refused to the Garve and Ullapool Railway did not go unnoticed; it might not be far-fetched to infer, as some contemporaries did, that some form of collusion had taken place between government officials and the directors of the Highland Railway. And the engineering difficulties envisaged for the Ullapool line were just as great on the ten-mile Kyle extension. Construction of the latter started in September 1893 and the line opened for traffic in November 1897 – an average rate of progress of a little over two miles per year. (Because of these delays, the promised £45,000 did not get paid to the Highland until the end of March 1898.)[20] It took a little longer for the Mallaig extension to be authorised on the West Highland Railway: although construction was authorised in July 1894, it took two years, and considerable wrangling in Parliament, for an Act to be passed confirming a generous grant of £30,000. The line opened in 1901.

In a rather sad ending to all his heroic work, in November 1897 Patrick Campbell Ross found himself in lodgings right beside the newly opened railway extension from Strome Ferry to Kyle of Lochalsh, and had to swallow the bitter dregs of the failure of the Ullapool proposal. 'Dougall's Folly', he muttered grumpily, referring to the Highland Railway general manager.[21]

For the Garve and Ullapool Railway Company, as for the local people, there was nothing more to be done. On 24 August, just over three years since the heady days of the 1890 Act, the Garve and Ullapool Railway (Abandonment) Act was passed. It did more or less what it said on the tin: the Garve and Ullapool Railway project was to be abandoned. Having not received any 'subsidy or pecuniary aid' from the Treasury, and no capital shares having been issued, and no land having been purchased within the stipulated three years, there was little hope of salvaging anything at all from the wreckage. The final paragraph of the Abandonment Act stated: 'All costs charged and expenses of and incident to the preparing applying for obtaining and passing of this Act or otherwise in relation thereto shall be paid by the Company' – a rather obscure, if worryingly all-inclusive, statement. Did 'this Act' mean the Act of 1890 or of 1893?[22]

The Highland Railway certainly interpreted 'this Act' as meaning that they could claw back all expenses relating to the 1890 Act. Thus, in November 1892 Stewart, Rule & Burns, their solicitors in Inverness, sued the Garve and Ullapool Railway Company for the sum of £470

5s 9d, plus interest at 5 per cent per annum, plus legal expenses, being the costs of preparing the Bill to promote the railway. The lawyers noted that the Ullapool company had 'no known office or place of business', but named individuals would do nicely – to wit, the Rt Hon. Earl of Cromartie at Tarbat House; Donald Matheson of Hyde Park, London; J. A. Fowler of Braemore; Major Matheson, now governor of Her Majesty's Prison at Ipswich; James Houston at the Army and Navy Club, Pall Mall; and Lady Mary Matheson of Stornoway Castle. The defendants in the case brushed off the claim, stating that they were not liable, since they had never employed the pursuers for their professional services: presumably their argument was that the Highland Railway engaged these services. In the event – maybe because of the high profile of some of the defendants? – the case was dismissed by Lord Low in January 1893.[23] As a postscript, we will remark that the Highland Railway Board resolved in October 1894 'to charge the sum of £320–14–2 incurred in connection with the Garve and Ullapool Line and also of £435–8–5 in connection with the proposed Lochinver Line to the Premium Account'.[24] A couple of undesirable debts just had to be written off. But the Highland Railway Company could afford it.

Thus did end the first attempt to construct a railway from Garve to Ullapool. With no result, and with the galling sight of a rival railway to the coast passing well to the south – and, as we have seen, with the Directors of the now-moribund Company being a little out of pocket.

And none of the publicity and none of the campaigns appeared to have done much to improve the welfare of local people. Mr Weir MP asked the Chancellor of the Exchequer in May 1893

whether, in view of the fact that in and around Ullapool a large number of families are absolutely without seed oats and potatoes, and are unable to find employment at or near their homes, and have no means to go elsewhere in search of work, he will place at the disposal of the Scottish Office sufficient money to provide employment for these persons on public works, or re-consider his decision with regard to granting a subsidy for the construction of the Garve and Ullapool Railway, or make other provision to open up communication with this populous and inaccessible district?[25]

The Chancellor dodged the question by swiftly passing it to the Secretary for Scotland, who dodged it in his turn by announcing (a) that £400 had been allocated for road-building around Loch Broom and (b) that fortnightly official reports had never flagged up any poverty in Ullapool, so no further measures were required. (That £400 was not necessarily for 'roads' – a memo from the Liberal Association of Loch Broom, of March 1893, states that the grant of this money was 'to make paths through dangerous districts to public schools'.[26] Roads, paths? In any event, not a railway.)

8

'A Railway Terminus on the Moon'

The Loch Maree and Aultbea Railway

The reader's attention has already been drawn to the Aultbea Railway zealots. It is now time to examine their campaign, for it was as hopeless as Ullapool's.

The Aultbea railway proposal was to construct a line which branched off from the Dingwall to Strome Ferry line at the village of Achnasheen, headed north-west up Glen Docherty, followed the south shore of Loch Maree and terminated at Aultbea on the eastern shore of Loch Ewe. In an initial plan, the line would also have taken in the village of Gairloch, but that idea was dropped quite early on. The total length of the line would be just over 37 miles, mostly flat; and the scenery along Loch Maree quite splendid. This proposal was first made in or slightly before May 1889, and it almost certainly post-dates the public announcement of Ullapool's aspirations; but it was fully fledged by the summer of 1889. We know all this because of the acrimonious war of words which thereafter raged between the Aultbea champions and the Ullapool champions. A war of words and of public meetings, letters to newspapers, skulduggery and petitions to government.

THE PROMOTERS OF THE AULTBEA RAILWAY

'Where Could You Find a Wealthier Man?'

Like the promoters of the Ullapool scheme, the promoters of the Aultbea railway were distinctly well off. Probably more so. We must remain unsurprised at this: power, after all, lay with wealth and land-ownership. Little has changed. No fisherman or crofter or teacher or church minister, despite their undoubted enthusiasm and energy, would ever be able to promote a railway. But while most of the promoters of the Ullapool line had only a distant connection with the land through which that railway would run, the promoters of the Aultbea railway were very closely involved, due to the location of their estates. In a letter sent to the Chancellor of the Exchequer in 1891, which also cited the full support of 'the leading business men of Stornoway', four rich gentlemen were named as proprietors. They owned practically all of the land across which the railway would run.[1] Who were they?

First and foremost, there was Sir Kenneth Smith Mackenzie, the 6th Baronet of Gairloch (1832–1900). He was the owner of over 170,000 acres of land in the Highlands, Lord Lieutenant of Ross and Cromarty and for some years chairman of Ross-shire County Council. Although he was appointed as attaché to the embassy in Washington, he never took up the post, preferring to stay at home and look after his estates.[2] In 1883 he was appointed a member of the Napier Commission. For most of the year, his residence was Conan House near Dingwall, but several weeks in summer would be spent in picturesque Flowerdale House by Gairloch. Here the estate covered 162,319 acres, with an annual rental of £8,297 6s 3d.[3] The land was split to 43,348 acres of arable and grazing land for 448 crofts, 77,648 acres in fourteen large sheep-farms, and the remainder in three deer forests.

His younger half-brother, whom we shall encounter briefly in this chapter, was the landowner and horticulturalist Osgood Hanbury Mackenzie, whose estate at Inverewe is now in the hands of the National Trust for Scotland. Osgood's evidence to the Napier Commission contained some useful remarks about timber, in which subject he was by then an expert; he also confirmed that sheep gradually deteriorated pasture land; but he was not optimistic about giving employment to local people. The only exception to under-employment came in the shooting season: 'Do they get much employment from shooting tenants? – A good deal, for a short time.'[4] (Oh, the fatal lack of a hyphen . . .)

The second promoter was the Earl of Lovelace (1805–1893), who owned Ben Damph Lodge (now a hotel) and its 12,000-acre estate at the east end of Loch Torridon. The estate had been purchased in 1886 as a chunk split off from the neighbouring Torridon estate, owned by Duncan Darroch; the house was completed in 1887. After a youthful Grand Tour in the eastern Mediterranean, the earl had settled down and proceeded to do at least three useful things in his life: he made architectural improvements to the various properties he had inherited; in the course of these home improvements he became an expert on roof-trusses (much to Isambard Kingdom Brunel's admiration) and also in polychrome brick-making (for which he won a medal at the Crystal Palace Exhibition of 1851);[5] and finally, he gave his name to his first wife – Ada Lovelace, daughter of Lord Byron, who became the world's first computer programmer. The earl himself was a Fellow of the Royal Society from 1841, probably on the basis of his innovative bricks. (As a minor piece of family trivia, his daughter married the poet and horse-breeder Wilfrid Blunt, and thereby inadvertently became the great-aunt of the Soviet spy Anthony Blunt.)

A third member of this group of extremely wealthy promoters was Paul Liot-Bankes. He was a Frenchman who had made one excellent decision in life: he had married Maria Ann Bankes, second daughter of the coal magnate Meyrick Bankes of Lancashire. Meyrick, with wealth partly inherited but mostly accumulated in the exploitation of mines and miners in England, had purchased the Letterewe and Gruinard estates in 1835, the former from a Mackenzie who had fallen on hard times, the latter from the Davidsons of Tulloch.[6] The combined estate (70,000 acres) encompassed the north shore of Loch Maree and Aultbea. Maria was a life-renter of the estate, living with her husband at Ardlair House by Loch Maree; her widowed mother continued to live in Aultbea (Drumchork House) after Meyrick's death in 1881.

The entire family seems to have fallen out in 1882: the usual thing – Maria and Paul disputing the inheritance in the Court of Session against the widows of two brothers who had followed their father to the grave in short order. Meyrick Bankes had effectively cut most of his children out of his will in a codicil of 1880. Disinherited were Maria's first husband, now divorced, as well as the daughter of that marriage; his own son Thomas, 'a confirmed drunkard and unfit to inherit any of his properties'; William Murray, husband of daughter Eleanor, as he had 'gone out of his mind and was confined to a Lunatic Asylum'; and he revoked previous legacies to two daughters.

The elder Bankes was a nasty piece of work, and was widely hated. Between 1835 and 1871, he expended considerable energy in evicting crofters and in dragging others through the courts. One old woman whom he evicted was obliged to take up residence in a cave; Bankes had her evicted from the cave.[7] One Donald Mackenzie, giving evidence to the Napier Commission, had nothing at all good to say about him or his works; when asked if Bankes was a wealthy man, he replied, 'Where could you find a wealthier?' Further: 'Did Mr Bankes do you any favour or any good in other respects to make up for it? – Nothing.' Evictions had taken place, cottages were demolished, cattle attacked with dogs, and three particularly unpopular factors were described as 'these inebriate three'.[8] By contrast, however: 'We have nothing against our present proprietor, P. L. Bankes, Esq.', citing a case where Liot-Bankes had provided them with potatoes and seed in a time of need; the witness slightly ruined the picture later by admitting that the crofters had had to pay back in full the charitable donations. Nonetheless, Mr and Mrs Liot-Bankes were said to be 'benevolent and truly kind to all on their estates'. (Their Letterewe estate, after several changes of ownership, in 1978 came into the hands of Dutch million-aire Paul van Vlissingen, an estate owner with ideas which bore no relationship to those of previous generations.)

The last of the main promoters was Duncan Darroch of Gourock and Torridon (1836–1910), the fourth in the line of chiefs of Clan Donald. His great-grandfather had made a pile of money in the plan-tations of Jamaica. Duncan purchased the 32,000-acre Torridon estate on the north shore of Loch Torridon in 1873 (from a man named MacBarnet, whose father had also made a fortune in the West Indies: profiting from slavery was clearly a *sine qua non* for Highland estate ownership), removed all the sheep and converted most of his lands to deer forest. In the process, he did also return crofting land to such crofters as had been cleared in previous decades to make room for the sheep, and thereby unusually earned the praise of John Murdoch's *Highlander* newspaper. By Darroch's own account to Napier, the number of cottages, tenants, cattle etc. on his estate had actually increased (and the rent arrears had vanished) in the ten years of his ownership; by the account of one of his tenants, 'our proprietor is the best in the whole north' – admittedly, said proprietor was sitting just behind him; but other evidence seems to confirm his praise.[9] Torridon

Figure 8.1 Part of the Ordnance Survey map supplied with the plans showing the
Achnasheen to Aultbea railway in 1892 (National Records of Scotland RHP14292)

House was built for Darroch in 1876; he later sold some of the estate to Lovelace. And in 1960, the house was also acquired by the Lovelace family.

At a late stage in the process of agitating for a Bill for the Aultbea railway, probably in 1892, Duncan Darroch lost all enthusiasm and dropped out; his place was taken by William Ogilvie-Dalgleish of Coulin. This was the chairman of Baxter Brothers, linen manufacturers of Dundee. He was made 1st (and last) Baronet of Coulin in 1896. The Coulin estate was – and remains – a 15,000-acre deer forest spanning the hills between Kinlochewe and Achnashellach; it changed hands several times during the nineteenth century, finally being sold to Ogilvie-Dalgleish in 1888 by Sir Ivor Bertie Guest, a wealthy Welsh industrialist.

All in all, the wealthy men promoting the Aultbea line were probably far wealthier than those promoting the Ullapool one. Even their self-appointed Secretary was a wealthy man.

AND OTHER SUPPORTERS

'A Reputed Croesus'

John Henry Dixon (1838–1926) was the main agitator for the Aultbea Railway; his fellow promoters were by and large quite happy for him to get on with it, only being wheeled out for important or decorative occasions. A solicitor from Wakefield, Dixon had retired due to ill health in 1871, at the age of thirty-three, to the north-western end of Loch Maree. His ill health did not stop him carrying on, and taking an active interest in community affairs, until he was eighty-eight years old. And evidently he was not a poor man: he lived in the house and extensive grounds of Inveran (near Poolewe) as a long-term shooting-tenant of Sir Kenneth Mackenzie, and had his own piper – William Boa, who won the Gold Medal at the 1888 'Northern Meeting' of pipers. A contemporary (admittedly one with an axe to grind) described Dixon as 'a reputed Croesus'.[10] Reputed or not, and despite having only worked for about ten years of his life, he evidently had enough ready cash to be able to promise the purchase of £2,000 in shares in the Aultbea Railway. He also wrote the book *Gairloch in North-west*

Ross-shire: Its Records, Traditions, Inhabitants, and Natural History with a Guide to Gairloch and Loch Maree (1886), which to this day remains a classic guide to the area. Much in the manner of Baden-Powell, Dixon took a keen interest in the moral education of young men. He remained a bachelor throughout his life but, after retiring – for the second time – from Poolewe to Pitlochry in 1902, he adopted a son (later killed in the war); he also enthusiastically organised Scout groups and 'Young Men's' clubs. At the age of eighty-five, he earned the title of 'the oldest Scoutmaster in the world'. In 1921, he was planted firmly centre stage in his kilt when Crown Prince Hirohito of Japan came to visit Perthshire.

We have already seen the main arguments put forward by Dixon, and refuted by Ullapool; but let us recap them here – as, indeed, the occupant of Inveran House did on every possible occasion over the course of three years. The arguments all demonstrated that Ullapool was Very Bad and Aultbea was Very Good. We can do worse than quote Dixon himself, in a letter to *The Scotsman* in June 1889:

> That Ullapool is distant some 15 miles from the Minch, and more than 50 miles from Stornoway; that the mouth of Lochbroom is narrow and closely surrounded by lofty hills, which must conduce to squalls and calms, so that access by sailing vessels must be (as it is) often tedious and difficult; that the approach through the archipelago of the Summer Isles is intricate (so that those not acquainted with the navigation require a pilot), are all facts that your readers can verify by looking at a map . . .
>
> That Lochewe is directly opposite to, and only some 34 miles distant from Stornoway; that it is the nearest inlet on the mainland to the Lews; that it opens directly from the Minch, and has an entrance a mile and a half wide; that there are no islands between Stornoway and Lochewe, nor any hills surrounding the mouth of the loch; and that Aird Point at Aultbea is only about 38 miles from Stornoway, are also facts that your readers can verify by the map . . .[11]

The words 'directly opposite to Stornoway' maybe needed some refinement; but he made a good case for the sheltered accommodation of Loch Ewe. We know, however, that all these claims were as a red rag to the bull in Ullapool. Dixon finished off this letter by asserting slightly prematurely that the Garve and Ullapool Railway was, 'as we believe, virtually defunct'. It was almost certainly this very public provocation which triggered the Reverend Macdonald's 'Ullapool Refutation' pamphlet noted above. (Dixon also used this letter to castigate those correspondents from Ullapool who hid behind such pseudonyms as 'Truth', 'Justitia' and 'Pro Bono Publico' when writing their letters to the editor; John H. Dixon, he, never hid behind any such pseudonym. Alas, his side was let down by an Aultbea supporter who in January 1890 wrote a letter to the newspaper and could not resist signing himself 'X'.)

The Scotsman's letters page was the arena for the controversy between May 1889 and March 1890. It would be tedious to document all the correspondence – suffice to say that we have already paraded all the arguments, and that there was more heat than light generated. To every letter from Loch Broom, there was an energetic riposte from Loch Ewe, repeating the several advantages of the latter; these arguments were used even when they were not called for – in a scathing reply to P. Campbell Ross's lament about the Great North of Scotland's *locus standi* objections (discussed above), John Dixon blasted that Mr Ross 'takes care to repeat two contentions . . . which are fallacies' – i.e. that fisheries would banish destitution in Ullapool; and that Ullapool lay nearest to Stornoway. In fact, Ross wisely had not mentioned either of those items in his letter. But Dixon did have one shot that accurately hit the mark: 'Mr Ross appeals to the public in *forma pauperis*. How does he reconcile this with the fact of his railway being promoted by so many wealthy proprietors?'[12] Perhaps true: but there is also a proverb about kettles and pots.

Dixon was so busy writing letters that he even had special notepaper printed up with his address and a subject line, 'Proposed Fisheries Railway to Aultbea for the Lews' – a veritable manifesto. These informative letters, most of which were addressed to Whitehall, were interspersed with reports of public meetings taking place both on the mainland and on Lewis. Before we make account of these, let us quote from one letter sent to *The Scotsman* by the Reverend Hector Cameron, Free Church Minister of Back on Lewis; he wished it to be known that his own congregation, 'consisting of not fewer than 500 families, are dead against Aultbea as a railway terminus for this island'. The Reverend's view of Aultbea was not a Christian one:

In one word, Mr Editor, I venture to assert, without fear of contra-
diction, that should a census be taken to-morrow of the entire
population of the Lews . . . we should henceforward hear as much
or as little of an agitation for a railway terminus on the moon as for
one at Aultbea.[13]

Public meetings sprouted thick and fast on the ground, attended by all
interested parties. On the west coast and on Lewis, every crofter and
fisherman worth his salt would have signed at least one petition, preferably two or three, either for Ullapool or for Aultbea. In May 1889,
for example, there were meetings in Poolewe, Gairloch and Aultbea;
and representatives from each (landowners, merchants, hoteliers,
ministers and sundry Mackenzies, 'besides all the fishermen from each
of the committees') came together in Poolewe on the 14th to constitute a grand-sounding Joint Committee, chaired by John Dixon. The
unanimous decision of this meeting was to recommend a railway from
Achnasheen to 'such a point in the parish of Gairloch as would best
develop to their utmost extent the fisheries of the Lews, and of the
North-West Highlands and Islands of Scotland generally'.[14] The presence of two hoteliers suggests that there were high hopes of tourists
sharing trains with the fish. A subscription list was opened to defray
expenses; one wonders who contributed how much, but – alas – such
details were not reported. This, in short, was the beginning of the
Aultbea campaign. Resolutions were duly passed, including one 'to
approach the Highland Railway Company with a view to their being
induced to make a "flying survey" of the proposed railway'. The
Highland received this request in early June, but its Board resolved to
defer taking steps until 'it is ascertained what the Government is
inclined to do'. Everyone would have a long wait, then.[15]

In November 1889, there was a 'large and enthusiastic meeting of
fishermen' in Aultbea; fishermen for the most part, although the Joint
Committee was clearly directing operations (Bankes chaired the meeting, Dixon took the minutes). To much applause, Dixon noted that a
competent engineer 'had given his opinion that the Aultbea railway
could be constructed for something like £5000 per mile, without rolling stock'. A whole host of local fishermen supported all the relevant
motions, which included drumming up support from the fish-curers of
Stornoway ('the best friends of the fishermen', proclaimed Dixon), and

writing to Lord Lothian. The railway would also attract, and be financed by, increased tourist traffic. A number of fishermen from small townships in the area stood up and spoke in favour of the proposed railway – 'if they got a terminus here, the fishing could be thoroughly worked. This could not be if Ullapool were chosen.' Satisfyingly: 'The proceedings lasted over three hours, and most of the speeches were in Gaelic.'[16]

John Dixon's fraternisation with the ordinary people of Gairloch was not always felicitous. According to a report in the *Inverness Courier* of 23 March 1888, Dixon had addressed a meeting of the Gairloch branch of the Highland Land League. He appealed for compromise and discussion on land matters; arguing that hunting and shooting benefited the whole community. Murdo Maciver (opposing) maintained that 'the land ought to be as free as the air we breathe'. To which Dixon replied sternly that 'Mr Maciver's views appeared to be the same as those of Mr Henry George, who was now discredited in America, and if such socialistic views were pushed, no line of demarcation could be fixed, and they must soon spread to personal property, as had been the case in France.'[17] Dixon's reasoned arguments concerning one (which?) of several French revolutions were coolly ignored by the Land Leaguers, and he beat a retreat.

Not to be outdone, or outmanoeuvred, by their mainland colleagues, the fishermen and crofters of Lewis spent long dark winter evenings at public meetings on the matter. In December, the men of Back, Tolsta and Tong on the east coast convened to 'denounce' Aultbea: it was their considered view that that scheme was only supported by 'fish-curers, landlords and sportsmen' (an interesting social coalition, and a neat reversal of Dixon's view that the fish-curers were the friends of the fishermen); a proposed meeting of the Aultbea faction, in Stornoway itself, was condemned, and counter-demonstrations outside the meeting-place were exuberantly promised. 'Dissentients' – those supporting Aultbea – were deemed to be but a small fraction of the population. But up at Barvas, on the same night, a meeting 'appeared to be distinctly in favour of Aultbea'. In early January, a crofters' meeting at Lochs came out strongly in favour of Aultbea and condemned those 'who are endeavouring to foist upon the fishermen of Lews the railway to Ullapool'. Ten days later, crofters over in Carloway met to vote in favour of light railways on Lewis, in favour of the Ullapool solution, and 'deplore and condemn' the Aultbea scheme.[18] Barely six months earlier, a minority faction in Stornoway was dead against Ullapool – but this time strongly favouring a railhead at Roshven, with direct connection to the West Highland line at Fort William.[19] Thus were communities riven.

For every petition, public meeting or letter in favour of Ullapool, there was at least one, preferably three, in favour of Aultbea. When P. Campbell Ross wrote proudly to Lord Lothian attaching a certificate from the master of a steam-yacht who stated that Loch Broom was entirely safe and navigable,[20] Liot-Bankes immediately followed with a letter to His Lordship gleefully enclosing seven – yes, seven – affidavits from yachtsmen and schooner-masters proclaiming that Loch Ewe was the calmest anchorage in the world; and then, as a killer blow, a further statement signed by twenty-two Isle of Man fishing captains, averring much the same thing, with added fish.[21]

LETTERS, MEETINGS AND PETITIONS

'An Epitome of Facts and Inferences'

Ultimately, however, both the Ullapool and the Aultbea campaigns had to convince Westminster. Aultbea's first opportunity to do this had come when Lord Lothian toured his domain; on 16 June 1889 he landed briefly at Poolewe and was 'made acquainted with the arguments of those who prefer that district to Ullapool as the terminus of the railway'. The newspaper report does not indicate whom he met, or what was said – but we can safely lay bets. Alas, the visit was frustratingly short, his Lordship having spent the best part of the day at Ullapool already and now anxious for his dinner.[22]

In the following months, Dixon kept up a campaign of facts, figures and petitions. In February 1890, he sent a letter and a lengthy printed attachment to Lord Salisbury (Prime Minister) and Henry Matthews (Home Secretary), and – for good measure – Lord Knutsford (Colonies Secretary); Lord Lothian had already received the same document in late November of the previous year.[23] This letter was interesting not for its nth iteration of the usual arguments, nor for the three pages listing the names of all those supporting the scheme, but rather for the map attached. This map was very simple: it depicted the north-west coast of Scotland, and marked on it – in red – were two alternative lines from Achnasheen to Aultbea; and – in blue – the proposed line from Garve to Ullapool. One red line travels along the south shore of Loch Maree, the other along the north shore, the latter rather an innovation given the bumpiness of the land. The blue line is fascinating: marked with the grim and accusatory word 'Tunnel' there is a wide curve to the south of Braemore – not merely a curve showing where the actual tunnel was to be, but a curve which effectively went on a six-mile detour around the south end of Loch a'Bhraoin, half-way to Loch Maree; and Ullapool is clearly marked in the position of Leckmelm. Could this be the provenance of the inaccurate map used by the first commission? Surely not.

A further opportunity to influence the great and the good arose when the first of the enquiring commissions (Walpole's) set out in April 1890: their first port of call was Ullapool, and their second was Loch Ewe. Arriving at Aultbea for luncheon on 5 April, they received a 'hearty welcome and a cordial cheer' from the assembled multitudes. 'Among the crowd were a number of the leading gentlemen of the parish' – Mr Dixon to the fore, and also Osgood Mackenzie, taking a break from cultivating his gardens at Inverewe. Dixon recited the usual list of advantages of Loch Ewe (possibly also slipping them a doctored map of proposed railway lines – 'this, gentlemen, will save you some time and trouble . . .'), others talked up the tourist trade, and various champions spoke of the benefits to fishing and crofting. Then, after lunch, they 'proceeded by boat up Loch Maree to see the course of the proposed railway . . . stayed at the Loch Maree Hotel and to-day, going on board the *Jackal* at Gairloch, they propose crossing over to Stornoway'.[24] Interestingly, the whole party returned to Gairloch on 26 May, having done the rounds of practically every island and coastal settlement known to Civilised Man; here they heard yet again from Mr Dixon; he listed the usual five advantages, just in case no one had been listening seven weeks previously. Not waiting this time for lunch, the Commissioners boarded their yacht and set off for Little Loch Broom where, possibly for the first and last time in its long history, the tiny settlement of Scoraig received important visitors.[25]

Doubtless some encouragement was given by this first commission, since a barrage of letters, petitions, resolutions and memoranda thereafter whistled southwards to London. These were dispatched most commonly by John Dixon, but occasionally Sir Kenneth Mackenzie also felt moved to write. Residents from various parishes and districts vied with each other for and against Ullapool or Aultbea; suspended uncomfortably between the two rival villages, the reckless crofters and fishermen of Little Loch Broom publicly came out for the Ullapool line. The office staff of the Secretary for Scotland, doubtless weary of letters from Ullapool and Gairloch, started making helpful annotations on the files; one read simply: 'This is the rival to Ullapool.'[26] The filing system at the Scottish Office groaned under the weight of incoming documentation. At length, however, something useful arrived in the post.

On 1 May 1891, John Dixon sent in a printed memorandum, in which he brought together all the relevant facts and figures and arguments.[27] Although printed commercially in Inverness, it is clearly marked 'Private' – possibly to keep it away from the prying eyes of Loch Broom spies. For a pleasant change it was addressed to the Chancellor of the Exchequer, George Goschen, it quoted at length the report of the 1890 Commission, extracting those words and phrases favourable to the Aultbea line.

So sanguine were the proposers of success that the services of an engineer had been secured to undertake a 'flying survey'. John Paterson of Fort William undertook this in April 1890, and he estimated costs of construction at somewhere between £293,000 and £325,000. There were to be four stations – at Kinlochewe, Slattadale, Poolewe and Aultbea. To the suggestion made by the 1890 report that a deviation be made via Gairloch, Dixon pointed out that this would add 15 miles to the route, require the ascent of two tricky summits (350 feet and 250 feet) and increase the total cost by £100,000: so that was rejected. Just how the line was to be routed to avoid Gairloch, we shall shortly find out. Finally, the revenues from working the line would not rely only on fish, livestock and steamer traffic: tourism was the thing. Ever since Queen Victoria's visit to Loch Maree in 1877, the lochside and Poolewe areas received some 4,000 visitors per annum, usually in July and August; the railway would admirably support the tourists and likely extend the visiting season by several months.

Neither Ullapool and Aultbea emerged victorious in the recommendations of either the 1890 Commission or the 1891 Committee. It was most likely in response to the first report, and to forestall the Ullapool promoters, that a deputation of Aultbea supporters was received in London by Lord Lothian in early 1891. Several gentleman were ushered into his Lordship's presence by Dr Macdonald MP: inevitably, John Dixon was there, as was a clutch of randomly chosen MPs with no obvious connection to the north-west Highlands. In a nod to the lower classes, a Glaswegian fish-curer and a building contractor from Edinburgh were permitted to attend; the Torridonian neighbours, Duncan Darroch and the eighty-six-year-old Earl of Lovelace, made up the numbers. The well-known arguments were rehearsed: fishing, crofting and tourism were talked up; the building contractor stated that he expected the construction costs to be about the same as for Ullapool, but that Loch Maree had much more attractive countryside for tourists to view; and Lovelace showed that he was in touch with the rebellious spirit of the times by stating that he was 'of opinion that an extension of railways would restore the sheep farming and potato culture in the West of Scotland to something like their former dimensions'. For all this they sought a guaranteed 3 per cent return on the entire capital costs, for a 'lengthened period'. The Scottish Secretary duly thanked the deputation for their information and promised faithfully 'to lay it before his colleagues in the Government'.[28] And closed his office door.

The second inquiry (Hutchinson's) eventually rolled into Gairloch parish, considerably more surly than the first. From the offices of the North-West Coast of Scotland Railways Committee, as the group preferred to be called, came an invitation of sorts, indicating that Hutchinson would be pleased to meet representatives from Loch Ewe in Inverness on 27 July – but sternly warning that no travel expenses would be paid. Failing that, they expected to be in the Gairloch area on the 29th.[29] In the event, no one could afford to go to Inverness, and the Committee arrived in Poolewe one day late, on the 30th, having previously called in at Ullapool. At Poolewe, Committee member Henry Tennant persuaded Dixon that some notes would greatly help their inquiry. Dixon went one better than that and, in a letter to the secretary of the Committee, J. Mauger Nicolle, on 3 August, he enclosed an eight-page handwritten memorandum grandly entitled 'Epitome of Facts and Inferences in Favour of the Proposed Aultbea Railway'. In much the manner of Goldilocks, Dixon's 'Epitome' appraised the rival railway schemes: Mallaig was too far south to service the fisheries, Kyle of Lochalsh too far out of the way, Ullapool too far inland, Lochinver and Laxford too far north. But Aultbea was just perfect.[30]

It was certainly fortuitous that Dixon had invested in his headed notepaper, for he found himself obliged to bombard the Committee with letters throughout the spring and summer of 1891. In an early letter in May, he provided some technical information concerning the surveyed railway line. This information sometimes strayed into the realm of alternative facts: he stated that the steepest gradient would be 1:45 'for only a short distance', which was not entirely true, since the plans show a gradient of 1:33 for three miles down Glen Docherty. No matter: he noted that the Devil's own Ullapool line had gradients of 1:40 for more than four miles. (It was slightly inconvenient that Dixon's 'Epitome' stated that the 1:45 gradient on the Aultbea line was also four miles long, not just 'a short distance'. By good fortune, he cannot have been aware of the cancellation of Ullapool's tunnel, which would probably have resulted in laughably steep gradients at Braemore.)

In another communication, he listed those persons who had given their word as gentlemen to buy shares in the Aultbea Railway Company: Sir Kenneth Mackenzie was ready to take up £5,000 worth; Darroch, Lovelace and Dixon £2,000 each; and the dowager Mrs Bankes was up for £1,000 of shares, while her son-in-law Paul opted for a very modest £500. Additionally, both Mackenzie and Liot-Bankes were prepared to give land for the railway entirely free of charge. A later report by W. C. Dunbar of the Scottish Office even suggested that the promoters would be prepared to find funds of £83,000 if the Government, for its part, was also prepared to assist financially.[31] It was all rather well organised. What could possibly go wrong?

Well, everything. Rather disconcertingly, the Aultbea proposal was dismissed in a very few words by the second commission: 'a terminus at Loch Ewe (on which Aultbea is situate) would afford but little practical advantage to people on the west coast of Sutherlandshire'.[32] That was all: two dozen words, and scarcely to the point, was all that Dixon's headed notepaper and many thousand words had bought.

THE ROUTE OF THE AULTBEA RAILWAY

'Pig Styes, Henhouses and an Islet'

This blatant snub does not seem to have discouraged the Aultbea supporters. But something serious had to be done to stretch Aultbea's nose in front of Ullapool's in the race for funding and investors. Lovelace tried a sneaky stratagem as soon as the second report was published, by writing to Lord Lothian to observe that the Garve and Ullapool Company had done nothing significant since the passing of their Act, and suggesting that their Act should be repealed and the Government should support the Aultbea line instead. Sadly, a comment on the file in Scottish Office records dismissively: 'It is hardly worth troubling his Lordship with this, as it is not a very practical proposal.'[33]

In May, the parliamentary agents whom the Aultbea group had appointed to pursue their interest in Whitehall produced a printed statement concerning the line, and presented it to the Scottish Office. The Government was asked to back the line by guaranteeing a 3 per cent return on £300,000 over thirty years. Revenues were calculated at £5 per mile per week – £10,235 per annum, against working expenses of £6,000 per annum: a tidy little profit. The statement talked of negotiations with the Highland Railway, which had apparently offered to work the line at the usual 2s 2d per train mile. But the promoters were not inclined to accept this generous offer, and 'propose to work it themselves' – an interesting, if rash, decision.[34]

The Ullapool Railway had achieved its Parliamentary Act in August 1890. It was high time for John Dixon and his Joint Committee to match this. In December of 1892, a notice appeared in the newspapers of an impressive collection of Private Bills due for debate in the coming parliamentary session; 172 in all, covering railways, electric lighting, tramways and water-works. For the whole of Great Britain, there were forty-three Bills which promoted new railways or railway-branches – a decline from a heady fifty-five in the preceding year. Among the forty-three, we find the Loch Maree and Aultbea Railway.[35]

For a Bill to be introduced, a proper survey had to be done, not just a 'flying' one. This was undertaken by Thomas Meik & Sons of Edinburgh. The Meiks were not the Highland Railway's normal surveyors, so the conclusion must be drawn that they were contracted directly by the Aultbea Committee to undertake the work. And they were probably not cheap; the two generations of the Meik family were noted engineers. Thomas Meik, the father, had designed several railways, mostly in Fife and north-east England, as well as a number of ports and harbours; he retired from the firm in 1888. His eldest son Patrick worked initially for his father, but then cut his teeth with Benjamin Baker and John Fowler on the Forth Bridge; in this, he had better luck than his younger brother Charles, who had the misfortune to be assistant to Thomas Bouche on his disastrous Tay Bridge. When Meik the father retired, the two brothers joined forces and went on to many other large projects together, in Scotland, England and Wales, as well as designing ports and railways across the Empire; at the peak of their career, they were commissioned to design the grand Kinlochleven hydroelectric scheme. But in 1892, little imagining the greatness of things to come, they designed a railway from Achnasheen to Aultbea.

Their 'Plans and Sections' document, like that of the rival Ullapool line, was a superior piece of work.[36] Slightly eccentrically, the plan identified not one, but three railway lines.

The first – confusingly labelled 'Railway No. 3' – ran south-westwards from Achnasheen station on the Dingwall to Strome Ferry line for a distance of 7 chains and 13 yards (about 155 metres). This took it clear of Highland Railway land and into virgin territory. The height above sea level at Achnasheen is 490 feet. The plan shows the Dingwall and the Aultbea lines separating at a junction 150 yards west of the station. In a fine piece of surveyor's exactitude, the 'Datum Line' – effectively, their own 'sea level' against which all vertical heights would be measured – is given as 'six hundred and thirty feet six inches below level of Ordnance Bench Mark on top of thirtieth Milestone from Dingwall at side of road between Auchnasheen and Loch Gown marked X on plan'. Modern readers anxious to find out more might seek this milestone about half a mile south of the station; but it has long since vanished into the undergrowth. (The difference between the Datum Line and actual sea level is around 140 feet; but this is not a mistake on the Meiks' part, simply a cautious surveyor's allowance for low-lying land.)

The second section, Railway No. 1, by far the longest at 29 miles, 4 furlongs, 8 chains and 5 yards, ran all the way to Poolewe. Rather than

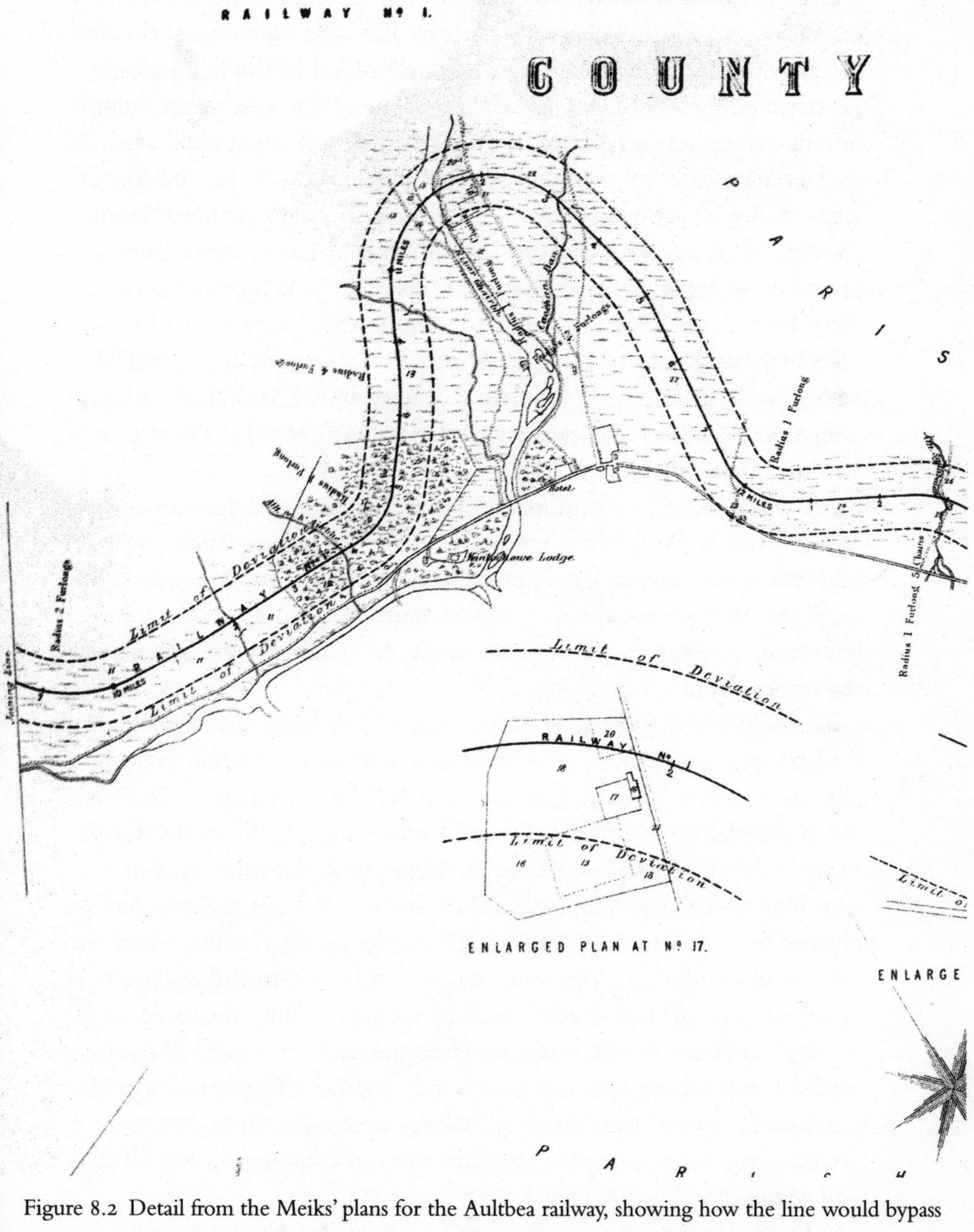

Figure 8.2 Detail from the Meiks' plans for the Aultbea railway, showing how the line would bypass Kinlochewe. A long viaduct would span the river Ghairbhe (National Records of Scotland RHP82306)

follow the road west out of Achnasheen, it circled round the back of Ledgowan Lodge, passed south of Loch a'Chroisg, and remained well south of the road to take advantage of the hillside contours, before looping in a reverse S-shape north, east and then west to enter Glen Docherty. There would be a struggle up the hill to the highest point on the line (750 feet); the line then descended the glen on the south side of the river at a gradient of 1:33 for three miles; swooped around the western end of the glen; circled just south of the village of Kinlochewe on a long viaduct; and then rejoined the road (the present-day A832). Then it hugged the south shore of Loch Maree as far as Slattadale. Where the road subsequently veers due west towards Gairloch, the railway instead heads north along the shore, straight for Poolewe.

Which is where it gets interesting. The southern shore of Loch Maree is by no means a level plain at the western end. Indeed, at grid reference NG880766 there are two major bluffs of rock which loom 300 feet above the waters. No problem: the Meiks envisaged here a tunnel – or rather, two tunnels, 100 yards apart. If nothing else, this demonstrated far greater chutzpah than the mere single tunnel (already abandoned) at Braemore. From his lawn at Inveran across the loch, Mr Dixon would just have been able to stand and admire Victorian engineering at its best, while his piper played laments in the background.

Railway No. 1 ends at Poolewe, and is immediately succeeded by Railway No. 2. This split may have been to allow for the line to terminate at Poolewe, should finances run dry. No. 2 heads northwards along the east shore of Loch Ewe, skirting round the back of Osgood Mackenzie's Inverewe estate and terminating at the shore end of the new pier at Aultbea. The total distance was 7 miles, 5 furlongs and 9 chains. A new pier would be constructed for steamer traffic – and no modest stubby thing, either: this one had to be 180 yards long so that, at the far end, its deck would stand 25 feet above the low water mark and 50 feet above the sea floor. A very respectable pier indeed; an estimate of cost was between £8,000 and £9,000. (The sea in a wide semi-circle around Aird Point at Aultbea is actually quite shallow; by contrast, there was a good 25 feet of water as soon as you fell off the end of the old Ullapool pier, length 75 yards.)

The total length of the railway, then, was to be 37 miles, 2 furlongs, 9 chains and 20 yards – just under 37.5 miles. But it had its fair share of

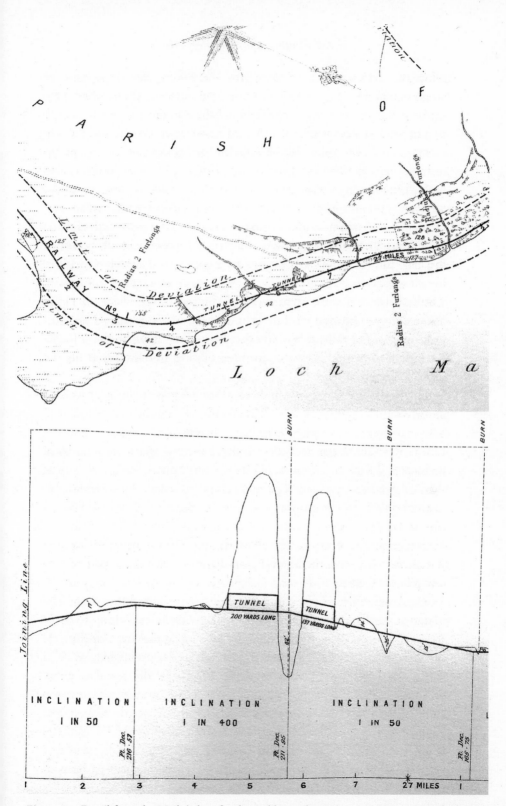

Figure 8.3 Detail from the Meiks' plans for the Aultbea railway, showing the two tunnels above Loch Maree – top as a map, bottom as a cross-section (National Records of Scotland RHP82306)

sensational bits. Over its whole length, there were thirty bridges to be constructed, of spans between 15 feet and 90 feet. There were three major viaducts – one across the glen behind Kinlochewe with a length of 325 feet (50 feet high), another of 200 feet across the inlet at Ob Gorm, about two miles east of Talladale, and a third of 315 feet across the inlet named Ob nam Muc, a mile further on, both about 35 feet high. (One railway viaduct seems to attract thousands of tourists to the west of Scotland; just imagine what we could do with three.) The railway would run within gawping distance of the renowned Victoria Falls. And then of course there was the magnificent double tunnel: the east tunnel would be 200 yards long approached up a long incline, the west tunnel 137 yards, both buried under 200 feet of mountain. The two tunnels were separated by a stretch of 100 yards above an 82-foot drop – no viaduct is mentioned here on the plans, so we must suppose that the railway would cling by its fingernails to the hillside. As indeed it would have to do after exiting northwards from the second tunnel.

The Book of Reference which accompanies these plans is, compared to the one for the Garve to Ullapool line, relatively straightforward. There are far fewer 'items' involved – barely 200, as opposed to the Ullapool scheme's 495. But there is more variety: apart from the usual pastures and houses, we have 'pig styes', hen-houses, 'swamps', a cart-shed or two, some stables, a peat-shed and an 'islet'. This islet was an engineering curiosity: it was a tiny rock about 50 yards offshore at Slattadale, and it came into the equation since the statutory 'line of deviation' would occasionally allow for the railway to stray into the waters of the loch. Fortunately, this deviation would have been an unlikely circumstance.

The ownership of the land was even more straightforward. The majority of the line (around 24 miles) ran over land owned by Sir Kenneth Mackenzie – most of Gairloch parish was owned by him. At the Achnasheen end, in the parish of Contin, lay about five miles of land owned by Hugh Cameron Ross, director of the Standard Bank of South Africa between 1885 and 1902. Then came the Mackenzie lands all the way to Poolewe; a long stretch of ten miles between Kinlochewe and Talladale was leased from Mackenzie by William Cazelet, the archetypical 'wealthy socialite' (two of his children became Tory MPs in the interwar years). At Poolewe, the Mackenzie domain

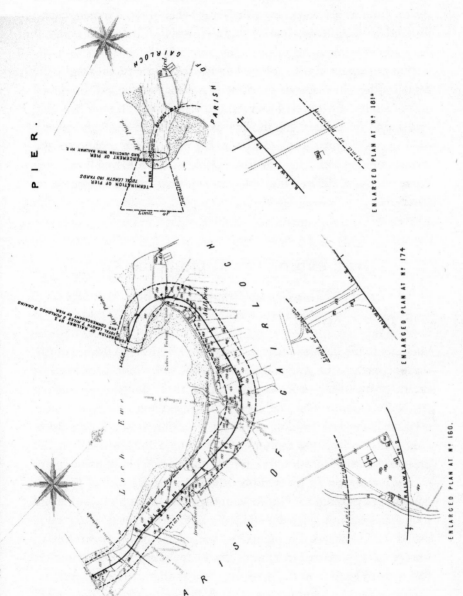

Figure 8.4 Detail from the Meiks' plans for the Aultbea railway, showing the terminus at Aultbea pier. The existing pier was to be extended to an impressive length of 180 yards (National Records of Scotland RHP82306)

passed seamlessly into the Inverewe estate owned by Osgood Mackenzie. After about six miles, we enter the estate of the Bankes family, with Maria Ann Liot-Bankes named as the owner – this land included Aultbea and its spanking new pier. Thus, when it came to negotiating for land for the railway, only Mr Ross – owner of Ledgowan Lodge at Achnasheen – was likely to be of any bother at all.

Not contained in these plans, but advised to the promoters by the Meik brothers in a separate financial document, was the estimated total cost of around £325,000 (if four stations were built).[37] If there was only one station, at Aultbea, and the line was constructed as a 'light' railway 'in a manner similar to those now being made at the instance of the Government in Ireland', then costs could be almost halved.[38] All these costs, of course, differed from the earlier 'flying' survey conducted by Paterson.

THE END OF THE AULTBEA DREAM

'What Can the Promoters Do, But Decide to Withdraw the Bill?'

Such, then, the detailed plans and sections. Like its rival further north, the document is of academic interest only, unless one is inclined to dream phantastically. For, by the end of 1892, things were looking decidedly gloomy. The Highland Railway extension to Kyle was as good as built. The London agents for the Aultbea line (Durnford & Co.) went through the motions of preparing a Bill. In the draft Bill presented to the Scottish Office for approval, a number of points are of passing interest: on the list of 'proprietors', Duncan Darroch of Torridon has dropped out, replaced by William Ogilvie-Dalgleish of Coulin; and John Dixon is now included. There was to be a capital of £315,000 issued in £10 shares. Locomotives were clearly of the 'light railway' variety, being restricted to 25 mph. To no one's surprise, the promoters had stepped back from the dizzy idea of working the line themselves, and went for the interesting solution of offering that contract to 'either' the Highland or the Great North of Scotland.[39] This particular suggestion went down like a lead balloon in Inverness: Andrew Dougall of the Highland was moved to write to the Scottish Secretary Trevelyan stating that his company would do everything it could to oppose the Loch Maree and Aultbea Bill.[40]

But one gets the sense that Durnfords in London had lost heart. In a further letter, they wanted to know the Government's intentions: was it worth the expense of proceeding with the Bill? Bitterly, the writer remarked that the Treasury did not even bother acknowledging letters from promoters of the Loch Maree and Aultbea line, let alone replying to them: 'What', the rhetorical question was asked, 'can the Promoters do, but decide to withdraw their Bill?' They could have saved their breath; a terse note was scribbled on the file – 'I do not see that this office has any more to say about these "Highland Railways".'[41] To add insult to injury, the Treasury, on being nudged by the Scottish Office, wrote a blunt reply to Durnfords, advising them that no financial support would be forthcoming.[42]

And yet, good money was thrown after bad: the Bill was submitted, and there is a report of the MP for Wick Burghs, Sir John Pender, giving the Lochmaree and Aultbea Railway Bill a second reading in the Commons on 21 April 1893.[43] A second reading is the point at which MPs may object to a Bill. (Curiously, although Pender's intervention was reported in *The Scotsman*, there is no record of it in the Parliamentary business published by Hansard. The Commons was occupied with the twelfth day of debating the Government of Ireland Bill. There was just enough time left over to discuss such matters as whether the Dog Tax should apply to crofters' dogs, and why Government messengers in Edinburgh were using their days off to work as waiters. But Hansard makes no mention at all of the Aultbea railway.) But this second reading, if it ever took place, was followed by a deafening silence, both on that day and thereafter. The Private Bill advanced no further. The dream of a railway line to Aultbea died.

By the end of 1893, both Ullapool and Aultbea had been rejected. As if to rub salt into the wounds, a popular 'Railway Tours' leaflet for 1896 offered – among many other highly attractive jaunts at very competitive prices – the following two excursions:

No. 4 – Achterneed by Rail to Strome Ferry, Mr Macbrayne's Steamer to Portree and Gairloch, by Coach to Loch-Maree and Achnasheen. Fare – 1st Class Rail, outside Coach, and Cabin

Steamer, 31s. None of the Tourist Fares via Loch-Maree include Coachman's Fee between Achnasheen and Gairloch, which is 1s 6d for one Passenger and 2s 6d for a party of two.

No. 8 – Inverness by Rail to Dingwall and Garve, by Coach to Lochbroom and Ullapool, Mr Macbrayne's steamer to Stornoway, Portree and Strome Ferry, thence by Rail to Inverness. Fare – 1st Class, 32s 6d. To Holders of Tickets for this Tour, the Fare by Coach from Garve to Ullapool, payable to the Coachman, will be 7s 6d, which includes his fee.[44]

No railways, merely coach and horses. But, on the plus side for Ullapool, Mr Macbrayne evidently considered the Loch Broom option to be the best for Stornoway.

9

'Zeal and Enterprise'

Plans for Other Railways

Continuing to rely on coach and horses was a dismal result for the people of Ullapool and Aultbea. But they could, had they wished, have taken some comfort from the very short histories of railway projects which were treated even more badly than theirs. Unbuilt railway projects might be categorised in three ways: those which had influential backers, but no money; those which had neither influential backers nor money; and those which existed only as lines sketched on the Victorian equivalent of a beer-mat – most commonly, a Bartholomew's railway map. In this chapter, we consider some of the schemes in the latter two categories.

OTHER RAILWAY SCHEMES FOR THE NORTH-WEST

'Poor Laxford'

Eight railway lines were proposed for the north-west of Scotland in the 1880s and 1890s: on the mainland, the branch lines to Laxford, Lochinver, Ullapool and Aultbea; the extensions to Kyle of Lochalsh and Mallaig; and in the islands, the railways on Skye and Lewis. The Kyle and Mallaig lines do not concern us here since they were built, they exist, they have had plenty of words written about them. The Ullapool and Aultbea railway schemes have been dealt with. The Skye and Lewis railways will not detain us here since, later on in this book, we shall plot their rise and fall in some detail. So now two railways remain.

Firstly and most northerly, the proposed railway from Lairg to Laxford. The plan here was for a branch line of the Far North Line operated by the Highland Railway, beginning at the small town of Lairg and following the present route of the A838. This would run along the north shore of Loch Shin, and then the south shore of Lochs Stack and More, before terminating at Laxford Bridge – a total distance of 37 miles. In truth, apart from potential fish-traffic, there was no great economic argument in favour of such a line. But this did not prevent local people from pursuing a campaign. Indeed, the campaign began well before anyone else on the west coast had even thought of a railway. In his submission to the Napier Commission, a retired fisherman by the name of William Mackay stated: 'If the railway was extended [from Lairg] to the head of Loch Laxford, it would form an admirable centre for the districts of Durness, and this parish of Eddriachillis [*sic*], and so the people would be able to send their fresh fish to the market. That is about all I have to say.'[1] Mackay's proposal was taken up by the next witness, the Free Church of Scotland minister at Eddrachillis, Duncan Finlayson, who testified that the people of the Kinlochbervie area suffered considerably from lack of communication with the outside world – the nearest doctor, for example, was 19 miles away, and secondary education was virtually impossible – but 'if we could get the railway . . . it would be of the greatest benefit to this district; and also a telegraph line.'[2]

Not much more was heard of this proposed railway until early 1890, when a flurry of petitions and letters were sent to the Secretary of Scotland; the people of the extreme north-west had, despite bad means of communication, got to hear of the campaigns running further south. At the very start of the year, the Reverend Finlayson sent a petition signed by the 'male inhabitants' of the parish of Eddrachillis, supporting a railway to Laxford. In his covering letter, the minister suggested – a little strongly, but not entirely without cause – that his parish was, with the exception of St Kilda, the most defective in communication with the south. A couple of months later, a petition signed by fourteen fishermen of Durness made its way southwards. At the same time William Mackay (not the retired fisherman this time, but a thirty-five-year-old schoolmaster of Kinlochbervie) wrote to the Secretary for Scotland, also suggesting a railway; he estimated that the annual loss of fish sales, due to lack of railway communication, was in the region of £288,000.[3] For good measure, Mackay also had his letter printed in the Aberdeen *Northern News* at the start of April; this was rather a cunning ploy, since one week after that he was able to write to the Prime Minister (Salisbury) citing an article in support of the railway which had just been printed . . . in the *Northern News*. 'The fisheries', stated Mackay, were 'the one practical means by which the population of the West Highlands and Islands can be raised from chronic poverty and be permanently improved'.[4]

The 1890 Commission took a cursory glance at the Laxford claim, but were scarcely enthusiastic. If a railway was to be built, it would cost an estimated £220,000 for the 37-mile stretch; but the Commission's preference seemed to be for a coastal steamer service, taking fish down to Strome Ferry. Evidently, the Commissioners had not understood a thing about the freshness of fish.[5] Mr Mackay was not one to give up; in early 1891, a petition slid onto a desk in the Scottish Office demanding rights for Laxford, and the under-secretary noted agreeably that it was 'a more modest proposal than others'.[6] After the 1891 Committee had made its rounds, Mackay wrote to the Scottish Office in November, arguing that 'in addition to fish traffic, sheep and cattle and general merchandise, Laxford is rich in gray granite and red granite abounds . . . It is estimated that a population of 43,000 or thereabout, would be benefited by this line.' He also claimed the support of North and East Coast fishermen.[7] Barely a month later, as word filtered out of the Great North of Scotland Railway company's attempts to build the Ullapool line, Mackay somewhat optimistically wrote again to London that the Railways Committee (i.e. the 1891 Committee, which as far as Mackay knew was still pondering its report) would have no alternative but to recommend the Laxford line against the Lochinver one, it being the furthest north. This claim was supported by a 'large representative meeting' at Kinlochbervie in early December.[8]

But money speaks, not people. It was clear to everyone in Whitehall that, without a personage of power or wealth, or both, to promote the Laxford railway, nothing was ever going to happen. Lord Lothian, meeting a deputation extolling the virtues of the rival Lochinver line in May 1892, was much amused that he had had the honour to greet many deputations in his office 'except perhaps poor Blackford [*sic*: this is a transcription error for Laxford]. Nobody came to me in favour of that particular terminus . . . it is quite out of the question from its position and the difficulty of getting to the harbour.'[9] Perhaps fortunately, the newspaper reports of this same meeting omitted these sympathetic words. Poor Laxford's blushes were spared. (That Laxford was no longer on anyone's agenda was painfully indicated by W. C. Dunbar's failure even to visit it in his assiduous investigations in 1892. In his otherwise excellent map, he also did not bother to mark any potential steamer route from Stornoway to Laxford.)

But by this time Mackay began to suspect that the lack of progress was not merely down to lack of interest. In a letter reporting on yet another public meeting in January 1893, he wrote: 'It is now an open secret that were it not for the opposition offered on account of the Reay Forest, Lochinver would receive bare consideration in the recommendations of the Commission and the Railways' Committee.' The 'Reay Forest' remark was repeated more publicly in the *Northern News* at the end of that same month, in an allegation that 'non-interference with the quietude, sport and amenity of the Reay Forest governed the Railways Committee'.[10] Reay Forest was a sporting estate owned by the Duke of Sutherland which lay directly on the line of the proposed Laxford railway; the allegation, therefore, was that the owners of the deer forest were utterly opposed to having noisy and smelly trains passing close to – or even through – their land and frightening off the deer before anyone could get a decent shot off. If the common people wanted a railway, they could do it a bit further south. How about Lochinver, for example?

None of which prevented Mackay from contacting the Highland Railway to ask if they would be prepared to help. Of course, replied Andrew Dougall of the Highland: 'Should the Government select the Laxford line as the proper one to the West Coast, I believe the Highland Company would deal with it in the same way as the Lochinver line.'[11] As a vague promise meaning absolutely nothing, this could not be improved on. Three years later, when light railways were being considered, the board of the Highland Railway was able to consider an 'application from a meeting held at Kinlochbervie in reference to construction of a Light Railway from there [*sic:* by 'there', Lairg is intended] to Laxford and it was agreed that the same reply be given to their application as had been made in June 1891, which was that the Directors of this Company would be prepared to work the line from Lairg to Loch Laxford, if made on reasonable terms'.[12] But by 1897, the Highland was far less amenable: in answer to a request from a 'public meeting' in Scourie for the survey of a line between Lairg and Laxford, the answer was a blunt 'No.'[13]

The Lairg to Laxford railway never progressed. A few years later, William Mackay took himself and his young family off to Canada.

The Highland Railway was always even-handed when dealing with minnows. In August 1896, the MP for Sutherland was able to inform Whitehall that the Highland Railway had offered to 'construct, work and maintain in perpetuity, such a line of railway, 38 miles long, from Culrain . . . to Lochinver, at a cost not exceeding £250,000, on condition that Her Majesty's Government shall for a period of 30 years pay . . . a dividend of 3% on the capital'.[14] But barely a month later, when a Mr Gordon of Lochinver wrote to propose that they work together on a project for building the railway from Culrain to Lochinver, the Highland's answer was again a straight no.[15] At least Mr Gordon then knew where he stood. But it was probably the final nail in the coffin for the Lochinver railway proposal.

This proposal was for a railway branching off the Far North Line at Culrain – the junction was sometimes referred to as Invershin – a few miles north of Bonar Bridge. Culrain has some claim to fame in the annals of crofting history: here it was, at the end of January 1820, that a battle took place between crofters and sheriff-officers delivering orders for eviction. A fearsome battalion of women armed with sticks, their men standing admiringly in the background, beat back the sheriff-officers and relieved them of the eviction papers. A second attempt to serve the papers, four weeks later, was likewise beaten off, the women this time armed with stones.[16] Seventy years later, Culrain was marginally quieter, emptied of crofters and fit for a railway. The branch line was to set off north-westwards along the route of the modern A837, turning northwards at Ledmore, looping around the top of Loch Assynt to approach Lochinver from the north-east, before terminating at Ardglash Point at the south-western tip of the natural harbour. In distance, about 42 miles. In cost, according to the 1890 Commission, about £260,000 – although in fairness, no proper survey had ever been done; the Commission members simply looked at a one-inch Ordnance Survey map and did some mental arithmetic.[17]

In terms of a campaign, Lochinver performed rather badly. Although Mr James Gordon of Lochinver announced himself as 'Secretary pro tem for the Lochinver Railway Committee' (and was doubtless the same Mr Gordon as later tried his luck with the Highland Railway), he did not seem to have the inclination to engage in the requisite frenzy of letter-writing. The Lochinver Railway Committee did manage a petition in March 1890, and some people in Tain wrote to the Scottish Office in June 1892, as did some 'fishermen from different parts of the Country and lying in Lochinver this the 3rd day of June'. (These fishermen were by and large East Coasters – from Buckie, Portsoy, Portknockie, Cullen, Cockenzie; the first name on the list was that of George Murray. A valiant attempt by the Scottish Office to write to Mr Murray acknowledging receipt of the petition ended in failure: the envelope addressed to 'George Murray, Fisherman, Buckie' was returned to sender with the words 'Insufficient address – several of name'.)[18] In January of 1893, the clerk of Sutherland County Council in Golspie felt moved to write in support. And in that same month, Mr Gordon wrote to the Secretary for Scotland announcing that the local fishermen all wanted a railway to Lochinver.[19]

Quite unexpectedly, despite a low-key campaign on the ground, the Lochinver proposal received a boost from the 1891 North-West Coast of Scotland Railways Committee. The Western Highlands and Islands Commission of the previous year had been prepared to envisage a line to Lochinver, but only if it was an extension of the one to Ullapool. Even then, they were not sure precisely what they were proposing but they did know it would be incredibly expensive. But now, having been scathing about virtually all the railway projects presented to them, Hutchinson's 1891 Committee stated that Lochinver 'affords the most convenient natural site for the establishment of a fishery centre and railway terminus'. Not only that but, in contrast to the fantasy dangerous rocks surrounding Ullapool, Lochinver's very own 'outlying dangerous shoals' were marked by warning beacons and lit by a bright lighthouse at Stoer, and so were quite acceptable. Hutchinson had even elicited some kind of promise from the Highland Railway that it was prepared to 'construct, work and maintain' a railway from Invershin (Culrain) to Lochinver – so long as Government guaranteed a 3 per cent return on the construction costs of £200,000.[20]

In May 1892, on the strength of this recommendation, Lord Lothian was honoured to receive a deputation in his Whitehall office of sundry persons seeking to promote the Lochinver Railway. Led by none other than the Duke of Sutherland (recall here that he owned the Reay Forest and was busily working against the Laxford line), the group comprised a ragbag of parliamentarians, including Angus Sutherland, one of the original Crofters' Party MPs. Mr Gordon was also in attendance. The group repeated the old argument that Ullapool was too far inland, so Lochinver was a far better bet. They talked up the fact that the Highland had made all the right noises about construction. It was all very persuasive. Lord Lothian replied in regally non-committal terms ('the Treasury and the Government were quite prepared and quite determined to do something') and ushered them out of the door.[21] On the following day, he received a similar deputation advocating the Ullapool Railway: a busy week indeed for the Secretary for Scotland.

None of this actually helped, however. As we have already seen with the fate of the Ullapool proposal, the Westminster Government was quite disinclined to entertain any new branch line, being content to stick with the less innovative (albeit more pricey) Mallaig and Kyle of Lochalsh proposals. And, in any case, no rich promoters stepped forward to assist Lochinver. As a final nail in the coffin, Under-Secretary Dunbar, in his report to the incoming Scottish Secretary Trevelyan in late 1892, was rather doubtful of Lochinver's credentials.

A few years later, some unfocused interventions by other supporters served only to bury the project even deeper: in 1896 a letter reached the Highland Railway from the clerk of Sutherland County Council, asking about the potential for railways from 'Invershin or Lairg to Lochinver or Loch Laxford'. The question was deemed too indefinite even to merit a reply.[22] In an admirable diversionary move by the Highland Railway, an 1897 resolution from Scourie to the railway company, asking for a survey of the Laxford line, elicited a negative reply and a suggestion that the people of Scourie contact the Lochinver supporters – who, of course, had already been neatly shunted to one side.[23] There is a tantalising reference in correspondence in March 1897 to a survey of the Lochinver route, undertaken by Murdoch Paterson; Mr Gordon wished to see the plans; but of this survey no more is known, unless it was the one which caused the Highland Railway's £435 write-off (already noted) back in 1894.[24]

And so, by early 1897, it was all over. As for James Gordon – if he is the same one honoured by a plaque inside Assynt Parish Church at Lochinver – then he subsequently devoted himself to far easier tasks than gaining funds for a railway: he was 'for 50 years a devoted member and elder of this church which by his zeal and enterprise was removed stone by stone from Nairn and re-erected on its present site in 1903'.

SOME IMAGINATIVE PROPOSALS

'Ingenious and Interesting Schemes'

For the people of Laxford, Lochinver, Ullapool and Aultbea, the rejection of their plans was a heavy blow. But their failure was only that of their respective campaigns; it was certainly not a result of social and economic problems suddenly vanishing; and least of all was it a failure of Scottish imagination. The history of railway construction in Scotland is littered with surprising ideas.

In 1845, no fewer than 248 Railway Bills were lodged with the Board of Trade. We were bang in the middle of 'railway mania' across Great Britain. In that year, one railway proposal stands out, partly for its lengthy name, but mostly for its proposed route. This was 'The Great National Direct Independent Land's End to John o' Groats Atmospheric Railway'. The name more or less told you everything. It was to run the whole length of Britain, and at least two engineering marvels would be incorporated: a viaduct a mile long over Loch Ness, and a tunnel boring right through the foot of Ben Nevis. Terminus to terminus, the total journey time would be a mere seven hours, with optional 'Steam Ferries to the Scilly and Orkney Isles' for onward travel. And it would be 'atmospheric' in the sense that the propulsion power would be compressed air.

Rather disappointingly, this was a spoof. Not even the most opium-addled of Victorian engineers was really chasing this fantasy. Which did not prevent Scottish businessmen, in the same year, from promoting a 'Scottish Grand Junction Railway', encompassing lines all the way up, down, and side to side across the Scottish mainland – but this plan was no hoax, merely well-intentioned hot air.[25] However, the seed had been planted for some highly ambitious ideas about railway networks.

Four decades later, the residents of Edinburgh were beginning to take an interest in the proposed railways of western Scotland. In May 1889, the short-lived Liberal newspaper *The Scottish Leader* was not content with this branch line or that short extension to a railway; it called for a 'bold, thorough-going, well-planned and comprehensive scheme' of railways up and down the entire west coast, as well as on Skye and Lewis.[26] In a lengthy article, it described a thoroughly joined-up network which would turn round the fortunes of the Scottish nation.

Building around the skeleton of the planned Glasgow and North-Western Railway – shortly to become the West Highland Railway – there would be a railway from Glasgow to Fort William, via Loch Lomond and Crianlarich. A branch would be built from Spean Bridge to Fort Augustus, which would extend all the way to Inverness; and another one (probably starting at Tulloch) to Kingussie – which would thereby become a hub for the transportation of cattle from the north of Scotland to southern markets. From Invergarry, a line would branch off west through Glen Shiel and make its way round the south coast of Loch Duich and Loch Alsh as far as Kylerhea, from where 'by means of a mole thrown across the narrow sound' it would cross into Skye; thence to Broadford and Portree; from Portree to Uig and Dunvegan, but also to Vaternish Point; from any of which there would be a steamer connection to Finsbay on Harris (just north of Rodel); and finally a railway up through Harris and Lewis to Stornoway. Pause for breath: there is yet more in the opposite direction. There would be a line from Fort William southwards to Ballachulish which would continue on to Oban; and from Oban a railway would lead all the way down the Kintyre peninsula to Campbeltown. Pretty much every base was thereby covered – except, rather glaringly, the north-west Highlands. The *Leader* ended with a pious hope: 'In order to carry out the scheme suggested, a vigorous and sustained effort, the abandonment of petty and local jealousies, suitable Government assistance, and the united and cordial co-operation of all interested in it, are absolutely essential.' Slim chance. But it was a call to arms. And was naturally and completely ignored.

In the same year and also from Edinburgh came a very odd proposal indeed. It was sent to the Scottish Office in June 1889, and received there by under-secretary R. W. Cochran-Patrick, who had been delegated the unenviable task of responding to this whole flood of unwelcome correspondence on the matter of Highland railways. He was by now inured to strange correspondence, but this letter lifted his eyebrows a good half-inch. It came from a perfectly respectable source – William Munro, Assessor of Railways and Canals (Scotland) in Edinburgh; Mr Munro hoped his suggestion would go some way to meeting the conflicting demands of the Aultbea and Ullapool lines. He proposed a railway which ran from

> Achnashellach to Torridon, thence to Gairloch, thence to Poolewe, thence to Dundonnell, and on to Inverlael and Ullapool . . . The whole of this distance . . . is about 56 miles, but even a part of it would do much good. A line along the coast thus, would not be so liable to snow-blocks, as the line through a hilly country from Garve to Ullapool . . . I attach a small Railway map in which I have coloured in light blue, the line I refer to . . . but which no doubt would require to be varied more or less according to the levels of the ground.

This light blue line was drawn on a Bartholomew's *Map of the Caledonian Railway* in a series of straight segments joining all the places mentioned. Some variation would indeed be required according to the levels of the ground: the blue line actually crosses the Torridon mountain of Liathach (3,456 feet) and passes over the high shoulder of An Teallach (3,483 feet). For sure, it would have knocked the Snowdon railway into a cocked hat. The file containing the letter has been annotated by Lord Lothian in cautious words: 'This is interesting. The line proposed would meet all requirements – but would I believe be physically impracticable, and too costly.'[27] His Lordship was not incorrect. To be fair to Mr Munro, as an Assessor of Railways and Canals, he would not have had much experience of the north-west, and so would be unfamiliar with the landscape.

A little later, another visionary improved on Mr Munro. John Struthers of Clarendon Square, London was a man on a mission. He had been pestering Whitehall since February 1891 with his plans for an integrated Scottish railway system. In March, he presented his ideas to the Philosophical Society of Glasgow. A copy of his lecture was sent to London. One of the under-secretaries at the Scottish Office spent some time trying to work out who on earth Struthers was ('This', he noted in puzzlement, 'is not Professor Struthers' – the Anatomy Professor at Aberdeen, a man justly famous for dissecting the 'Tay

Whale' in Dundee in 1884). The under-secretary duly summarised the ideas, which involved linking up various railways across the north of Scotland and down its west coast: 'His schemes', stated the summary, 'are ingenious and interesting but have no practical value.'[28] But Mr Struthers, buoyed up for sure by the enthusiasm of the assembled philosophers of Glasgow, was not easily discouraged. In the late summer of 1891, he wanted to know whether he could present his plan to Hutchinson's North-West Coast of Scotland Railways Committee; the Railways Committee rather thought not. Affronted, Struthers wrote to the *Glasgow Herald*, which unveiled his scheme to a startled world.

In essence, it was this: railways would be built on Lewis, Harris and Skye; linked by a steamer service across the Minch from Tarbert to Uig, this would allow fish landed at Stornoway to reach the foot of Skye swiftly and cheaply. From Glenelg on the mainland opposite Skye, a railway would run southwards along the coast to the mouth of Loch Hourn, then eastwards along the north shore of Loch Hourn, 'where, at the point at which it narrows, the ascent would be commenced of a steep ridge between the head of Loch Hourn and Loch Quoich'. Then it would travel due east past Loch Garry, turn right at the Great Glen and proceed southwards alongside the Caledonian Canal to join the West Highland line at the southern end of Loch Lochy. From Glenelg, it would be 50 miles in total and – contrary to all known facts – there would be 'only one minor engineering difficulty': the ridge at head of Loch Hourn.[29] The Scottish Office dutifully filed the proposal in a pigeon-hole and opened the next letter.

Railway experts of every type popped up with astonishing regularity in the last decade of the century, proposing this and proposing that. In 1890, a Stranraer gentleman by the name of H. Temple Humphreys suggested that good and practical railways could be built on Skye and Lewis, using a new type of 'timber railway' which he himself had recently successfully deployed in Italy (in a 'Petroleum Mine'), at a mere £500 per mile.[30] Mr Humphreys had indeed some standing – he was the celebrated inventor of the 'cycloscope', which allowed railway curves to be measured in tight spots where complex equipment would prove awkward of use; and had patented a 'post and rail-way' method of construction which he promised would dramatically cut the cost of construction over rough and hilly ground.

Sadly, there were no takers for his 'timber railway' on Skye; which may have been a good thing since, while timber rails might pass muster in hot and dry Italy, they were not noted for their performance in a wet climate. There is a cautionary tale from New Zealand's Southland province, where the timber rails on such a railway had to be turned and scraped incessantly to be of any use in the damp conditions. Ultimately they had to be lifted and thrown away – they were not even good for sleepers.[31]

On less slippery ground was the proposal of Charles Forman, which was delivered to Dunbar at the Scottish Office in October 1892.[32] Forman was a partner in the firm Formans and McCall, the engineers at that time supervising the building of the West Highland line between Crianlarich and Fort William. Forman outlined a plan for a railway leading from Spean Bridge on the new West Highland Line up to Fort Augustus (22 miles – a line in fact later built between 1897 and 1903), with a line branching off from this one at Invergarry and following Glen Shiel as far as Invershiel, then along the south shore of Loch Duich and Loch Alsh to Glenelg (44 miles). Either a ferry or – in the spirit of modernity – a bridge would take trains over to Skye, where a railway would continue to Portree (36 miles). A hundred miles of track, all for the cost, he thought, of £645,000. Ingenious indeed, and if any man was capable of delivering this line across inhospitable territory, it would have been Forman, at that time up to his knees in the bog of Rannoch Moor.

Forman was a very successful engineer with a fine clutch of challenging Scottish railways in his portfolio. One of his schemes was more ambitious than most. In 1893 he put forward a plan for a railway to the top of Ben Nevis. It was to be 4¾ miles in length, with a maximum gradient of slightly less than 1 in 3. The budget for construction was £30,000, which included a hotel on the summit for the exhausted traveller. Revenues from a projected 15,000 passengers per annum (at 1s 6d each) were £1,125. Profits perhaps came from the beer and pies in the hotel restaurant.[33] That it never came to pass, and Ben Nevis remains relatively unsullied, is probably something for which we may always be grateful.

10

'Imprisonment With or Without Hard Labour'

The Light Railways Act of 1896

Imaginative ideas for railways were there; the promoters were there; public meetings, petitions and begging letters – all there. What was not there, sadly, was a supportive government. While the Liberal administration of Gladstone might, in the early 1880s, have made a praiseworthy stab at improving the lot of crofters and fishermen, the solutions provided were half-hearted at best. Among the many panaceas offered were railways. But the Liberals were not particularly keen on financing railways, because it meant raiding the State piggy-bank. In any case, in the period after the collapse of the hopes of Laxford, Lochinver, Ullapool and Aultbea, the Liberals had other things to think about. Not least of these was the great internal dissent which tore them apart, with one faction favouring Home Rule for Ireland, and the other faction dead against it and siding with the Conservatives on the issue. The Liberals had been returned to power in August 1892, but lasted only three years until, with a huge majority, the Conservatives and Liberal Unionists formed a government which stayed in power until 1906. But in those later eleven years, some small crumbs of assistance were scattered before a starving flock of railway promoters. To the critical modern reader, it may seem counter-intuitive that the Conservative governments were actually more pro-active when it came to promoting transportation than the Liberals – but the record speaks for itself.

We have noted earlier that Ireland often benefited from helpful legislation over the second half of the nineteenth century, while people in the Highlands and Islands, afflicted by very similar social and economic pressures, got almost nothing. Whenever the problems of Scotland were addressed by commissions and Acts of Parliament, the template was usually something that had been deployed for Ireland a few years earlier. The template, but frequently without the truly effective bits. So it was with a Light Railways Act, which was passed – for England, Wales and Scotland – in 1896. Seven years earlier, the previous Conservative administration had pushed through a similar Act for Ireland. This allowed for the Treasury to grant up to £25,000 for each light railway in Ireland deemed necessary for the development of fisheries or other industries, but which required special assistance from the State for its construction. Moneys could be paid as a one-off capital sum or as annual subsidy, or both; and shareholders could expect the Government to guarantee them an excellent annual dividend of 3 per cent on their investments. No wonder that the desperate Scottish railway promoters kept asking for this same largesse. And so this Irish Act – but not all of it – became the model for a new British Act under the Conservative government elected in 1895.

Until 1896, the business of constructing a small railway in Britain was a lawyer's dream come true. All manner of regulatory hoops had to be jumped through, a Private Bill had to be presented to Parliament, an Act had to be passed and approved by Her Majesty; and only then, somewhat impoverished by legal fees and the necessity of buttering up appropriate parliamentary representatives, were you good to go. But on the 14 August 1896, all this changed, with the passing of the Light Railways Act whose aim was 'to facilitate the Construction of Light Railways in Great Britain'. With economic stagnation affecting the rural areas of Britain in the late nineteenth century, it was considered that opening up access to more remote places could be achieved by the swift construction of cheap railway lines.

The streamlining of the whole process was to be overseen by a commission appointed by the Board of Trade, whose job it would now be to accept, scrutinise and authorise proposals for building 'light' railways. Such applications could come from local councils (county, borough, etc.) and/or from private individuals or companies. In essence, the Commission took over all the responsibilities which until then had resided with Parliament. Almost to the exclusion of everything else, the Act focused on the regulation of the financial management of such railways, and stopped far short of actually providing any finance except as a loan (and only then under very specific circumstances). It was up to local councils to provide most of the finance, in conjunction with private investors; if this was achieved, then and only then would the Government provide loans of up to one quarter of the total amount required, at an interest rate of just over 3 per cent. If the railway was considered important for the development of agriculture or fisheries, and 'the railway could not be constructed without the special assistance of the State',[1] then a bit more government money could be forthcoming – but only up to the value of half the capital required and strictly regulated by Treasury penny-pinchers. These were undoubtedly terms of unprecedented generosity: only the Irish had seen such things before.

It is slightly disconcerting that the one thing the Act did not do was define what, precisely, was a 'light railway'. Although there were some stern words about the 'preservation of scenery and objects of historical interest', there were no regulations in the Act about the gauge of the lines, the size or weight of the rolling stock; nor were there any stipulations for signalling, level crossings, speed or similar niceties of health and safety. It was up to the Commissioners themselves to 'settle any draft order submitted to them . . . and see that all such matters (including provisions for the safety of the public . . .) are inserted therein, as they think necessary for the proper construction and working of the railway'.[2] However, in Schedule 2 of the Act, a dozen previous statutes concerning railway construction and operation were referenced, under whose sections all the requisite safety regulations could be found. The rather elderly Regulation of Railways Act of 1868 stipulated for light railways a speed limit of 25 mph and a maximum axle weight of 8 tons (8,130kg). Offenders who broke these limits were sternly threatened with 'Imprisonment, with or without Hard Labour, for any Term not exceeding Two Years'.[3]

Conveniently for those thinking of building a light railway, in 1896 there also appeared the authoritative book *Light Railways for the United Kingdom, India and the Colonies: A Practical Handbook*, by J. C. Mackay. His non-technical definition of a light railway makes perfect sense: it was essentially a small investment, starting from which, were it successful, a 'proper' railway could then be financed and built. From his wide survey of such railways in Europe, India, South Africa and Australia, he reckoned on construction costs of between £3,000 and £5,000 per mile, depending on the weight of rails and rolling stock. Limits on speed were dependent on the weight of the rolling stock and the strength of the rails.

The new Act attracted many proposals to build light railways. In the four years from 1896 to 1899, at least 200 plans from all over the UK were submitted to the Light Railways Commissioners in London. But in the event only around thirty light railways were ever constructed between 1899 and 1925, of which six were in Scotland: the Wick and Lybster (1899), the Lauder (1901), the Cromarty and Dingwall (authorised 1902, begun 1914, but never completed), the Dornoch (1902), the Leadhills and Wanlockhead (1902) and the Campbeltown and Machrihanish (1906).[4] The Wick and Lybster scraped through on the basis of a generous donation from the Duke of Portland, who owned land around Berriedale in Caithness; the various local authorities put their hands in their pockets; even the Highland Railway chipped in a miserly amount, albeit very unwillingly. The Cromarty and Dingwall line was beset by arguments with the Highland Railway and enjoyed the infamy of not starting in Cromarty and not finishing in Dingwall; nor, indeed, of ever operating – while still under construction in 1915, the track was sacrificed to the greater good of the war effort. The Dornoch line was only opened as a result of a hefty subsidy from the Duke of Sutherland, and was greatly welcomed by the philanthropist and multi-millionaire Andrew Carnegie; he had high hopes of an easier rail connection from the south, since Dornoch lay barely six miles from his castle at Skibo. However, his enthusiasm appears to have stopped well short of any financial contribution. Although most of these lines endured for a respectable number of years, none of them grew up to be a 'proper' railway such as J. C. Mackay might have hoped for, largely due to the slow death of the economic developments which the railways were intended to service.

Readers will observe that the Garve and Ullapool Railway does not appear in that list of Scottish light railways. But this was not for want of trying. The line had by no means been forgotten in the years since 1893's traumatic abandonment. In August 1894, the local MP, James Galloway Weir, asked the Chancellor of the Exchequer 'whether in the preparation of the Estimates for next year provision will be made for a guarantee to enable the Garve and Ullapool Railway Company to proceed with the line from Garve to Ullapool?'[5] To which the

Chancellor replied, regretfully etc. A full year later, Weir tried again. Fed up, the Chancellor was more forthright this time:

> Two successive Governments have, as the Hon. Member is aware, considered this matter; but neither of them have seen their way to support the proposed line, in view of the adverse reports of the Western Highlands and Islands Commission, 1890, and the subsequent Special Committee of 1891. The Government will, of course, consider any representations that may be laid before them, but I cannot help pointing out that the experience of this Government and their predecessors with regard to the proposed guarantee to the Benavie and Mallaig line, is not such as to encourage them to undertake more proposals of a similar nature in the Highlands.[6]

And in April of 1896, the Lord Advocate (at that time, Charles Pearson, MP for Edinburgh and St Andrews Universities), in response to a question from Mr Weir and other inquiring Scotsmen, declared that,

> with regard to the Ullapool Railway, it was not yet a realised fact. The Government had chosen one line, and a Resolution regarding it was only the other day on the Order Paper. The line to Mallaig was likely, he hoped, to prove a great advantage and boon to the district it served. He did not say that there were not advantages in forming lines in other parts of the country, and it might be that light railways might be constructed in some of the districts which the Hon. Member had in his mind, but he would be a little too sanguine if he thought that the Treasury would, immediately after passing a substantial amount for one of the best Highland lines, proceed to undertake another railway equally important.[7]

The very thought of the Treasury spending money on an 'important' railway line was clearly risible. (The funding of the Mallaig extension, in April 1896, had still not been agreed – there had been a delay of two full years between the authorising of construction and the authorising of absolutely critical government funding. Not everyone in Westminster agreed on the idea of even the smallest subsidy for a railway.)

The draft of the Light Railways Bill was being circulated in February 1896. And within days an ever-hopeful Arthur Fowler rode out from

Braemore once more. He wrote to the Highland Railway, almost as if nothing had happened in 1892 to make the company an untrustworthy ally; Fowler wanted to know whether the company would be interested in a joint venture to establish the branch line as a light railway. The general manager of the Highland, Charles Steel (Andrew Dougall had recently retired under something of a cloud, having been caught in dodgy share dealings) met with Fowler, and the meetings were minuted as follows:

> The General Manager reported that he had three interviews since last Board Meeting [3 March 1896] with Mr Fowler and Mr Manners, Engineer, in regard to the question of the Garve and Ullapool Railway and that he had informed Mr Fowler that subject to the approval of the Board, the only arrangement which the Highland Company would be able to make in connection with the Railway would be that they would work it on the terms mentioned in 1891, *viz*: a fixed rate per mile with an allowance of 10 per cent on traffic sent southward by the Highland Line and that the Highland Company could not incur any Capital responsibility. Approved.[8]

This was not the first light railway request to be considered by the Highland that year. At the beginning of March, the Board noted that a meeting at Kinlochbervie had asked the Highland to build a light railway to Laxford; the considered reply was to be the same as for Ullapool – not build, but work 'on reasonable terms'. At the same meeting, the Board also decided to delay replying to a request from Wick regarding a light railway from Wick to Scrabster; a month later, the Scrabster proposal was back on the table, this time in a request sent from Thurso – a reply was duly postponed, awaiting further information, costs, etc. The Highland could do delaying tactics in its sleep.

In order to keep up the momentum, the indefatigable P. Campbell Ross sprang into action. Still signing himself the Honorary Secretary of the Garve and Ullapool Executive Committee, in May 1896 he wrote to the new Secretary for Scotland, Lord Balfour, attacking the proposal for a railway from Culrain to Lochinver, but – in an unforeseen change of tactic – suggesting instead the construction of a line from Ullapool to Lochinver (32 miles: very hilly, if we recall). This would be a light railway.

This was not a Campbell Ross aberration, for in August 1895 yet another public meeting in Ullapool had supported the idea of a railway from Garve to Ullapool and then continuing on to Lochinver; the Government was being asked to provide finance. Which was particularly bad timing since, three days after the date of this petition, the Liberals in government were replaced by the Conservatives.[9] But that the idea of an extension to Lochinver had even surfaced was an indication that desperation had set in. The only conceivable rationale behind this was to ensure that the Culrain to Lochinver Light Railway never got built.[10] To speed things along, a few more petitions were definitely called for: in April 1897, Balfour received a petition signed by around thirty Glasgow businessmen who had interests in the north-west, encouraging Westminster to support the Ullapool railway. Barely two days later, Ross put pen to paper again, attaching a printed 'Memorial' (entitled 'A Brief Statement of Facts') and a petition signed by no fewer than 610 residents of the Loch Broom area demanding a railway.[11] In May, pestered to the limit by Ross, Balfour agreed to write out a Certificate, as recommended by Section 5 of the 1896 Act, which allowed for the Treasury to chip in some cash if the local authority did so first: this Certificate stated that

> the construction of a Light Railway . . . between Garve and Ullapool
> in the County of Ross and Cromarty . . . will benefit agriculture in
> the central districts of the county and will establish a necessary means
> of communication between the fishing harbour of Ullapool and the
> interior of the country, and owing to the exceptional circumstance
> of the District, I do not believe that this railway will be constructed
> without special assistance from the State.[12]

'The State' in this instance did not mean the Treasury alone; it meant the Ross and Cromarty County Council first, and then – just maybe – the Treasury. His Lordship's useless piece of paper was greeted by Campbell Ross and the obligatory public meeting with derision and the response that it was hopeless asking for any assistance from the Council.[13]

So, not in an unforeseen manner, Arthur Fowler's hobby-horse fell at the first hurdle. But at least the honour of Ullapool was saved by a similar failure for a revived proposal for the Achnasheen to Aultbea Railway. Had that rival proposal gone through – oh! how bitter would have been the gall in Lochbroom!

It is to Fowler's credit that he did not take no for an answer. In September of 1898, the Board of the Highland Railway was found to be debating the question of a light railway once more, with exactly the same resolution:

> The meeting considered an application from the promoters of the Garve and Ullapool Light Railway and it was resolved to inform them that the Highland Company can make no contribution to the proposed Line, but if it is sanctioned by the Light Railway Commissioners, this Company will construct and work it on terms to be agreed; and further, that if the promoters desire it, and will undertake to defray the expense, the Company's Engineers will be instructed to survey the proposed Line.[14]

Sir John Fowler died in November 1898; when his eldest son Arthur died unexpectedly four months later at the age of forty-three, leaving a widow and two young sons, the cause of the Ullapool railway was taken up by Liberal MP James Galloway Weir. Weir had made his money as an importer and manufacturer of sewing machines (the most popular model was 'the 55 shilling, with improved mesh gears'), and had first been elected in 1892 as one of five Crofters' Party MPs before transferring his allegiance to the mainstream Liberal Party in 1895. Slightly behind the pack, Weir wrote to Balfour in April 1899, also asking for a Certificate as proposed by Section 5 of the 1896 Act; an under-secretary wrote back, drily pointing out that his Lordship had already fulfilled that obligation two years earlier.[15] Weir then made himself a thorn in the flesh of the Highland Railway. In February of 1899, the board meeting was 'read [a] letter from Mr J. G. Weir MP regarding the proposed Garve and Ullapool Railway. The Board fully discussed the matter and instructed the General Manager to prepare a suitable reply.' Evidently this reply was unsatisfactory to Weir for, a month later, he was pestering them again: 'Read further letter . . . from Mr Weir MP regarding the Garve and Ullapool Railway. Resolved that an answer be given similar to that given to the promoters of other Light Railways.'[16]

The Highland Railway Company was finding it hard to put to rest the spirit of Ullapool.

I I

'Unsatisfactory from the Very Beginning'

Railways on Skye and Lewis

And now, lit by the warm glow of the Light Railways Act, we must settle back and hear the sorry tales of the proposed railway lines on the islands of Skye and Lewis. Despite impressive local public support for both of these schemes, they were completely incapacitated from the start by the lack of any wealthy promoters. The later intervention of a London–based band of gentlemen and accountants did nothing at all to move the islanders' ambitions forward.

RAILWAYS FOR SKYE

'A Serious Matter'

We begin with Skye. During Lord Lothian's visitation there in June 1889, there had been very adequate talk of railways across the island. His Lordship had been aware of proposals of railways from Dunvegan and Uig to Portree and from Portree to Kyleakin; in an unguarded moment in Broadford, he 'proposed taking a run along the road to Kyleakin to see if the suggestion for a light railway there was at all practicable or necessary'. He duly did so and returned in one piece, but without further comment.[1] In Portree, there was much debate with local people about the proposed lines to the west coast, and even suggestions of a direct line between Broadford and Isleornsay. The latter suggestion was interesting: a line terminating at Kyleakin would

205

perforce link to the Highland Railway's terminus at Strome Ferry (and later Kyle of Lochalsh), whereas a line terminating at Isleornsay would link with the North British Railway's proposed railhead at Mallaig or Roshven. Clearly, this was not just about stand-alone lines on Skye – larger interests were involved. Lord Lothian contrived to sound concerned about the effect of a Skye railway on the land – 'Would the tenants also give facilities for the railway, which would necessarily cut up their crofts and farms?' The reassuring answer, perhaps to be taken with a pinch of salt since it came from a factor of one of the large estates, was that 'there would be no difficulty in that respect'.[2]

The next visitors to the islands were the members of the 1890 Commission, who took the view that light railways of the sort discussed earlier could indeed be built; but they slightly muddied the waters by lumping together the railways for Skye and for Lewis, reckoning they would cost in total about £450,000. There was no attempt at any kind of cost analysis, and one is left with the distinct impression that the hard work was being left to others. In late 1892 an under-secretary for Scotland on a lightning tour of the West concluded that a Portree and Dunvegan light railway would be of great benefit, but he did not go so far as to estimate costs. The Skye Railway remained a sound-bite.

Only in 1896, after the Light Railways Act was passed, was there a renewed attempt to get things done. In the autumn of that year, the Highland Railway was approached by a deputation from Inverness-shire County Council asking about light railways on Skye, specifically terminating at Kyleakin; and also concerning a steam ferry across the strait capable of conveying railway trucks. 'The deputation expressed themselves highly satisfied with what was said to them.'[3] What was said to them remains undocumented; but we can probably guess. One of the things this deputation had requested was a survey. Such a survey was duly undertaken – but it was rather odd: the route surveyed ran from Kyleakin, via Broadford, to Torrin at the head of Loch Slapin on the west coast. This seemingly pointless route presumably (a) gave easy access between the east and west coasts of Skye and (b) supposed that Torrin could be developed as a port serving the Outer Isles. Maybe. Whatever the reasons, the Highland Railway remained unenthusiastic; in late April 1897, it was minuted that the General Manager had been over the route of the Skye railway and was 'unable to recommend taking any definitive attitude in regard to the matter'.[4] The

County Council changed tack: in June, this time with reference to the County Council's enquiry about a railway from Portree to Dunvegan, the Highland stated it was willing to operate the line, but not construct it; no survey was even discussed. And by April 1898, the Highland announced that it would definitely take 'no action' for any railway on Skye.[5]

Almost certainly, one of the triggers for this rather decisive 'no action' was the most unwelcome sound of a competitor sniffing around Skye. The competitor was the Hebridean Light Railway Company (HLRC), established in February 1898. You knew things had taken a turn for the worse when a London company came up with a grand scheme for a huge railway across both Skye and Lewis. The HLRC had registered offices in Cannon Street, London; indeed, this was exactly the same address as that of the locomotive and tram manufacturer Dick, Kerr & Co. The directors were a motley selection of accountants (probably employed by Dick, Kerr), lawyers, stockbrokers and respectable gentlemen of no known profession. (For a list of the directors, see Appendix 7.) According to the articles of the company, they all earned £250 per annum; their duties were light. And not one of them had any connection with Skye or Lewis. Clearly, the cunning plan of the HLRC was to organise the construction of a railway and then sell the operator its own locomotives to run on the lines. This was not necessarily a bad thing – Dick, Kerr & Co. were at that time beginning to develop electric-powered locomotives specifically for the light railway sector. Had they succeeded in their plans, perhaps new-fangled electric engines would have been purring across some of the more spectacular landscapes of the Western Isles; there would have been plenty of hydroelectric power available, after all. (Much later in its existence Dick, Kerr & Co. became a constituent part of English Electric, known for its locomotives and aircraft during and after the Second World War.) For the moment, sadly, locomotives were to be powered by steam.

When first launched in April 1898, the HLRC had capital of £5,000 which it proposed to cover with the issue of £1 shares. The registration documents clearly stated that 'Capital is merely nominal at present and subscribed for by Dick, Kerr & Co. Ltd, Contractors';[6] and, indeed, in the several years of its existence, no one other than the locomotive company seems to have acquired any shares. This did not prevent the directors from doing all the sensible things in preparation for building a railway: having a survey done, estimating costs, paying themselves and passing round the hat for contributions from others. The first step was to issue a formal notice of their intentions; this appeared in the newspapers in April 1898, with the useful advice that 'Notice of any objection to the proposed Railway should be made in writing to the Light Railway Commissioners on foolscap paper, to be written on one side only.'[7]

The HLRC commissioned plans from Sir Douglas Fox. They had gone straight to the top, for Fox was one of the most prestigious railway engineers of the time; he had designed a number of railways and associated infrastructure across Britain and its Empire. The most famous was perhaps the Snowdon Mountain Railway, completed in 1896 and still running to this day (despite a fatal accident to a paying passenger on the opening day). Fox was later elected president of the Institute of Civil Engineers. Doubtless a busy man, he sub-contracted the Skye and Lewis surveys to an Irish engineer, William Barrington, who was based in Limerick. Barrington had been the principal engineer for the South Clare railway in the west of Ireland. One West Coast railway being much like another West Coast railway, he was dispatched to the north-west of Scotland in late 1897 or early 1898 to see how the land lay. As one would expect from a man who, in later life, served as a member of the Senate of the Irish Free State, he did his work with great efficiency and swiftly produced two sets of plans – one for Railways 1 and 2 on Skye and one for Railways 3 and 4 on Lewis; we shall examine the latter shortly.[8]

Railway No. 1 was most ambitious. It was to run from Isleornsay at the top of the Sleat peninsula on Skye and lead all the way to the pier in Uig in the north-west of the island. Its total length was to be 52 miles and 7 furlongs; it would have numerous bridges and no fewer than fifteen level crossings, each with its own gatekeeper's house. The total cost was, with some precision, estimated at £325,285 18s 4d. The railway was to be a light one, with a 3.5-foot gauge. A notable feature of the railway was that it was to start at a point on Skye whose closest mainland railway terminus was that of the West Highland line at Mallaig (then still under construction); and it would completely bypass Kyleakin, which was a stone's throw from the Highland Railway's new terminus at Kyle of Lochalsh. The board of the Highland Railway would have been most unamused by this plan; hence its decision to have nothing to do with any railway on Skye.

The route was to follow the line of least resistance up the east coast of Skye; this entailed a great deal of weaving in and out along the coastline. Leaving Isleornsay, where a brand new pier would be required (£20,000), the proposed line would head up the shore of Loch na Dal (through two short tunnels right at the start: £7,000), making its way towards Broadford – essentially following the modern A851 road. Once Broadford had been reached, a steep climb was required to ease the line around the coast and along the shoreline of Loch Ainort; it passed through the village of Luib, and eventually arrived at the head of the loch. At this point, the road heads steeply uphill, but the railway line would follow the flatter route along the coast, via Moll, before eventually rejoining the road at Sconser, and so onwards into Sligachan. Then came perhaps the trickiest part of the route: a viaduct 80 yards long and 63 feet high (£16,000) was required to bring the line round the back of Sligachan before it struggled up and down Glen Varragill, with some steep inclines on the way, until it fetched up in Portree. From Portree, where doubtless many passengers might choose to disembark, the railway headed to Skeabost and passed through Snizort and Kingsburgh until it reached the hill above Uig. An interesting and swift descent, which included two three-span bridges, brought the line down into Uig and across the foreshore, before the train finally halted on the pier (required strengthening: £2,000), from where Mr Macbrayne's steamers could be boarded for Harris and Lewis.

Back at Skeabost, there was a junction with Railway No. 2. This led over to Dunvegan, at that time a frequently used port for Oban and the Western Isles. The proposed line followed the present A850 road towards Edinbane; just short of that settlement, it headed round in a long curve south-westwards to maintain its height on the contour before rejoining the road; then, at Upperglen, it struck off southwards up the Red Burn and into Glen Eoghainn, and so on southwards to join the road from the south (A863), just between Roskhill and Lonmore. Finally, it rattled down into Dunvegan and terminated at the pier. The total length of this branch line was 21 miles, 4 furlongs and 2 chains, and the estimated cost was £138,449 5s 11d. Four gatekeepers' houses were included in the price.

For the two railways, then, a total of £463,735 4s 1d was required. Quite a tidy sum. How on earth was such an amount of money to be raised? We have already seen that the Light Railways Act of 1896 stipulated that the greater portion of the funding should come from local authorities and/or a private company prepared to put its hand in its pocket. In this situation, then, the HLRC turned a benevolent smile upon the Skye District Committee of Inverness-shire County Council. The gentlemen of the District Committee duly convened on 27 April 1898 to see what could be done.[9] Councillor Alexander Macdonald of Portree was the moving spirit; he pointed out that the funds of the Light Railways Commissioners were running out and that the people of Skye had best be quick to profit from the Government's unprecedented generosity. Rather bullishly, not to say over-optimistically, he suggested that 'it was a serious matter to offer opposition to the proposed light railway. The district would benefit from competing routes, and a consequent reduction of rates, while the poor people would be able to dispose of their produce in small quantities.' He proposed raising money by a rates levy 'not exceeding 6d per £1 charged on the valuation' and expressed the sanguine hope that the crofters would be unanimously in favour. Macleod of Macleod seconded the motion, with the proviso 'that the railway should go to Dunvegan as well, where there was a large population' (and there also, quite by chance, the Macleod's ancestral home).

Two opposing voices were heard – one from Glendale and one from Kilmuir, clearly still hotbeds of dissidence. The representative of Kilmuir argued that the fish-curers of Stornoway would not use the new service. His argument had a strong logic: any fish sent from Lewis to Mallaig by the new railway would have to be loaded and then unloaded two times more than necessary – from steamer to train at Uig, and from train to steamer at Isleornsay, all to save perhaps 50 miles of sailing. In those days before advanced humankind hit upon the idea of the intermodal container, each trans-shipment of perhaps hundreds of barrels of fish would be a lengthy, expensive and labour-intensive task. The fish magnates of Stornoway might not be easily tempted. The councillor therefore 'thought there was very little prospect of the railway ever paying a dividend'. And both he and the Glendale man worried that the present steamer services might be withdrawn, should the railway actually prove its worth, thereby

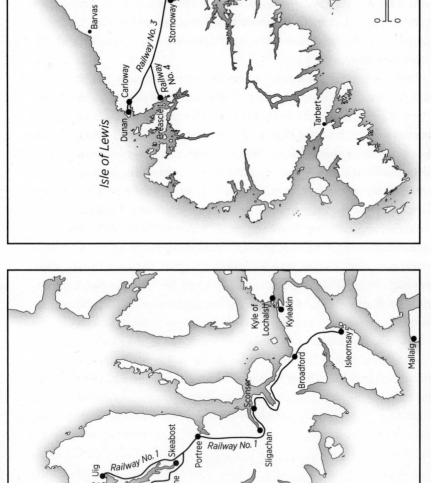

Figure 11.2 In 1898, the Hebridean Light Railway Co. drafted plans for a short railway which simply traversed Lewis from east to west, for the transportation of fish.

Fiugre 11.1 For Skye, the Hebridean Light Railway Co. proposed two lines covering much of the island and skirting around some very hilly terrain. Note that Kyleakin, the ferry port for Kyle of Lochalsh, is not served at all: Mallaig was to be the mainland port of choice.

leaving the people without a flexible transportation option. The councillor for Braes, that other sink of dissent, promptly stirred things up further by suggesting that the railway should proceed from Sligachan to Portree via Braes; evidently this man was deluded enough to imagine that the Highland Light Railway Company wished to build a railway for the convenience of the local population. Or perhaps there was a little rivalry between rebellious communities – Glendale would profit from a fine railway to Dunvegan, so why should not Braes have one too?

Nonetheless, the motion to raise money through the rates was passed, some said by a majority of eight, others said unanimously;[10] Councillor Macdonald's trust in the crofters was repaid by their elected representatives. But the HLRC had hoped for at least £35,000 to be raised by the people of Skye[11] and the District Council's open-handed support fell far short of that; so the overall target of at least a quarter of a million pounds still lay quite beyond the grasp of the HLRC. Things got desperate: Barrington appealed to the Highland Railway. In June 1899, he wrote to the board asking if it would work and maintain a narrow-gauge light railway from Dunvegan to Portree – 25.5 miles – for 60 per cent of gross receipts, diminishing to 50 per cent when the glorious threshold of £9 per mile per week in revenues was attained. Most of Railway No. 1 had clearly been jettisoned in an attempt to salvage something. The Highland's board remained unmoved. Six weeks later Barrington pestered them again, so: 'The General Manager was instructed as to the reply to be given to Mr Barrington.'[12] In this way the plan for the Skye railway, like so many before it, crashed into the buffers.

RAILWAYS FOR LEWIS

'Once This Light Railway Was Constructed,
It Would Not Stop There'

With the plans for the Isle of Lewis, matters went little better. The first hints of the ambitions of Lewis railway enthusiasts had come in Caldwell's letter to Joseph Chamberlain in May 1889; his comments are worth quoting at length:

The railway from Stornoway to Ness might take one of two directions. It might proceed *via* Barvas, thence along the west coast to Ness, a distance of 22 or 24 miles . . . The other direction of the proposed railway would be from Stornoway to Ness *via* the more populated villages of Back, Gress and Tolsta, thence through the moor or along the east coast to Ness. The distance by this latter route would be about the same as by the other route – *viz.* 22 to 24 miles; and the expense of construction would be much about the same whichever route was selected . . . It is satisfactory to know that, so far as regards the proposed harbours and railway communication in the island of Lewis itself, there is the most perfect unanimity of its inhabitants in their favour.[13]

Caldwell noted approvingly that those local people who had no money were quite willing to labour on construction instead – one hears an echo of the arrangements for building the famous Big Quay at Stornoway some seventy years earlier. He could foresee advantages to general communication, education, fisheries and tourist traffic. He then made an interesting remark: the proposed harbours and railways 'will [also] benefit the chief proprietor of the island to a very large degree, and the chief proprietor ought to take some considerable stock in the proposed railways'. The 'chief proprietor' was none other than Lady Mary Matheson, at that time busily promoting the Ullapool Railway; but in respect of a railway on Lewis, on her very doorstep, not a peep was to be heard from her, nor – later – from her nephew Donald. Perhaps because it was indeed on her very doorstep, running perilously close to deer forest and sheep-farm and the sacred pleasure grounds?

Caldwell was at that time passing comment on a proposal which had recently emerged from yet another official inquiry into Highland poverty. In January 1888, Malcolm MacNeill (erstwhile secretary to the Napier Commission) toured Lewis, observing for himself the appalling conditions endured by crofters and cottars.[14] He did so amidst extraordinary scenes of civil disobedience by those very crofters and cottars: deer-raids, the demolition of walls and fences, the diversion of salmon rivers, mass trespass, Lady Matheson under siege and being obliged to shake hands with deputations of crofters and worse; it all led to military occupation, arrests and trials. The root cause of all this upheaval was in plain sight, as MacNeill shortly reported to the Scottish Office:

privation and starvation caused by loss of land and the complete lack of wage-paying work. Even *The Scotsman*'s correspondent was obliged to state that the endemic destitution was 'most deadly in its effects'. The reverberations of the report were most likely the trigger for the spate of later visitations by MPs. And buried amongst MacNeill's recommendations were proposals for a railway from Stornoway to Loch Roag in the west, and to Ness in the north: transport infrastructure as the basis for economic relief.

Stepping boldly in the footsteps of Caldwell came Lord Lothian. Much of what he had to say on the subject has been filtered through the prose of newspaper reporters,[15] but it was clear that his Lordship spent a considerable amount of his precious time in hearing proposals for light railways across Lewis. Some people were talking up Carloway as the future 'centre for a great fishing district, embracing all the banks between Lewis, St Kilda and the Flannen *[sic]* Islands; but this will to a large extent depend on the facilities afforded for conveying the fresh fish to Stornoway and thence to the southern markets'. In Carloway, Lothian 'entered into conversation with the fishermen, and heard their views with regard to a harbour at Carloway, and railway communication between Carloway and Stornoway . . . After leaving Carloway, the party entered conveyances and drove to Stornoway by Breasclete, Callernish, and Garynahine, Lord Lothian being enabled in the course of the drive to form some idea of the route of the proposed railway.' According to *The Scotsman*, while 'the urban and rural population are by no means agreed as to what railway scheme would most benefit the island', its own reporter judged that 'opinion seems to agree that light railways may be constructed . . . in Lewis from Stornoway to Ness and Carloway, perhaps also including other principal fishing stations to the north and west of the island'. Lord Lothian summed up the situation very nicely for the populace: 'what you wish for most of all is a tramway or light railway going to the outlying districts'. Summed it up, and then neatly sidelined it: 'Well, you know it is not possible for me to give any opinion upon any of these schemes and projects.'

Two years later, a deputation from Stornoway visited George Goschen, the Chancellor of the Exchequer (a Liberal in a Conservative government), to give him their views on the fishing industry. They 'observed, with respect to the scheme to construct a line of railway from Stornoway to Carloway, that they desired to draw the attention of the Government to the fact that the Commissioners [i.e. those from Walpole's inquiry of 1890] were favourably impressed with that scheme, and, in consequence, had a survey made of it for their further information'. So, a survey of some sort had been done: it is quite probable that this survey was for a road, as we shall shortly learn. But now the difficulty was to find 'parties locally interested' to raise capital. Throughout the meeting, Goschen kept muttering that all these remarks should have been made earlier, to someone else, and certainly not him; but promised to pass on their views. Then he impatiently shooed them out and got on with some proper work.[16] The following year, 1893, Mr Dunbar from the Scottish Office did 'not hesitate to recommend the proposal to build a light railway in the Lews . . . although no immediate return can perhaps be expected'. Dunbar had listened to talk of spending £15,000 on a new road to Carloway, but it was his considered opinion, and that of the chief magistrate of Stornoway, that the money would be better spent on branch roads and a railway.[17]

All well and good. Everyone was agreed that railways would improve the condition of the people. But nothing was done. Well, not quite nothing: plans for a road were instead much debated and acted upon.

There is now a single-track road stretching across most of the fifteen bleak miles that separate Stornoway and Carloway, named the Pentland Road. It had a long and difficult birth.[18] The Western Highlands and Islands Commission of 1890 made note of a plan to build a railway along this route, and had been sorely disappointed by the unwillingness of locals to come up with any money. But the following year, somewhat out of the blue, a generous offer was received from the Scottish Office: it was prepared to pay up to £15,000 on improving the road from Stornoway to Carloway. On receipt of this offer, the Lewis District Committee thanked the Scottish Office politely, but stated that they would much rather spend the money on a light railway over the same route.[19] This smart diversionary tactic clearly failed for, one month later, the same local councillors were to be found reviewing plans for a road to Carloway, and unanimously accepting the £15,000 on offer. The only point of debate was a proposal to include in the scheme a branch road cutting down to Breascleit. In May of 1891 a local engineer, Alexander Macdonald of Stornoway, was instructed to draw up plans for the road; six weeks later, he duly delivered and was paid the grand sum of £29 12s for his efforts. This was the last thing to go smoothly on the project.

In October, the District Committee wrote to Lady Matheson, asking for a small piece of land for the road; she does not seem to have bothered to reply. In May of 1892, invitations to tender were issued to build the four sections of road and seven associated bridges. Eleven bids were received, ranging from £1,567 to £4,080 for the first section of the road, and around £1,416 for the bridges. Another seven months then elapsed; there was some debate about abandoning the bridges, but far-seeing minds pointed out that bridges would be required should a railway ever be built. Should, then, the bridges be of concrete construction? There followed a debate about where to find sufficient sand and whether concrete would survive a 'moist climate'. Just to spice things up, another letter was sent off to London, asking for a railway. And in the interim, a cold dose of real need broke into the proceedings: a delegation of the residents of Carloway petitioned the District Council about the 'ill success of East Coast fishing and comparative failure of their crops', and begged for work on the construction of the new road.[20]

At last, the contract to build the road was let. The successful contractor was Charles Mackay & Co. of Inverness. A bright start was made in February 1894; but already by June there were complaints of shoddy workmanship and the use of inferior materials, not to mention the fact that the contractor had failed to issue regular status reports. By September, things had gone completely sour: only one short stretch of road had been completed near Carloway, no one was happy with the quality, the contractor filed for bankruptcy and Mr Macdonald the engineer was chastised for not exercising sufficient supervision. In October, Macdonald resigned; and then the contractor for the bridges asked for more money. A new engineer was appointed: John Paterson of Fort William, the same man who had once done a flying survey for the Aultbea railway. But by then the damage was done, and work on the road shuddered to a complete halt. Nothing more was done for a good sixteen years.

This, of course, only spurred on the champions of a railway. At the start of 1897, the prospect of a light railway was being discussed with the general manager of the Highland Railway.[21] The board of the Highland pondered awhile, then agreed that there was insufficient information and voted to do nothing. And then, in a surprise move, the Hebridean Light Railway Company approached the North British Railway company; the nearest the North British had come to this part of the world was in their construction of the railway to Fort William, which at that time was being extended to Mallaig. Apart from one border skirmish with the Highland over the matter of a railway to Fort Augustus, the North British had steered well clear of the Highland's domain. It is possible that the HLRC had already approached the North British in the summer of 1897, since the minutes of the board indicated discussions 'with parties interested in the construction of Light Railways in Skye and Lewis'; the General Manager was instructed to keep negotiating.²² By October, he was able to report back, and the board very circumspectly 'agreed to offer to enter into working agreements with the promoters . . . based on a sliding scale varying from 50 to 65 per cent of the receipts'.²³ It all began to look very satisfactory.

It was now down to Mr Barrington, engineer of Limerick, to do the honours: he prepared the plans and sections for Railway No. 3 and Railway No. 4. Given the nature of the landscape he encountered on Lewis, it is well that Barrington's strengths included both light railways and arterial drainage.²⁴

Railway No. 3 was to run from Stornoway to Dunan Pier, slightly to the west of Carloway. It set off from the pier at Stornoway and headed, a little disconcertingly, eastwards. But a long circular curve took it past the present Council offices on Sandwick Road, up towards Goat Hill, across the top of the town, westwards to Laxdale and then out past Marybank, before joining the route of the 'new road to Carloway'. Thereafter, it simply followed that same road all the way westwards, passing through Carloway and terminating at Dunan Pier next to Borghastan. This railway would be 18 miles and 7 furlongs in length, costing £110,765 4s 1d, with eight gatekeepers' houses.

Back in the middle of the moor, at grid reference NB267363, was the junction where Railway No. 4 began. This was a simple enough railway, again following the planned branch roadway, and ending up, 3 miles and 7 furlongs later, at the pier at Breascleit. A mere £24,477 1s 5d was the estimate for constructing this desirable branch line, with just a single level crossing and its lonely gatekeeper.

From almost every angle, these were far easier railways to build than the ones on Skye. The land was more or less flat, and few settlements and fewer crofters stood in the way. With commendable enthusiasm, the Lewis District Committee got right behind the plan. At much the same time as their colleagues on Skye were voting for a levy on the rates, the Lewis District Committee did likewise. At a special meeting in Stornoway in early May 1898, the councillors proposed to levy 4d in the pound to raise £6,000 to part-finance the building of the railway. Barrington was in attendance at the meeting. But the debate was by no means frictionless. No one seemed to know in any detail the conditions of the proposed ratepayers' loan. So Barrington kindly explained: 'No portion of the funds of the Light Railway Company would be applied towards the repayment of the loan to be advanced by this Island until the revenue of the district exceeded the sum of £9 a week per mile per annum.' He reassured his audience that this was perfectly normal in Ireland. The councillors did some quick mental arithmetic; several pursed their lips. This was not what they had understood from earlier discussions. There was a motion to go back and consult the electorate. But when someone said that the Light Railways Commissioners only had £170,000 left in their coffers, delay was deemed ill-advised and the 4d levy was pushed through: five votes for, three abstentions, none against.[25]

Their resolution was forwarded to the full Council in Dingwall for approval. With some understatement, Dingwall noted that the road 'had given a great deal of trouble to the County Council, and was a source of a great deal of irritation to other bodies'; but the motion was approved. The proposer welcomed the decision with the hazy, but doubtless visionary, words that 'he had no doubt that once this light railway was constructed, it would not stop there'.[26]

The bold resolutions of Lewis and Skye, ratified on 6 May by their respective county councils, attracted the attention of the relentless P. Campbell Ross. In a letter to *The Scotsman*, and now signing himself as the 'Hon. Secy. Executive Committee, Garve and Ullapool Railway Scheme', he tore into the plans to build railways anywhere else on the west coast or islands, Ullapool being the most logical and desirable terminus. He spared not the Highland Railway, but urged the board thereof to 'come forward and make reparation for the injury done us seven years ago. It has no time to lose.'[27] Barely four days later, taking full advantage of a small typographical error in the printing of his first letter, he returned to the fray and mocked the 'unfledged

"Hebridean Railway Company"'. Recapitulating an argument raised on Skye itself, he wrote:

> Consider that, if the Hebridean line were completed, what would be the value of herrings landed at Carloway, trucked to Stornoway, then shipped to Uig (Skye), thence carried by rail to Isleornsay; there shipped for Mallaig and trucked there, when all the fish reach Edinburgh, Glasgow or London after all the handling required? Schemes of the Hebridean Railway kind look well on paper and until tested.[28]

Ross's letters excited the wrath of the Provost of Stornoway, who quite rightly pointed out that it was 'very amusing' for Ross to urge the Highland Railway to consult its conscience. The letter from P. C. Ross

> clearly proves what every person in the Highlands and Islands (not blinded or thirled to the Highland Railway Company's interests) has known for many years, that that Company is simply acting 'a dog in the manger policy'. It pretends to be interested in every scheme proposed . . . survey the proposed lines, and then promise reports which are never forthcoming, and by these means hope to divert other railway companies from occupying the ground.[29]

What Provost Anderson, the writer of this riposte, failed to point out was that he himself was allegedly 'the local agent for the promoters' of the Hebridean Light Railway Company.[30] Evidently public office and private interest were perfectly compatible in those distant times. Very different from today, of course.

Like the Skye contribution, the generosity of Lewis still fell far short of the HLRC's expectations; they had hoped for £20,000 from Lewis and were promised less than a third of that.[31] And whereas, in 1897, the North British Railway had tentatively agreed to work with the Hebridean Railway, by 1898 they were not so keen. In May of that year, the directors considered 'further correspondence with, and plans prepared by, the promoters of Light Railways in the Hebrides'. The board agreed to apply the conditions already arranged 'to the modified lines'. Quite what had been 'modified' in the plans is not clear: it was surely too early for Barrington's excellent plans to be altered – the ink was scarcely dry on them; perhaps this related to earlier ideas? And by July, the North British was back-pedalling furiously: the board resolved 'not to guarantee any return upon capital investment'.[32] By early 1899 it was all over:

> The General Manager reported on position of negotiations in regard to the proposed Hebridean Light Railways, and submitted an amended proposal by the promoters as to a working agreement. It was resolved to adhere to the former decision not to give any financial assistance and also that the proposed working agreement should not be applied to the modified scheme suggested.[33]

Once more, that word 'modified' haunts us: was this a modification to the overall plan, covering Skye and Lewis, or had we been reduced to simply a stripped-down route on Skye? For, in June 1899, William Barrington was found writing a rather despondent letter to the Highland Railway asking if it would work and maintain a light railway from Dunvegan to Portree for 60 per cent of receipts; there was no mention of any longer line on Skye; even less of a railway on Lewis. The Highland minutes noted very neatly that this application was 'not agreed to'.[34]

The ambitious plans of the Hebridean Light Railway Company ultimately foundered. It continued to issue financial statements each year until 1906 (each of them showed that only 1,007 shares had ever been purchased – one by each director, 1,000 by Dick, Kerr & Co.). A despairing letter was written by a secretary at Dick, Kerr in 1903: addressed to the Registrar of Joint Stock Companies, it stated bluntly that 'the Company never got beyond registration, and a partial survey . . . No meeting of Directors has taken place since 26th May, 1898' – and some of the directors 'are not now alive'. Rather pathetically, the writer would 'esteem it a favour if you would kindly advise me what I ought to do under the existing circumstances'.[35] In October 1908, a formal request was made to remove the HLRC from the register of companies since 'for 10 years it has lain quite dormant' and, to everyone's relief, the company was finally dissolved on 25 February 1910.[36]

But the idea of a direct link between Stornoway and Carloway never slept. The people of Lewis were made of sterner stuff than the gentlemen of Cannon Street. Within months of the project fizzling out, the

Congested Districts Board was made aware of the situation. We shall discuss the Congested Districts Board (CDB) in the next chapter – it was a government body charged with funding small improvements in the economy of the Highlands and Islands. In its annual report for 1898, the CDB commented that the work on Carloway road 'has been unsatisfactory from the very beginning'.[37] The gentlemen of the Board then received a request for £1,985 to complete the Carloway end of the road; the Board agreed and was able, two years later, to report a rare success: 'This has been done in a very satisfactory manner.'[38] The road now ran for all of four miles – from Dunan Pier to a point about three miles east of Carloway, in the middle of nowhere. Not much, but it was a start.

Then, in a move that few would have predicted, the CDB in 1904 came out to 'strongly urge the completion of the Carloway Road, and the construction thereon of a Light Railway from Stornoway to Carloway . . . and [we] submit that a grant, in accordance with the Light Railway and other Acts, be given for the entire cost'.[39] An added incentive, it seems, was the arrival in Loch Roag (between Carloway and Breascleit) of the 'Home Fleet, consisting of Eight Battleships, Four Cruisers, and a Torpedo Gunboat . . . It is probable that Loch Roag will become an annual rendezvous.' A training battery was also proposed by the Admiralty – it is not recorded quite what the local fishermen would make of that kind of noisy disturbance. The CDB even went so far as to calculate the likely annual revenues for a railway (£4,350, almost half of it from the transportation of fish; the total was less than half of Barrington's wild promises of '£9 per mile week'). But not much more happened for several years until, in a generous final flourish in 1910, the CDB handed over £8,000 for the road to be completed; as indeed it was, to everyone's satisfaction, within two years.

On the 6 September 1912, the Liberal Secretary for Scotland, Thomas McKinnon Wood, arrived on Lewis to open the road. It was to be named after his immediate predecessor, Lord Pentland, also a Liberal, who had been instrumental in pushing the project over the finishing line. (Mr Wood's arrival was inauspicious: he sailed into Stornoway aboard the fishery cruiser *Minna*; the harbour was crowded with a destroyer flotilla and numerous fishing boats; in the congestion a cargo boat crossed the *Minna's* bows and carried away her bowsprit;

it was all rather upsetting, and reminiscent of Napier's *Lively* incident.) Wood and the official party made their way to Carloway in six motor cars (the principal landowner, Duncan Matheson, was conspicuous by his absence) and Mrs Wood gracefully opened the Pentland Road. Her husband then made a speech which finished with a truly underwhelming paean to success:

> He sincerely trusted that the road that day opened would for many years carry the produce of the sea and of the earth, that it would help on the commercial prosperity of that part of the island, and that it would be, as roads had been through all the ages of the world, one of the greatest means of advancement and improved civilisation. (Loud applause).[40]

Just imagine that, if you can: a road, here in Great Britain, in the twentieth century! Astonishing achievement. A local JP slightly spoiled the triumphant atmosphere by daring to suggest that the road might one day be superseded by a railway. Shame on you, sir!

If the Secretary for Scotland thought he could spout platitudes and then move on swiftly, he was much mistaken. The following day he met a delegation of leaders of the crofters, cottars and fishermen of Lewis. The meeting made it perfectly obvious that, in some three decades, very little had changed on either side. As always, the crofters and fishermen had their demands and the Government had no adequate response. It is worth quoting the demands in full:

> The deputation urged the necessity for (1) the extension of crofters' holdings on their own grazings and the formation of new holdings for cottars by the breaking up of the large farms and deer forests; (2) the construction of a road from North Tolsta to Ness and the settlement of cottars along that route; (3) grants for the fencing in of crofting townships in order to further the development of the live stock industry; (4) State loans for motor fishing boats; (5) the suppression of trawling on the spawning banks and the extension of the trawling limit to thirteen miles all round the coast.[41]

To all of which, Mr Wood replied in the time-honoured formula of government ministers that 'several of the matters referred to were meantime being specially inquired into, and that when the reports . . . were received they would be very carefully considered with a view to formulating a policy'.

Road or no road, railway or no railway, the fundamental questions of land ownership and economic underdevelopment remained completely unresolved. And the Westminster government remained without a strategy that would help.

12

'The Luxury of a Steam-Tramway'

Tramlines and Electricity

The Congested Districts Board for Scotland was established in 1897. It was part of the continuing government effort to breathe some life into rural Scotland. The fact that it had to be set up at all suggested that the initiatives proclaimed by the 1886 Crofters' Act were not doing the job. And, as always, the Irish had got there first – their Congested Districts Board had been established in 1891, as part of the strategy of killing Home Rule. For Irish purposes, there was a complex calculation to determine what was a 'congested district': it was any part of an electoral division where there lived more than 20 per cent of the population of that electoral division, and whose total rateable value, when divided by the population, gave a sum of less than £1 10s. The Irish legislators could have saved time and effort and simply said 'the entire west coast'. By contrast, the definition for Scotland was far less complex – as Lord Balfour, the Secretary for Scotland explained when the Act was passed:

> a congested district should mean any crofting parish or crofting
> parishes, or any area in a crofting parish or crofting parishes, which
> the Commissioners, having regard to the population and valuation,
> should determine to be a congested district. They had found that,
> to adopt the definition in the Irish Act would, owing to the
> disturbing element brought in by the large amount of sporting
> rents, have excluded some districts which stood most in need of
> assistance.[1]

'The disturbing element of sporting rents' – if nothing else, there was a touch of realism here concerning land use in the north-west of Scotland.

The Congested Districts Board for Scotland (CDB) was incorporated into the Board of Agriculture in 1912. In its brief fourteen years of existence, it did some good, but by no stretch of the imagination did it ever come close to emulating the transformation of the rural economy which took place in Ireland over the same period. The major difference was that the Irish scheme was generously funded by Westminster and the churches in Ireland, and was linked to ongoing land reforms, while the Scottish one was run on a shoestring: a civil service budget of £35,000 per annum. The Scottish CDB's remit was to provide expertise, advice and loans or grants for improvements to agriculture, fishing and 'home industries', as well as for transportation and communications infrastructure (roads, bridges, piers, telegraph lines, postal facilities). For agriculture, the Board could distribute seed for potatoes and oats, and provide loans for dairy equipment. For fishing, it could finance the building of piers, jetties and even cottages for fishermen. The Board had the nominal authority to make purchases of estate lands for redistribution to landless crofters and cottars. Rarely could it afford to do so. It was also encouraged to promote the movement of people from the more deprived areas of northern Scotland to the less deprived.

As required by statute, the CDB issued an annual report.[2] These reports make for slightly depressing reading. In the 1900 report, for example, much space was taken up in describing efforts to do something for 'young men' – but the best that could be suggested was that they join the Royal Navy. (For young women, the CDB was proud to promote the career of domestic servant. Under the circumstances, it may have been better than nothing.) The CDB managed to spend £2,172 on potato and oat seed – but crucially expected to have £1,400 of that money repaid by the recipients: this was clearly no charitable enterprise. In that year also, the Commissioners lamented the difficulties they faced in ordering and distributing seed; and described their futile attempts to get crofters to keep hens in fenced enclosures. Adverse comments were made about the high railway charges for conveying eggs to market. However, they did manage to encourage two crofters on Coll to set up beehives to establish the viability of apiarism. It all seemed rather low-key.

The advantage of not having achieved much in the first few years was that they had failed to spend all their annual budget, and so entered 1903 with £86,000 in the bank. In that year, things began to look a little more lively – more beehives and hens laying eggs, but also the purchase of land on the island of Vatersay for growing potatoes, and the construction of some roads, bridges and piers. A fecund bestiary of rams, bulls and 'high-class stallions' was also purchased and distributed. 1904 was a triumphant year: the CDB managed to buy three large farms and prepare them for crofts of around 10 acres each. One was the infamous Glendale estate on Lewis, scene of so much trouble twenty years previously. Also on Skye, the troublesome Kilmuir estate was purchased; and on Lewis, the Matheson farm at Aignish was acquired, through the suspect kindness of Major Matheson (this was Duncan, who had by now inherited all of Lewis via his father after the demise of Lady Matheson). It is noteworthy that all three of these estates had been major scenes of action during the 'Crofters' War' of the early 1880s – their owners now saw a chance to divest themselves of property with a troublesome history and a potentially troublesome future. For Glendale, the CDB paid £15,000; for Kilmuir, £80,000.

As the Commissioners remarked rather forlornly, these purchases ate up almost their entire bank balance. Indeed, by 1906, the Board had to report that it had effectively run out of money: 'Owing to the state of our funds and our commitments, we have been unable to undertake any further purchases of land.' In the nine years to 1906, the CDB reported that it had expended £6,700 for fisheries, £93,000 for roads, bridges, piers and lighthouses and £36,000 for miscellaneous agricultural improvement: £136,000 in total. In the same period, the total amount spent acquiring land was £175,000. In short, they had spent almost every penny of their budget to date. And its analysis of its own achievements was not starry-eyed: the CDB considered that the task of encouraging cottars to establish themselves as crofters with land was never going to succeed, the cottars being so impoverished that they could not afford to move, even had they the inclination so to do. Which, it appears, they did not. Nor had would-be crofters any cash to stock their new farms, and they were understandably wary of borrowing from the CDB. As a final obstacle, if a man's status changed from tenant to landowner, his rates bill would increase dramatically and he would lose all the safeguards offered by the Crofters' Act.

The activities of the CDB, while doubtless well-intentioned, could not be considered a resounding success. Their most expensive land purchase, Kilmuir on Skye, got bogged down in difficulties arising from a standoff between the crofters and the Crofters' Commission about the value of their rents. This situation was not properly resolved until 1910 – and even then, the crofters chose to become tenants of the CDB rather than landowners in their own right. All this left a huge amount of the Board's money tied up in land. And not every attempt to acquire land made it past the initial stages: in 1901, the Lord Advocate was forced to admit to the Commons that an early application to a Lewis landlord for land at Aignish 'was quoted by the Congested Districts Board to the proprietor, who simply regretted his inability to accede to the request, without assigning any reasons'.[3] This landowner was Duncan Matheson, who was in the enviable position of being simultaneously a landowner and the chairman of the local board which negotiated with landowners on behalf of the CDB: no conflict of interest there, apparently.

James Weir, MP for Ross and Cromarty, was frequently outraged at where the CDB was spending its money. In 1909 he wanted to know why, of 55,000 acres of land acquired for new holdings, 42,000 were in Inverness-shire (i.e. Skye) and only 240 acres in Ross and Cromarty (i.e. Lewis). Further, he wanted to know, 'would the Board endeavour to arrange the land scheme on a more equitable basis in the future?', to which the swift and very smug reply of the Lord Advocate was: 'That is impossible, because it was arranged on an equitable basis in the past.' But the truth was simply that the CDB had no money, no compulsory powers and very few friends. On the plus side, it provided the opportunity for at least one person to discover the pleasures of beekeeping.

In a curious final fling in the year before the CDB vanished into the Board of Agriculture, the Commissioners decided to increase the number of 'congested' parishes from 65 to 148, which aligned with the same area as the Crofters' Commission; quite how they hoped to deal with twice as many parishes on the same budget is unknown.[4] (The Crofters' Commission, too, vanished in 1912 – into the Scottish Land Court.)

Back when the CDB was young and hopeful, in November 1901, a letter dropped through its letter-box.[5] It came from a Major E. W. Blunt, resident at Tarbat House near Invergordon on the east coast.

Major Blunt had a proposal: he was planning to build a 'tramway' running from Garve, as far as Ullapool, and then some – it was to lead all the way to the shore opposite Isle Martin, another three miles to the west of Ullapool. The purpose of this tramway was to facilitate the transportation of freshly caught fish to the railways which converged on Inverness. Blunt considered that Isle Martin was 'a perfect natural harbour for fishing boats'; it would avoid the 'narrow entrance' at the mouth of Loch Broom, which he considered to be a tricky one for fishermen. He had obviously read all the relevant Commission reports of the 1890s.

A 'tramway' was to be preferred to a railway line, light or otherwise, because it could run on the road which already linked Garve to Ullapool. Historically, a tramway is the most primitive type of railway, bearing only relatively light loads and rarely fit for passengers. It could be laid quickly and cheaply. What Major Blunt sought was the widening of the road by around 50 per cent, so that the trams would not unduly interfere with road traffic; but he conceded that some of the river crossings for the road would have to be supplemented by additional bridges for the tramway. He further backed up his proposal with reference to the light railway at Grenoble in France, which had many steep gradients, but ran on a 1-metre gauge line with 2-metre wide rolling stock. The French example was only to show that it could be done – Blunt would use good British standard rolling stock and '50-pound' rails in Ross-shire. Finally, he indicated that he proposed to use steam power for the tram-engine but was prepared, should circumstances prove conducive, to use the hydroelectric capacity of the district to power the whole affair.

All in all, he felt that the plan was a capital one, worthy of some financial assistance. What he failed to do, however, was give any indication of estimated costs.

The members of the CDB discussed the proposal amongst themselves with some scepticism, and were not impressed. One doubtful gentleman expressed the thought that: 'This is a proposal to supply the luxury (so to speak) of a steam-tramway alongside of a good carriage road.' In its reply, at the end of December 1901, the Board pointed out that, firstly, much of the route did not in fact run through a 'congested district'; and secondly, that the road was already there, transporting fish as required from the fishing boats on the west coast to Garve and beyond – so why would anyone need a tramway? The request was turned down.

We should highlight something that Major Blunt himself did not: Edward Walter Blunt-Mackenzie, to give him his full name, was the husband of the Countess of Cromartie. Not an impoverished man, and possibly not the average beneficiary for whom the Congested Districts Board had been designed. His wife, the young Countess of Cromartie, was Sibell Lilian Blunt-Mackenzie (1878–1962), who, over the first three decades of the twentieth century, produced an impressive list of historical romances concerning gloomy Celtic heroes. Titles included *The Web of the Past*, *Zeo the Scythian*, *Heremon the Beautiful* and *Sons of the Milesians* – and we must not forget *Parting Song*, a musical composition 'in F and A flat', with words by the Duchess of Sutherland. The Countess was a person of some talent.

As was her husband, a man eighteen years her elder. For this was not his first attempt to persuade the CDB to part with its money.

Seven months earlier, in April of 1901, he had written to the CDB, this time from his army base at Woolwich, with another first-rate scheme. This was to 'establish a line of motor cars' which would run between Garve, Ullapool and Badentarbet (near Achiltibuie). 'There seems no chance of a light railway being helped into being,' he noted – a fact he had conveniently forgotten by the end of the year. 'This line will help the fishermen and shepherds of the West Coast' – to judge from the handwritten letter, the 'shepherds' were something of an afterthought; the hill-men might have been astonished and honoured at the inclusion. Blunt calculated that a motor car would cost about £670, 'a small outlay compared to a railway'. A grant from the CDB was required to improve the road surface and ease some of the gradients. In a follow-up letter a week later, he revised his costs to £600 per motor car, with 32 shillings and 6 pence as daily running costs. A motor car carrying a five-ton load would travel at 5 mph, one with three tons at a hair-raising 8 mph. Thus far, and no further, his business plan.[6] Badentarbet, quite coincidentally, was a part of the vast Cromartie estate; a few years later, it was home to Edward Blunt's brother, Charles (who, at the outbreak of the First World War, was also the commander of the famous Ullapool Volunteers).

The CDB was not greatly enthused. They perceived that the road did not run through a 'congested district' until it reached the parish of

Lochbroom – about 14 miles west of Garve – and pondered aloud the crucial question that would occur to any one of us: 'how big a catch of herring a motor car could drag over such a road?' (The answer is, of course, twenty-four barrels of herring in the three-ton load and forty barrels on the larger one.) They did not even begin to ask about the sheep. A reply was sent to Major Blunt in May, regretfully turning down his application and helpfully pointing out that new-fangled motor cars were in any case unreliable: they called his attention to a meeting of the shareholders of the Edinburgh Autocar Company, which had concluded that same month that

> motor cars as at present constructed could not be run profitably in the public service . . . In public service, cars would not last more than two years, and long before the end of that period the cost of upkeep had become so great as to make them unprofitable.

(Amnesia was evidently rife in the north of Scotland: just as, seven months later, Blunt had forgotten that any form of railway was unlikely, so the CDB in the same period managed to forget that they thought little of motor-cars, since there was a perfectly good carriage road to Ullapool. Or were they perhaps recommending horse and cart?)

Blunt was not at all discouraged by two rejection letters. Over the next few years, with money that we must suppose was provided by the Countess, he dabbled in aluminium smelting and hydroelectricity. Famously – at least locally – his small hydroelectric scheme lit up the front of the Raven's Rock Hotel near the spa town of Strathpeffer in 1903. This scheme was subsequently expanded to bring illumination to Dingwall, under the auspices of his Strathpeffer and Dingwall Electric Lighting Company. The coming of the new source of light was a wonder of the age. The local newspaper reported on the transformation effected on the High Street:

> In anticipation of the completion of the scheme several establishments in the town had the necessary fittings introduced some time ago, and on Monday, ex-Bailie Frew and Mr Alex. Ross, solicitor, in the same building, were able to take advantage of the connection. Ex-Bailie Frew's jewellery establishment, in the High Street, was brilliantly lighted up, and attracted a great deal of attention.

On the following day the premises of Messrs C & J Urquhart, iron-mongers, were connected with the system. Mr George Souter, bookseller, completed his arrangements, and his shop is also lighted with electricity . . . So far Messrs R Mackenzie & Sons, electrical engineers, Dingwall, have been responsible for the fitting up of the different establishments, and they have performed their work to the complete satisfaction of those concerned. It is interesting to note that it is over three years ago since electric light was first introduced into Dingwall, Lemon's Ærated Water Factory and residence in connection therewith having been lighted with a private installation.[7]

This was surely the dawn of a new age in Dingwall, heralded a few years earlier with the passing of the Electric Lighting Acts of 1882 and 1888, which simplified the application process for generating and selling electricity. Even before this, hydroelectricity had been generated on small rivers across the Highlands: the Fowlers' Braemore House had had electric lighting since the 1880s, and a sawmill on the estate was powered similarly.[8] Larger local electric companies were all the rage at the turn of the century, and Cromarty was not going to be left behind. In 1909, Blunt turned his enterprise into an incorporated company ready for shareholder investment – the first three shareholders, each with a single £1 share, were Blunt himself, his wife (occupation: 'Countess in her own right'), and his sister ('Spinster') who lived in Banbury. According to the requisite legal documents, the purpose of the company and all its many assets and licences was 'to produce and accumulate electricity and electro-motive force and transmit it for use in lighting, heating etc'.[9]

Sadly, a week after the inauguration of electric lighting in Dingwall in 1903, a dreadful accident occurred, which was reported by the local newspaper:

Yesterday afternoon, Kenneth Mackenzie, 70, labourer, Auchterneed, had his left leg fractured at the corner of Tulloch Street and High Street. While he was driving a horse and cart along Tulloch Street, the horse took fright at a coil of electric cable which was being rolled along the street, and bolted, coming into contact with the lamp at the corner of Mr Frew's shop. Mackenzie, who was sitting in the cart, overbalanced himself and fell out, one of the wheels passing over his leg. He was conveyed to the Infirmary in the ambulance.[10]

Sometimes technology simply defies human – and animal – understanding. Just like the railway to Ullapool.

13

'Pestilential Robber Barons'

Social Upheaval, 1918–1919

By the time the idea of a railway to Ullapool was put forward once more, the world had almost entirely changed. It was in early 1918 that the railway proposal was again being seriously considered: by then all nations were trapped in a horrific global war, and the spectres of communism and revolution had been made flesh in the largest country in the world.

The effects of the war on the communities of north-west Scotland were many and varied, but all were largely negative. The most obvious and tragic consequence can clearly be seen in practically every settlement up and down the west coast and on the islands, in the shape of the ubiquitous war memorials inscribed with the names of young men who never came back from the fields and seas of war; or who, without memorial, came back severely wounded or traumatised. The loss of these men, and women, had a longer-term impact on the viability of the fragile economy, both in the crofts and fisheries. And there was an impact also on the estates owned by the rich: scions of the rich and famous also fell in huge numbers, and suddenly there was no one to inherit the estates and, coincidentally, no one to labour on them. At Braemore, the two sons of Arthur Fowler were both killed in 1915 and, as we shall see, the estate passed to another branch of the family.

Another effect was economic and more immediate: the seas around the north of Scotland were effectively off limits for four years. With much of the North Sea seeded with mines, and both it and the Atlantic Ocean dangerous places to be afloat, fishing was no longer an enterprise to be conducted with any enthusiasm. In the four years of war, the harvesting of the seas dropped to barely a third of pre-war levels, made a brief partial recovery in 1919–20 thanks to state subsidies, and then slumped again. Additionally, the traditional export markets around the Baltic vanished completely. What was surprising was that any fish at all were harvested. The number of registered fishermen had also fallen dramatically – one major cause being the transfer of men into the Royal Navy, many of whom never came back.[1] The fishing boats, too, found other uses during the war – a good proportion of those re-deployed as mine-sweepers did not survive unscathed. With the principal source of income choked off, the economy of the north-west Highlands and Islands came to a sudden standstill.

But with death and the horror of war came revolution. In Ireland, things had already come to such a pass in 1914 that the Home Rule movement was finally forced to agree to a parliament based in Dublin. That the agreement was not actually carried out immediately was because the war interrupted proceedings. But the war with Germany did not stop the juggernaut of the Irish independence movement, nor that of republicanism. The abortive Easter Rising of 1916 attempted to capitalise on the chaos and uncertainty of the war, but failed to set the island alight: if anything, the British government had more ideas on how to deal with Ireland than with Germany and Austria. Nevertheless, when the war had ended and a general election was called in December of 1918, Sinn Fein republicans captured almost all the available Irish constituencies, refused to sit in Westminster and moved firmly down the road towards independence, which goal – after a guerrilla war against the British state – was finally achieved in December 1922. The valiant and extended efforts of the unionists to head off the demands of the Home Rule parties had come to naught. Westminster might well have learned some lessons from this experience.

Meanwhile, the workers and peasants of Russia had also found their political voice after centuries of oppression. In the fateful year 1917, first in February and then more dramatically in November, the Russian people were introduced to Western democracy and then opted for communism. The subsequent civil war in Russia lasted eight years. The political effect of this revolution upon the working class of Britain and Europe was huge. And with the unilateral withdrawal of Russia from the war, neither Imperial Germany and Austria nor Britain and the USA quite knew what to do next. One thing was certain, however: the working classes and the rural poor needed to be monitored carefully – at the very least, they would need to be appeased. One major result of any war is that men and women from vastly different backgrounds come together in a pressure-cooker atmosphere; ideas, frequently dangerous ones, are transmitted far more readily, and new ideas emerge from conflict, argument and day-to-day experience. These new ideas not only infected men conscripted into armies and navies, but also women who replaced men in the factories, on the railways and in the dark satanic mills.

After a war there will be demands ranging from electoral reform, through nationalisation of industries, all the way up to the conquest of state power. After its defeat in 1918, Germany was not in a position to keep its working class in its proper station and soon faced revolutionary upheavals of its own. In Britain, an effort to stem the tide was made by the Coalition government when it passed the Representation of the People Act in February 1918, extending the vote to all men above the age of twenty-one, and to women older than thirty owning a house which was rateably valued at £5 per annum. It was a concession which was later to backfire against the Liberals and Conservatives of the coalition. But what else were they to do?

LAND RAIDS AND THE BREAKING UP OF ESTATES

'Idlers and Useless Aliens'

Predictably, in the north-west of Scotland, men returning from war were no longer content to see the land retained in the hands of large estates. Promises had been made during the course of the war about returning to plentiful land.[2] And when these promises did not bear fruit, men took the law into their own hands. Land raids, as we have seen, had already become an activity of choice for frustrated cottars as early as the 1880s. Sporadically in the early years of the twentieth century, there were incursions on to unused land – mostly, but not exclusively, in the islands: in 1900, on Barra and neighbouring Vatersay, and Sconser on Skye; on Uist in 1904; again on Barra in 1909 and 1917; Tiree in 1918; Gress on Lewis in 1919; and the Uists and Raasay in

1920. The Raasay events generated considerable publicity: some of the raiders were servicemen who had returned home and found no land available to them (the island was by then owned by William Baird & Co., the iron-masters, who had profited hugely from the war and operated an iron-ore mine there, courtesy of German prisoners of war), and the others were people from the desolate island of South Rona, who had been cleared out of Raasay in previous generations. Despite sympathy from the Scottish Land Court and the general public, the Raasay tres-passers were arrested and subsequently fined; but their cause was deemed just, and eventually they got their land.

Land raids (or 'grabs') took place all over the north-west. Some were more successful than others – especially those which took place during or just after the war years, for the very simple reason that there was huge public support for men taking land to grow food, just as the Government had advised. It was notable that many of the localities involved in these 'grabs' were the same ones as had seen cottar and crofter agitation twenty or thirty years earlier.

On Lewis, things were further complicated by the sale of the island to Lord Leverhulme in 1918, Duncan Matheson doubtless heaving a great sigh of relief to have got rid of it. And Leverhulme's grand plans for the island did not countenance the transfer of land back to the crofters, most of whom were simply not interested in becoming part of his proletariat; hence the continued land raids there. Leverhulme's refusal to compromise with agitating crofters ultimately led to the complete failure of his plans and – rather unexpectedly – to the hand-ing back to the community of 70,000 acres of land around Stornoway.[3] Fittingly, part of the 'Soap Man's' fanciful vision for Lewis involved the building of those very railways out of Stornoway which had been mentioned on and off for the preceding thirty years. But no: they were not to be.

The land raid was a rural echo of the struggles and aspirations of the urban working class in Britain, where socialism had been gaining ground throughout the last decades of the nineteenth century and into the twentieth. The Marxist Social-Democratic Federation had been established in 1881, and various left-wing groupings inherited its mantle over the next few years. Meanwhile the Scottish Labour Party had been founded in 1888, the Independent Labour Party in 1895 and the Labour Party itself in 1906. In Scotland, in January 1919, the famous

'Battle of George Square' took place in Glasgow, an event which saw British Army tanks take to the streets of the city, and the deployment of the military at strategic places in lowland Scotland. 1919 was a year during which strikes in Britain peaked – thirty-five million days lost due to strike action, a figure shortly to be eclipsed by the 162 million of 1926.[4] One such strike was the national railway strike which ran from 26 September to 5 October, and disrupted most of Britain – even, lest it be doubted, on the Highland Railway: 'Business Paralysed in Inverness', reported *The Scotsman* newspaper, headlining a report that the last train to reach Inverness only ran because it was bringing striking railway workers back from Perth to their homes in the north. In Inverness 1,500 men came out, and the strike was solid in more rural Ross-shire: 'The Highland Railway workers appear to be practically unanimous in support of the strike.'[5] (*The Scotsman* was also greatly concerned about the fate of parties of golfers who were stranded at Lundin Links after the Scottish Foursomes Tournament; an Edinburgh group only managed to get safely back home by hiring a charabanc at the rather preposterous cost of £28.)

This was also a period when the Scottish republican and inter-nationalist John Maclean was most active. He had been a member of the British Socialist Party, one of the offshoots of the Social-Democratic Federation; he was elected chair of the All-Russian Congress of Soviets in January 1918, and was shortly thereafter tried and sentenced for sedition. In August 1920, John Maclean was to be found on Lewis, 'representing certain Trade Union organisations'; he visited Gress and Coll, where the land raids had just taken place; he was apparently made very welcome, and later addressed a public meeting in Stornoway.[6] This visit by a champion of the urban working class to the landless rural poor formed a pleasing mirror image of the day in 1888 when John Murdoch, the champion of the landless rural poor, had chaired the pre-foundation meeting of the urban working-class Scottish Labour Party. On the same day as Maclean's visit was reported, there was also printed an extract from the Highland Land League's annual report; it is splendid – *The Scotsman*'s readership must have been quite appalled:

Another year's work has appreciably advanced our ideal of that glorious commonweal in which the twin abominations of landlord-ism and capitalism shall cease from troubling, and where liberty and justice shall abound for all. Our fight for Scotland's green and purple land continues to be against her rapacious land-hoarders – the pestilential robber Barons . . . aided and abetted by a confederacy of tyrants, jobbers and knaves calling themselves a Coalition Government.

The League went on to praise the land-raiders and condemn the deer forest set aside for the 'cruel sports of idlers and useless aliens'. While the language was blustery and the insults exquisite, the sentiments were merely reflective of a population which had grown beyond weary of promises and legal procedures. Returning servicemen were no longer prepared to wait for reforms. They simply took what they felt was long overdue.

PRE-WAR INQUIRIES AND LEGISLATION

'Loss of Life, Hardship and Misery'

Westminster and Whitehall were not unprepared for any of this. It has been argued that Asquith's government had spent a large part of the war pondering how best to manage the expectations of men returning from service.[7] The popular disturbances were not about new issues – the war simply brought the problems into sharper focus, and everyone was aware that the ending of the war would bring massive challenges to the rule of law and property. The Liberal Party had been back in power since 1906, and in the years up to 1914 had continued its attempts to resolve the land problem in the Highlands and Islands. In 1911, for example, the Small Landholders (Scotland) Act came into effect, setting up a new body to replace the Crofters' Commission and giving it a reasonable budget to permit loans to crofters seeking to purchase or increase their holdings. The Act was desperate to replace the words 'croft' and 'crofter' with the buzz-words 'holdings' and 'landholder'; it sounded a little like a rebranding exercise. In any case, the Act still left the putative landholder with a fundamental problem: that he was given no assistance to actually stock his holding.

It was only in December 1919, with the Land Settlement (Scotland) Act, that loans could be handed out for seed, livestock, fertiliser and tools. This Act also specifically stated that preference was to be given to women who had some agricultural experience and who could also be considered for the role of landholder; and 'to suitable persons who have served in the forces of the Crown in the present or in any previous war'.[8] (The words 'present war' strongly suggest that the legislation was drafted some considerable time earlier – or else someone was unaware the war had ended.) Under this Act, powers of land acquisition and development were signed over to county councils.

At the end of the Victorian era, there was a huge legacy of social and economic problems in the Highlands and Islands. We can concede that the Liberal and Coalition governments since 1906 had been trying hard to resolve these. As well as faltering attempts at land reform, there had been investigations into health and poverty: in 1904 it was reported by the Medical Relief Committee that 'the want of sufficient medical attendance and nursing have a most prejudicial effect on the well-being of the district. The loss of life, hardship and misery which this implies cannot be calculated'; and in 1909, the Royal Commission on the Poor Laws determined that medical provision was 'deplorably insufficient, and affects not only the physical well-being of the paupers, but also that of the whole population'.[9] But it took the third such report, that of the Dewar Committee of 1912, before something positive was done about the situation. Sometimes it seemed that the Government, far from being the 'lady with a great many lovers' of Lord Lothian's fond idyll, was more like a deaf dotard who need to be bawled at several times before he heard.

Dewar set a welcome precedent: his committee of nine included a woman. Admittedly, she was a Marchioness (of Tullibardine) and Duchess (of Atholl), and was firmly against the notion of women's suffrage; but she also championed social reform, and later, despite her earlier convictions, became an MP. Later still, her firm opposition to fascism earned her the soubriquet of 'the Red Duchess'. Both male and female members of the Committee took their work seriously: somewhat in the mould of Napier, they issued questionnaires to the medical profession, then toured the main towns of the northern Highlands, as well as the Outer Hebrides and Skye. All of this was after overcoming an initial hurdle – no one had actually told them where to go: 'in the absence of definite indication in the remit as to the exact area to which the enquiry was to be confined'.[10] The lack of clarity sounds familiar. And you could tell the Committee was largely made up of medical professionals – of the 258 witnesses, '170 underwent oral examination'. Noteworthy in the medics' commitment to the task was a trip made to Ireland to discover how the 'Dispensary System' of medical provision in that island might inform: another dreadful case of Skyemen imitating Irishmen?[11] Also in the mould of Napier, there was a hefty companion volume to the main report, containing, in 500 pages, the testimony of all witnesses – amounting to 23,558 questions and answers. One thing was stressed several times in the report: the absolute inadequacy of transportation provision, which prevented patients from visiting doctors and doctors from attending emergencies; on occasion doctors had to walk 20 miles to reach a patient, or risk their lives on snowy mountains and stormy seas. Bold young men had acquired motor-cycles to cope, 'which, however, were far from suitable on Highland roads'.[12]

Some good came of the Dewar inquiry. As a direct result, the Highlands and Islands Medical Service was set up in 1913, and given adequate funding and equipment. If it still did not provide totally free health care, it acted as a practical proof of concept for the National Health Service established thirty-five years later.

The only thing that was missing from a great basketful of commissions, committees and legislation specific to the Highlands and Islands was something to do with railways. Given all the muddy waters the last railway commissions had stirred up, this was perhaps not surprising. But that oversight was soon rectified.

During the war, the lines of the Highland Railway Company had unexpectedly become of global strategic importance. Since the seas around the north of Scotland formed a major theatre of war and gave passage to and from the North Atlantic, the Royal Navy stationed its battleships at Scapa Flow on Orkney. One drawback of this location was that it could not readily be supplied from the south by sea: the whole point about the Scapa Flow base was that the surrounding seas were dangerous. Although the essential tons of coal were transported by ship from Grangemouth, timber, food, munitions and men had to come from England and central Scotland by rail to Inverness or Thurso before being ferried across to Orkney. And since the Highland Railway owned the fastest route north – from Perth to Inverness and all points northwards – it fell to the Highland Railway to become central to the military defence of Britain and its seas. Throughout the war, provisions, mail, personnel, newspapers, even reels of cinema film were sent north; tired men came back south on leave, as did timber from the rapidly felled forests of the north. The trains operated under the generic name of the 'Jellicoe Express' from 1917, in honour of the First Sea Lord. The full journey of over 700 miles from the south of England to Thurso offered an unforgettable experience of discomfort and stench which few naval personnel could possibly forget; the trip typically lasted twenty-one hours.

Clearly, the single-track lines which the Highland had built in the preceding decades were pushed to their limits – on occasion, the Admiralty had to construct additional crossing loops to permit more trains to use it as war demanded. Clearly, also, passenger traffic was shunted right to the back of the queue. Frequently the line was so congested that lower-priority trains had to detour via Aberdeen and Elgin. Thankfully, the Highland shareholders were not out of pocket: the company negotiated a deal with the Government, under whose terms, for each passing year of the war, it was guaranteed the same annual income that it had earned in 1913. On top of that, the Government also paid for the additional maintenance of the track and supplied engines and rolling stock as required.

Such was the importance of the north of Scotland and the route to Orkney that, in July 1916, all of the mainland north and west of the Great Glen was declared a restricted area, access being by permit only. There was massive disruption in the movement of basic supplies to the north-west. For people on the islands, matters became a lot worse when the United States finally entered the war in April of 1917. As a major part of its contribution, the USA agreed with Britain to construct the 'Northern Barrage', a 235-mile-wide barrier of mines which stretched across the sea from Orkney to Norway, its primary purpose being to prevent German ships and submarines from reaching the North Atlantic and wreaking havoc on freight and passenger shipping. The barrage was a munitions industry's dream come true: some 100,000 mines were required for the full scheme (70,000 were actually laid), and 15,000 miles of steel cable to anchor them to the sea-floor. Everything – mines, cables, explosives – was manufactured in the US and shipped over to Scotland for assembly and deployment.[13] Many of the American ships offloaded at Kyle of Lochalsh, and their cargoes were transported along the railway to Dingwall and then to a depot at Invergordon. Another unloading point was established at Corpach, by Fort William. Had there been a railway up beside Loch Ness, transport to Invergordon would have been so simple; as it was, the Americans had to use Telford's 100-year-old Caledonian Canal. In late 1917, the village of Kyle of Lochalsh and the entire railway line to Dingwall were commandeered by the Admiralty, and passenger traffic virtually ceased. Worse still, the steamer routes from Oban and Mallaig were also halted, so that anyone wishing to travel to Stornoway either had to bluff their way to Kyle and hope to board the small Macbrayne steamer there, or else had to endure the danger, discomfort and joylessness of an endless sea journey from Glasgow.

(That the journey via Kyle was not impossible was amply demonstrated by Lord Leverhulme, who, with his entourage, travelled this route in the high summer of 1918 to make himself known to his new subjects on Lewis. Almost certainly, Leverhulme had beforehand ensured that no obstacles would impede the progress of his party: a Lord passing through to survey his domain could not reasonably be halted. Lesser mortals would have found the journey more challenging.)[14]

Whether the Northern Barrage was successful is a matter of debate – it is generally agreed that fewer than a dozen U-boats were sunk by the mines. But perhaps many more were discouraged. What is certain is that a fair number of civilian lives were lost when ships hit the mines in the years immediately after the war; but by then the American industrialists had made their profits, so no real harm was done. The clearing of the minefield began in December of 1918, proceeded slowly (several mine-clearing ships were damaged in the process) and was not completed until well into 1920. Throughout that time, there was a huge impact on the fishing industry.

One lesson the Government could draw from all this was that railways had major importance in the conduct of war. That much should have been clear since the Franco-Prussian war of 1870; and it became painfully evident from the ease with which German troops arrived in Belgium by train in the first days of the war in 1914. In the mud of Flanders, both sides found that laying light railways was more efficient than convoys of lorries, which tended to bog down. In France itself, the wide-ranging railway network proved of enormous value to the British war effort, when large numbers of men had to be moved safely towards the Turkish and Middle Eastern theatres of war. The role of railways across Britain was also of the highest importance, since troops and equipment had to be taken from centres of industry and population to the major ports. What the situation cruelly exposed was that the railway network north of Scotland's central belt was woefully inadequate. Although there was an alternative route to Thurso from the south via Aberdeen, one single act of sabotage (or, more likely, a landslip or a heavy snowstorm) on the Highland's lines would have jeopardised the entire British naval strategy for the North Atlantic. And vast areas of the coastline were virtually inaccessible by any defence force, leaving the country exposed to possible enemy invasion.

It was in part to address these weaknesses that yet another body of men was sent forth in 1918 to suggest how to improve transportation in the north of Scotland.

14

'Difficulties in Paying the Fare'

The Rural Transport (Scotland) Committee of 1918

At the start of 1918, the war still raged and, leaving aside Russia, social upheaval and revolution were still perceived only as a distant threat; but this was the moment at which the Secretary for Scotland, Robert Munro, appointed a Rural Transport (Scotland) Committee which was instructed to report back to him on

(a) the rural areas most in need of transport facilities for agriculture, forestry and other rural industries;
(b) the means of improving communication in these areas, either through improved or new roads, light or narrow-gauge railways, motor transport and steamer services.[1]

The Committee comprised a number of senior civil servants; it was chaired by Sir T. Carlaw Martin, a Liberal newspaper editor and director of the Royal Scottish Museum in Edinburgh, and included two engineers, two forestry specialists and someone with a wide knowledge of the Scottish Poor Laws – so not necessarily a group of men with transportation expertise (for a full list of members, see Appendix 8). The first action of the Committee was to split itself into two parts: one to investigate and report on the north and west of Scotland, the other to concentrate on the east and south. Even despite this very sensible division of labour, the report covering the Orkney and Shetland Islands did not appear until a full year after the main report, which itself was issued in April 1919.

The members of the Committee undertook their mammoth task conscientiously. They travelled the land, visiting every corner, meeting with parish and county councils, examining roads and harbours, comparing steamer and railway timetables; some members even crossed the Channel and visited the ruined, stinking battlefields of France and Belgium, as well as the rather more sweet-smelling Jura mountains. And it cannot have been an easy journey: the north of Scotland was still a restricted area, and Orkney even more so. Fortunately, the navy came to their assistance on several occasions. Their main report ran to over sixty pages, and was admirable in its level of detail. Welcoming the report, Robert Munro advised the first annual meeting of the Edinburgh-based Association for the Betterment of the Highlands and Islands (that title tells us much) that: 'In no part of Scotland was improvement [to transportation] more possible and more urgently required than in the Highlands and Islands. In this matter the system was really a generation behind. (Hear, hear.)'[2] Munro had by then received the Committee's report and was about to publish it.

There was a breath of fresh air in it. Possibly the civil servants had done their job rather too enthusiastically. The report repeated the argument, for example, that the citizens of Scotland had the right to cheap transport, just as they had the right to cheap postage – an argument which indeed led to its logical conclusion: that the transport network should be under tight national control, and subsidised in the remoter areas.[3] Not only the railways: 'we are of the opinion that the steamer service of Messrs David Macbrayne Limited, should be taken over by the State upon equitable terms'; a suggestion that took almost exactly another fifty years to carry through.[4] Had even a tiny part of the recommendations been followed through, the infrastructure of rural Scotland might now look quite different.

THE LOCHBROOM EXECUTIVE COMMITTEE

'A Munificent Offer'

We shall return to these findings and recommendations shortly. First we must turn our attention to Ullapool, where, on 5 March 1918, the parish council and school board convened jointly to consider a letter which had been received three days earlier. It had come from the Rural Transport Committee, and invited the elected representatives of Loch Broom to make proposals for improving transport in the area. Under the leadership of Sir Montague Fowler of Braemore and Kenneth Cameron, chairman of the parish council, a special Executive Committee was swiftly established to pursue this matter with the utmost vigour. Fowler was appointed Chairman, and Mr D. S. Ross (no relation to P. Campbell of that ilk) was to be its secretary. (For a full list of members, see Appendix 9.)[5]

Sir Montague Fowler (1858–1933), fourth (and last) Baronet of Braemore, was the third son of Sir John Fowler. Coming from the family of a very wealthy and eminent engineer, he might have been expected to pursue some career along the same lines, or go into politics, or even – as his younger brother Evelyn seems to have done – become expert at doing nothing. Instead, he entered the church. He attracted public approbation for several charitable acts before the war and was rector at various churches in London; but the high point of his ecclesiastical career was his appointment as chaplain and purse-bearer to the Archbishop of Canterbury. And he wrote books: *Some Notable Archbishops of Canterbury* (1895), *Church History in Queen Victoria's Reign* (1896), *Christian Egypt* (1901), *The Morality of Social Pleasures* (1910) and others. In 1913, he founded the Church Imperial Club in London, which had 'an imposing list of divines and Church dignitaries as patrons'.[6] In 1889 he married his first wife, Ada Dayrell Thomson, a niece of the Archbishop of York. She too was an author, a bit like the Countess of Cromartie, but more racy: her several works written under the pseudonym 'Dayrell Trelawney' included *The Revolt of Daphne*, *The Robbery of the Pink Diamond* and *The Secret of the Haunted Road*. She also wrote several plays under the nom de plume 'Gaston Gervex', and a marvellously patriotic poem, '*Femina Imperialis 1900*' ('Awake! Imperial daughter of a race/That rules the sea . . .'), appeared under her own name in the *Revelstoke Herald* of British Columbia in 1900. Ada died in 1911. In 1914, Montague married his second wife, Denise Chailliey, a Frenchwoman thirty-four years his junior; she wrote neither novels nor church histories, but produced two daughters, bred toy spaniels and outlived her husband by sixty years.

Montague had come to be baronet of Braemore by the dictates of Fortune. His elder brother Arthur Fowler had succeeded his father, Sir

John, as baronet upon the latter's death in 1898. But Arthur himself had died at a young age in 1899 and been succeeded by the eldest of his two sons, John Edward, then aged fourteen. John and his only brother, Alan, were both killed in France in the summer of 1915 – in this they shared the tragic fate of a large number of the sons of the ordinary people of the area. Sir John's second son, Percival, had already expired childless in 1904; the then-existing law of male primogeniture kicked in, despite a perfectly adequate supply of Arthur's daughters. And so it was that in late 1915 the third son, the Reverend Montague, found himself baronet of Braemore. He wasted no time. Arthur's widow, Alice, still grieving for her two sons, went to live in the more cramped surroundings of an Inverness hotel. Sir Montague installed his new young wife as mistress of the Braemore estate, and settled down to the life of a wealthy laird engaged in quite moral social pleasures – a task he took up as if born to it.

Montague was a tall, straight-standing man, someone you would probably trust in affairs both religious and lay. By all evidence he was perfectly self-confident. Somewhat in contrast to his earlier charitable works, in 1917 he raised a court case for complete control of the family trust fund (£40,000) and the entire contents of Braemore House; arrayed against him were several surviving members of other branches of the Fowler family, including the Dowager Lady Alice. Clearly, Alice had not willingly given up Braemore or the rights of her immediate family. With impressive hard-headedness, Sir Montague successfully pressed his own claim and inherited the lot.[7] The other Fowlers picked up the legal costs. In 1920, he was to be found suing – again successfully – a seasonal shooting-tenant of Braemore for the sum of £153 9s 1d, in respect of unpaid rates. But, in common with other landowners after the Great War, he seems to have found himself in possession of an estate which leaked money at an alarming rate. Much of the family finance was tied up in railway shares and Russian stock – a portfolio which did not come out of the war in a healthy state.[8] Two attempts to sell the Braemore estate (1920 and 1923) failed, but in 1928 he finally managed to offload the larger part to a brewing magnate (John Calder of Alloa, later managing director of Ind Coope). This did not seem to stem the outflow of money. In his will of 1933, Montague asked that 'mementos' be given to loyal servants and friends: 'I regret that the enormous expenditure caused me by the years of litigation in regard to the disentail of Braemore and other cognate matters prevent me from leaving legacies to many who have served me so loyally.'[9]

With the baronetcy, the big house and a reasonable collection of debts, he also inherited the Ullapool Railway project. Montague was not a man to sit back idly. And so the first meeting of the Lochbroom Executive Committee in 1918 took three decisions: firstly, to promote the Garve and Ullapool Railway; secondly, to seek funds to improve the pier at Coigach (Badentarbet); thirdly, to write to all the local landowners and invite their co-operation and support for the railway. All of this was duly done, and Montague went back up to Braemore House to review his assets and put together his arguments in favour of the railway beloved of his brother and father.

On 1 June 1918, the members of the Lochboom Executive Committee reconvened. Another letter had been received from the Rural Transport Committee, indicating that its members would be in Ullapool on 4 June and would like to arrange a meeting. It was also minuted that various letters of support had flooded in, some from the local landowners, others from the 'East Coast Fishermen'. Almost certainly, some of the enthusiasm of the East Coast fishermen was because they were obliged to fish far from home, off the west coast, until such time as the North Sea was safe again.

A week later, the local committee members met once more. Much had been done, much was reported. The meeting with the Rural Transport Committee had taken place in the Royal Hotel of Ullapool, and on that occasion Sir Montague had made the following points to the inquiring visitors:

1. The railway would enormously increase the food supply of the country by opening up markets for a healthy fishing industry. Having to offload catches at Kyle or Mallaig meant that northern fishermen could only fish two days a week and had to spend two days getting the catch to a railhead; with a railway at Ullapool, they could fish four or five days a week. Any objections about the suitability of Ullapool for fishing boats (*vide* the infamous 1890 report) were no longer valid – 'even had they been well founded' – since all fishing was now done by steam boats.

2. The timber industry would be opened up. For the duration of the war, Braemore (i.e. Sir Montague's estate) had been busy selling huge amounts of timber to the government's Timber Supply Department. And now the estate could sell huge amounts more. Hillsides between the 200-foot and 900-foot contour lines could be planted, and mature timber loaded directly to trains.

3. More agricultural produce could be sent to towns – 'hay, straw, oats etc. and even milk'. Given the low number and breadline status of the crofts in the area, this argument sounds a little desperate.

4. All the plans etc. were in place for building the railway, and 'no difficulties would be found in the way'. Someone forgot to mention the descent at Braemore. A questionable estimate was mentioned of £3,000 per mile for construction.

5. There were no railways north of Kyle which opened on the west coast. A railway to Ullapool would open up the steamer passage to Stornoway (40 miles, as opposed to 70 miles from Kyle). Aultbea had by now been completely forgotten. And 'this railway could easily be extended northwards along the west coast' – a claim which depends on a rather broad interpretation of the word 'easily'.

6. With the war still not over, it was proposed that Ullapool could become 'an admirable coaling-station for the Fleet'; and a railway to Ullapool would also permit troops to arrive quickly to fend off hostile incursions on the north and west coasts ('or', the argument continued, a little fantastically, 'in the event of possible disturbances in Ireland' – nothing could have surprised the Irish Republicans more than a government force sailing from Loch Broom).

7. The area was also very promising for the development of hydropower, which itself would facilitate the timber industry, and could also be used to power the railway.

Sir Montague also wished it to be minuted that he, as chairman, had been to London recently and talked to the War Office, the Admiralty, the Timber Supply Department and the American Embassy, as well as influential MPs. He had found great support for the railway in the capital. The Timber Supply Department had sent two engineers to Loch Broom at the start of June, to investigate options for generating electrical power 'by which the railway could be worked'. All of which sounded very promising indeed. Even the Americans were on board.

Intriguingly, the minutes of this meeting also record that Messrs Tait and Ferguson ('two eminent engineers') of the Rural Transport group had carefully examined the route from Loch Droma westwards and expressed the opinion that the proposed route of the railway (keeping to the east side of the Strath at Braemore and along Loch Broom) 'would present no engineering difficulties'.[10] Now this was something new: as we know, the original proposal from 1890 had been for the line to descend on the west side of the Strath, via that tunnel. The tunnel had since been struck firmly off the menu by Sir John Fowler, but the line was probably still planned for the west side of the descent. So someone, somewhere, some time in the intervening three decades, had come up with an alternative. Or was this just Messrs Tait and Ferguson themselves, suddenly put on the spot? It is not known whether either of them had any experience of building railways: Tait, indeed, seemed to be an expert on hydropower. In any event, this was a clear indication that the proposed railway was to be 'light', given that only lighter rolling stock could conceivably master the 1 in 22 gradient here. Maybe. Or, just maybe, no one had seriously thought things through.

To crown a memorable meeting, Fowler then announced that 'he was prepared to grant free of charge the ground necessary for the way leave of the proposed railway from Garve to Ullapool so far as it passed through his lands, on the understanding that the other proprietors along the route did the same'. The Committee unanimously recorded their appreciation of this 'munificent offer', and instructed the tireless Mr Ross, Secretary, to send out more letters.

There still exists an example of one of the letters which were sent out to the landowners. By happy chance, it is the one sent to the Countess of Cromartie, wife of Major Blunt. It was a short letter, much to the point. It begins by reminding her Ladyship of the 1890 scheme which 'unfortunately, however, owing to a hitch at the last moment . . . was dropped for the time being' (an amusing spin on the facts). It pointed out that the presence of a railway 'enhances the value of a deer forest' – always a valid concern, although the Duke of Sutherland might have disagreed – and mentioned also the advantages accruing to fisheries, forestry and so forth. Finally, it asked the Countess to consider emulating Fowler's generous example by donating land for free for the building of the railway. This request was backed up by the rather questionable assertion that

> the Rural Transport Committee . . . clearly indicated that the prospects [of the railway] would be enormously strengthened if the local Committee were in a position to assure them that the landowners through whose properties the line would pass were willing to give way leave free.[11]

This particular letter is annotated in the handwriting of a recipient other than the Countess, who was presumably far too busy parting the dark mists of the Celtic past. The note indicated that there should be no difficulty in acceding to this request, but urged that, instead of a railway, a tramway should be built, which would avoid any trouble with level crossings, fences, signals and so forth. The writer also recommended that 'the line should run to Kannaird Bay [i.e. Isle Martin] if it is to help the fishing industry'. The annotation is dated 4 July 1918, from 'HQ IX Corps' in London; and the signature is, of course, that of E. W. Blunt-Mackenzie.

Other recipients of these letters included a select gathering of the rich (mostly named Mackenzie, as was the Countess of Cromartie). There was: Mr Mackenzie of Farr (factor to King George V); Major Stirling of Strathgarve; Sir A. G. R Mackenzie, 11th Baronet of Coul; Mr Mackenzie of Dundonnell; the Marquis of Northampton (a grandson and heir of the flighty Lady Ashburton, once a Mackenzie); and Mr Mackenzie of Catton's Trustees. Some of these we have come across before; clearly, not much had changed in terms of estate ownership since 1890. (Catton's Trustees is another steamy tale altogether, of disputed land, illegitimacy, Australian claimants and lengthy court cases. The land involved was centred around Dundonnell and the Fannichs. And yes, there were plenty of feuding Mackenzies at the heart of it.)[12]

In July, Fowler undertook to write to Mr Ferguson, the engineer on the Rural Transport Committee, 'to ascertain the probable route of the Garve-Ullapool railway should it be constructed'; this is suggestive of some doubt and confusion, and certainly of a change from the original

route. A lengthy gap then appears in the minutes of the Lochbroom
Executive Committee – more likely representing a problem with document preservation than a lapse in activity. The next meeting on record
is dated 5 September 1919, several months after the Rural Transport
Committee had published its main report. The minute of the Railway
Committee, as it now described itself, stated rather laconically that 'the
inch to mile maps, having been obtained, Mr Ingham [Deputy Chief
Surveyor of the Board of Agriculture] and Sir Montague Fowler agreed
to draw a line of rail, as requested'. The implication was that, despite
various attempts and the actual existence of detailed plans and maps, no
one yet knew where the line was supposed to run.

THE REPORT OF THE RURAL TRANSPORT
COMMITTEE, 1919

'Boxes of Live Lobsters'

After much uncomfortable travelling and serious deliberation, the
Rural Transport Committee issued its first and main report in April
1919. It is a little difficult to summarise in a few words, but I will try.
In essence, the report stated that rural transport in Scotland was sham-
bolic. The 25,000 miles of public road were poorly maintained, leading
to high transport costs and delays. The railways were quite insufficient
in number and range to handle the loads any better than the roads. The
steamer service up and down the west coast left much to be desired. In
comparison with other European and Scandinavian countries, transport provision was 'very inadequate'. None of the basic needs of
forestry, fishing, agriculture, hydropower, education or the transmission
of news were being met.

A graphic example of the difficulties of transport was provided,
showing quite clearly that things had not greatly improved since the
last time anyone bothered to look into the matter, in the 1880s:

> The journey, for instance, from Durness to Lairg – a distance of
> fifty-four miles – costs 16s. The first twenty miles are traversed in a
> horse-drawn waggonette in which passengers are surrounded by
> mail bags, boxes of live lobsters, live calves tied in sacks, personal

luggage, etc. At Rhiconich an addition of the same sort is received from Kinlochbervie. At Laxford everything is transferred to the waiting motor mail-car which has arrived from Scourie. At this stage it may be found that the motor mail-car cannot contain the accumulation, and there is loss of time and temper and some heart-burning before it is determined what goods and passengers can be taken, and what must be left. Valuable consignments of lobsters and salmon are lost when thus delayed, being unfit for food before reaching the market. From Laxford to Lairg the motor mail, with its varied and congested freight, proceeds at an average speed of eight miles per hour. The climate of the north-west is notoriously bad, and through rain, sleet, or snow the passengers, destitute of protection, must sit still with such patience as they can exercise . . . The expense of travelling is to dwellers in these parts a serious item . . . and constitutes a heavy burden.[13]

As a picture calculated to boost the case for improved transportation, this could scarcely be bettered. The sum of 16 shillings (arguably equivalent to £60–£80 now; and the best part of a working person's weekly wage) for such luxurious transport even makes some of the more outrageous twenty-first-century privatised rail fares seem modest. A railway would, at the very least – surely? – separate lobsters and calves in sacks from the rest of the travelling public; anything else would be a bonus.

The Committee's recommendations for improvement were many and varied. As we have already noted, there was a shameless call for railways and steamer operations to be placed under State management. Steamer services were considered to be hopelessly poor: Ullapool, for example, received a steamer once a fortnight, and places further north might see a steamer every six weeks. Arterial public roads were in a very poor state and should be supplemented by 'concrete wheel tracks' running alongside to bear the load of the new heavier vehicles and prevent further deterioration. The Crinan Canal was to be replaced by a much larger 'ship canal'. And railways should be built or extended – railways, plenty of them. The capital cost for building railways should be met out of the public purse, and their subsequent management would be the responsibility of the State. Only in this way, asserted the Committee, would transport improve and bolster rural industry and fishing, and thereby drag local communities into the twentieth century. There was a very strong implication that landowners and landowner-ship in general were at the root of many of the problems; the report stated that several landowners refused to let roads and railway have passage across their land, and that: 'By far the greater part of the in-terior of Inverness-shire is reserved for sport. It contains some of the largest and most highly-rented deer forests in Scotland.'[14] One pithy sentence in the report expresses the Committee's view of settlements on the mainland: 'The contrast between congestion and desolation is rather remarkable.'[15]

Worse was to come: in discussing a new road between Deeside and Speyside, the Committee blithely argued, 'Though it may appear to some to be a retrograde step to suggest the imposition of a toll, we see no reason why one should not be levied upon motorists using a road of this description for touring purposes.' The revenue thus gained would assist in the maintenance of those roads. A hundred years on, the hard-pressed officers of the Highland Council Roads Department may even now be viewing the North Coast 500 route with similar dark thoughts in their minds.

If, between the lines, the Committee expressed dangerous socialist views on landowners, private steamer companies and tourists, then two of its members appeared to be out-and-out Bolsheviks. In their 'Reservations' – minority reports tacked on at the end – George Mackay and H. M. Conacher went several steps further. Mackay, a man who clearly knew his own mind, argued that transport would only improve if agriculture and industry were first improved. 'There is small utility in giving a man the possibility of a good railway or steamer service if his conditions of life are such as make it difficult for him to pay the fare,' was his sound argument. He pointed out that no railway so far built in a rural area of Scotland had ever led to an increase in population – indeed, quite the opposite: with a railway nearby, rents increased and the poor found it even more difficult to live as tenants. Mackay also stated that 'the condition of the Highlands . . . is wholly the product of the arbitrary action of the landowners during the last 110 years' – a view every land reformer would endorse.[16] Conacher was of similar mind: 'it remains true that a small class of men is responsible for the fact that the social economy of the Highlands of Scotland stands in tragic isolation apart from the general development of the mountainous districts of Western and Central Europe'.[17]

Among the many recommendations for improvements to the transport network, seventeen railways were proposed. Some of these would now bring tears of joy to the corporate eyes of Visit Scotland: a 75-mile line on Skye, between Armadale, Portree and Dunvegan; on Lewis, a 40-mile railway between Stornoway, Carloway and Ness; and on Arran, between Whiting Bay and Blackwaterfoot. A host of new mainland lines was also advocated – one of these was that old favourite, the 40-mile railway from Culrain to Lochinver. But standing out above them all, the Garve to Ullapool route, which would be termed, in twenty-first century parlance, a no-brainer.

> We are impressed with the arguments in favour of the construction of this line . . . We are further impressed by the existence of large reserves of water-power, and the consequent prospects of manufacturing industries being established in the neighbourhood of Ullapool . . . Apart from these considerations, the great argument in favour of this line is that it would give the shortest through connection between a port on the west coast and the existing railway system.[18]

Sir Montague and his team had done their work well.

Sadly, the steam had by now run out on the rival Aultbea proposal. The Committee did not 'feel justified in recommending the construction of a railway from Achnasheen to Aultbea on Lochewe'. The best they could suggest, discounting a boat service along Loch Maree, was a 'road motor service' to Achnasheen, there to meet the Dingwall–Kyle railway. And it was not for want of lobbying by the Aultbea supporters: although John Dixon had long since departed for Pitlochry, the new Mackenzie of Gairloch had evidently submitted plans and documents to the Committee.[19] A similar road-based proposal was suggested as a landward escape route for the inhabitants of Torridon, lest they felt forgotten in all of this. But an improved road to Loch Ewe had to wait until the next war, when one was hastily constructed to service the Royal Navy base there.

So sanguine was the Rural Transport Committee of having its recommendations implemented that, in January 1919, several of its members set off for the still-smoking battlefields of France to take an inventory of spare rolling stock, rails and other paraphernalia of the light railways which had been deployed by the British Expeditionary Force during the war. They concluded that the Government should snap up these bargain-basement items (one careful owner and barely affected by mud, blood or ordnance) for use in the proposed railways in Scotland.[20] On a subsidiary visit to examine rural transportation in the French Alps and Jura mountains, two committee members learned to their surprise that the French government heavily subsidised the local railways.

The 1919 report of the Rural Transport (Scotland) Committee was, even viewed from a century further on, an astonishing document to be produced by a team of senior civil servants. It was in stark contrast to the railway reports of 1890 and 1891: two decades and a war had swept away a great deal. One might say the report was far ahead of its time, were it not for the fact that the actual social, economic and infra-structure conditions were far beyond their sell-by date.

THE END OF THE DREAM

'Bridging the Gulf'

As the position of the Rural Transport Committee became clear, the members of the Railway Committee of Ullapool felt encouraged to even greater efforts. Possibly some of the growing revolutionary mood of those days was beginning to rub off on them. In a printed 'Petition' simply dated '1918', their case was summarised.[21] The document began:

> Among the numerous promises held out to their electors in December, 1918, one of the most insistent was the assurance that the Coalition Government, if returned to power, would open up and develop the Highlands by improved rail, road and sea communication.

It pointed out that 'nearly 100 miles of the north-western seaboard is inaccessible to the railway system', and proceeded to list some bullet-points for an easy appreciation of the case for the railway. It would:

- facilitate the development of the fishing industry

- promote tourist traffic (the grand sights of Corrieshalloch and Strone were, of course, mentioned)
- promote – and use – hydroelectric power. A calculation was provided here, indicating that 'at least 10,000 h.p. continuous could be generated at a cost of about 1/4th penny per BOT unit – sufficient to supply several large industries at Ullapool'. ('BOT unit': Board of Trade unit = 1kwh)
- encourage – and exploit – forestry
- increase cattle-stock to help feed the nation
- improve mail and passenger traffic to Stornoway.

The document ends by citing several worthy supporters – the local MP Mr MacPherson, the Duke of Sutherland (statement dated 1890), the Chairman of the Highland Railway (statement of 1908: evidently, the company had mellowed), and *The Scotsman* editorial of 6 July 1891 (although, in truth, *The Scotsman* did not specifically champion the Ullapool route, merely a properly run railway somewhere in the north-west.) It was not, if one looks closely, a very impressive list.

At some point in 1919, a letter signed by Montague Fowler and Kenneth Cameron was sent to Ian MacPherson, the Liberal MP for Ross and Cromarty between 1911 and 1935 – at around this time MacPherson had become Chief Secretary for Ireland, and doubtless had things on his mind other than a minor railway in his constituency.[22] The writers 'ventured to ask you to use your influence with the Government' to authorise the immediate construction of the railway, for the following reasons:

1. it had been recommended by the Rural Transport (Scotland) Committee;
2. it could be built easily and cheaply;
3. at Inverlael and Braemore there were 'a large number of splendidly built huts, capable of accommodating 300 men, which will shortly be vacated by the Canadian Forestry Corps and the German Prisoners, who have been operating on the Braemore timber, and will likely be leaving within the next few weeks. These huts would at once be available for the men to be employed on the railway';

4. there was an excellent pier at the head of Loch Broom, erected
   by the Canadians – at which all construction materials, rails,
   trucks etc. could be landed;
5. there was ample timber at Braemore and Leckmelm;
6. the Ministry of Labour was anxious to find employment for
   'several hundreds of men . . . for a considerable period'.

Since Sir Montague has drawn our attention to it, some words here
about forestry and timber. The Canadian Forestry Corps was an army
of around 10,000 Canadians mustered to answer the Old Country's
call for help in 1916. A crisis was already looming in the UK's timber
supply for the war effort, since most of the timber used in peacetime
had come from abroad; that source had effectively been cut off by the
German Navy. Matters were made worse in late 1917 by the revolution of the Russians, whose endless forests had supplied much of the
world. So a mass army of Canadian lumberjacks turned up in Britain:
3,000 of them to start felling trees with admirable efficiency in
Scotland, the remainder to do the same in England and Wales and
even, as military advances permitted, in France. The Canadians were
assisted in their efforts by around 830 PoWs from Germany (as at the
head of Loch Broom), and more willingly perhaps by Finns (many
rescued from torpedoed ships) and Portuguese workers. Overall, in
the UK, some nine million cubic feet of timber was harvested and
sawn up, with the Canadians supplying the muscle and expertise for
around one quarter of the total. The wood was used primarily for
railway sleepers (2.5 million of them) and pit-props (50,000 tons
thereof).[23] And while the Canadians sawed and chopped and then
stepped back to a safe distance, the various large estates providing the
timber grew rich.

The overall effect on Scotland's forests was not far short of devastating. By 1924, it was calculated that over 20 per cent of Scotland's
woodlands had been felled; and since Scotland had not been well
afforested in the first place – only 5 per cent of the total land area
pre-war, the smallest percentage in Europe – huge swathes of land now
stood desolate and treeless. But yet another lesson was learned by the
Government from this experience: along with a hundred and one
other new bodies, the Forestry Commission was set up in 1919 to
replant the hillsides and glens in case of another war.

On the face of things, the case for the Ullapool Railway was a shoo-in. But there was a nervous tone in Fowler's letter to MacPherson:

> The report will, we presume, be passed to the Minister of Ways and Communications. In the colossal powers entrusted to him, and among the multitude of schemes submitted to him, the Garve–Ullapool Railway may be in danger of being overlooked . . . All that is required is a bridge by which the gulf between the recommendations of the Rural Transport Committee and the authority who can order the construction of the railway, and finance the operation, can be crossed.

The rather revealing use of the word 'gulf' suggests that the Lochbroom Executive Committee was beginning to realise that the recommendations of a group of sympathetic civil servants did not necessarily cut much ice in the harsh and ill-defined realities of post-war Britain. In any case, responsibility for transport was about to pass to a completely new government ministry – an ideal moment for racing certainties to be knocked on the head and buried.

And what, indeed, was the lasting result of the report of the Rural Transport (Scotland) Committee? At the end of the day, there was not much to show. Of the seventeen railway lines which were proposed across the length and breadth of Scotland, not a single one was actually built. There were several reasons for this, but the primary one without doubt was what the London *Times*, during the 1919 railway strike, hailed as 'The Triumph of the Lorry'.[24] During the war, thousands of lorries had been built to move the British Army from place to place, and thousands of men had been trained in how to drive them. When the war ended, the lorries became surplus to requirements; the men needed jobs; there were virtually no regulations surrounding road transport companies. It was a perfect storm as far as railways were concerned. Any ex-serviceman able to acquire a lorry could, without any further expense, go into the business of moving goods and people around – albeit on some rather precarious road surfaces (towards which they paid little or no maintenance fee). If you wanted a railway to do the same job, you had to jump through far more hoops. The development of road-based transport also got the Government out of a sticky situation – railways were at the mercy of the trades unions, as events in 1919 had shown, but privately owned lorries offered no such challenge to authority. 'Out of evil,' preached *The Times* on the subject of strike-breaking lorries, 'good may come.'

As Montague Fowler feared, there was no appetite in Westminster for rural railways away up north. Although the Ministry of Transport Act of August 1919 set up a single amalgamated ministry to plan and manage transport across the UK, it did little to implement the recommendations of the Rural Transport Committee. The new Ministry's remit was to take over 'all powers and duties of any Government Department in the relation to (a) railways; (b) light railways; (c) tramways; (d) canals, waterways, and inland navigations; (e) roads, bridges and ferries, and vehicles and traffic thereon; (f) harbours, docks and piers'.[25] Rather too hopefully, railways were at the top of this list; in reality, and for decades to come, this was effectively the Ministry of Roads.

The only meaningful piece of legislation which the new Minister of Transport put forward to improve railways was the Railways Act of 1921, which amalgamated about a hundred railway companies into the 'Big Four' to cover all national railway operations from 1923 onwards. The Highland and Caledonian Railway companies now formed part of the London, Midland and Scottish Railway, while the Great North of Scotland and the North British companies came under the wing of the London and North-Eastern Railway. But while this Act took a faltering step away from anarchic free enterprise towards central planning and collaboration, these new companies were still businesses driven by shareholder interests. The Act fell far short of nationalising the railways, in stark contrast to other major powers in Europe which had already brought their railways under far tighter governance, up to and including outright nationalisation, years and even decades before. A Select Committee of the House of Commons had in earlier years proposed the complete nationalisation of the railways 'from the standpoint of efficiency and economy, and with due regard to the interests of the proprietors, the railway staffs, and the general community'.[26] But that was a step too far – and might have been grievously misinterpreted by the socialistic working class in those dangerous post-war days. It was far too little, far too late. And naturally, by the same lack of logic, there was no nationalisation of steamer services.

Thus, notwithstanding the efforts of the Lochbroom Executive Committee of 1918, the Garve and Ullapool Railway, which had seemed an odds-on favourite, was now just another shattered dream.

15

'Not an Economic Proposition'

Major Vyner's Idea

In the 1930s, Commander Clare Vyner RN bought Isle Martin, just north-west of Ullapool, and took up residence in Keanchulish Lodge on the mainland opposite. He already possessed a number of large estates up and down the country, both in England and Scotland. We should not be totally astounded to learn that he was a great-nephew of the colourful Lady Ashburton, whom we encountered previously, or that he married a daughter of the Duke of Richmond. The land-owning fraternity then (as now?) encompassed a rather tight and inbred circle of families; Vyner was also a great friend of the Queen Mother.

But he also had a small reputation as a philanthropist, and had grand plans for developing Isle Martin and its local economy. In 1938, he founded the Lochbroom Trading Co. Ltd, a 'land and industrial development company'; his business partner was Ullapool entrepreneur Kenneth Cameron, and they had offices in Inverness and Thurso (close to one of Vyner's other estates), as well as premises in Ullapool. (Kenneth Cameron died in 1951, aged 86. He had been the chairman of the Parish Council at the time of the 1918/19 proposal. And he may well also have been the same Kenneth Cameron, owner of the wool-mill in Ullapool, who, with Arthur Fowler, wrote a stern letter to the Scottish Office in 1892, 'disposing of the objections' in the Hutchinson committee report. A man, therefore, who managed to support all three significant attempts to build that longed-for railway.)

In 1938, the trading company converted the old herring-curing station on Isle Martin into a flour mill. It was a bold move: the island had no grain (it came by ship from Liverpool, and originated in Canada), nor had it any residents (but it soon would, along with a small school), and the flour had a distant market (it had to be taken by ship back to Liverpool; the ship was also owned by the Trading Company). There was even a light railway from the island's pier to the mill – the only one to come geographically close to Ullapool; it was, alas, powered merely by human muscle. The mill closed temporarily in 1942, re-opened in 1945 and then closed permanently in 1948. The island was sold by Vyner in 1965, but he continued to live at Keanchulish Lodge. The subsequent owner of the island sold it to the RSPB in 1979, and it passed to community ownership in 1999.

Just how little the character of landownership had changed in 1945 is reflected in the Valuation Rolls for the wider Loch Broom area. At that time, Coigach was still owned by the Cromartie family, Braemore was being run by a trust managing the remnants of Montague Fowler's estate (he had died in 1933 at his home in Hertfordshire) and the estates of Leckmelm, Strathvaich, Strathgarve and Inverlael were still firmly in the hands of sundry earls, majors and commanders. As a small concession to modernity, some land was now owned by the Forestry Commission, tiny patches were in the hands of the National Trust for Scotland and parts of Ullapool were owned by the Lochbroom Trading Co. Ltd.[1]

In the late summer of 1945, Commander Vyner contacted the Scottish Committee of the London, Midland and Scottish Railway (LMS), which now managed the railways of the north Highlands. Not much else had changed, though: the LMS Traffic Committee of 1945 comprised four gentlemen with the title 'Sir', one viscount, three colonels, one 'Colonel Sir'; and a pair of lesser beings. In the twenty years which had elapsed since the creation of the LMS, neither it nor any other railway company of the 'Big Four' had done anything to expand or improve the British railway network. Such lines as had been built either served the suburbs and satellites of London, or had been constructed in haste during the Second World War (in Scotland, for example, to service the naval bases at Faslane and Cairnryan). Conversely, small branch lines had been closed down on a regular basis: 3,200 miles closed even before Dr Beeching had his bright idea.

And yet, paying absolutely no attention to the historical trend, Vyner came to the LMS with a proposal for a new railway. Intriguingly, given his interest in Isle Martin, the railway was simply the original route between Garve and Ullapool, and was not to be extended further west. There is no indication that his proposal was specifically to benefit the fishing industry – his case seems to have rested solely on general 'development'. The proposal was duly discussed at a meeting of the LMS board in Glasgow on 18 September.[2] It was the last item on the agenda. A preceding item was unquestionably of more import: the monthly discussion of 'Claims exceeding £100' – a miscellany of lost, damaged or stolen goods, such as cardigans (979 of them), whisky (several instances), ladies' coats and costumes, concentrated orange juice, scarves, more whisky, cigarettes, cloth in various shapes and forms. And whisky. (In June 1945, as a change from the usual litany of pilfered spirits and tobacco, there had been a claim for 249 face-powder compacts lost in transit between Beith and Birmingham: wide-boys with some welcome imagination, or just poor complexions?)

It had evidently been a long day for the Committee, for the final agenda item was swiftly dealt with:

Reported . . . that Commander Vyner, a landowner in the Ullapool area, has revived this proposal and has asked whether the Company would consider the construction of a railway from Ullapool to Garve for the development of that area.

Commander Vyner had meetings with the Company's Officers following on which he addressed a communication to the Scottish Committee, setting out his proposals and suggesting that a small sub-committee of the Company and himself should be invited to produce a scheme, possibly in conjunction with the Scottish Economic Council, showing the requirements, the probable cost and how the scheme should be financed.

Estimates have not been prepared of the cost of constructing such a railway, but assuming a figure of £25,000 per mile, the cost would amount to at least £850,000, but would probably be nearer £1,000,000 before the work was completed. This figure is double that quoted by Commander Vyner and is more in relation to the authorised capital and borrowing powers of the original Company of £320,000 (having regard to the value of money in 1890 as compared with 1945) than the figure of £500,000 quoted by Commander Vyner.

> The Executive Committee are of the opinion that the revenue from the proposed railway would not meet working costs and renewals, apart from the cost of providing the capital required, and that Commander Vyner should be informed that no economic justification can be found for his scheme, it being considered a road motor service more likely to be suitable to serve this area.

And, in capital letters lest anyone should miss the point, the members of the Committee 'AGREE THAT THIS IS NOT AN ECONOMIC PROPOSITION'.

At this time, the LMS was more concerned with closing down its unprofitable lines than opening up new ones. Money was going out faster than it came in: at the Hotels sub-committee meeting on the same September day, they discussed a serious fire which had resulted in the total destruction of the 'Male Staff House' in Kyle, which would now have to be rebuilt. In any case, the LMS was not long for this world: the landslide victory of the Labour Party in July 1945 had paved the way for the long-overdue passing into State control of the debilitated transportation, mining and heavy industries of the country. The LMS was swept up into the nationalised British Railways in January 1948, along with the other 'Big Four' members.

Note the reference in the minutes of the LMS to the Scottish Economic Council. This was established in 1936; in its first composition, there were fifteen male worthies (no women). One early member, rather surprisingly, was Willie Gallacher, the Communist Party MP for West Fife; he was greatly outnumbered by an assortment of industrialists, JPs and senior civil servants, but at least they were all Scottish. The Council was set up by the Secretary of State for Scotland to 'examine the possibilities of improving economic conditions in Scotland. It will also consider questions affecting the extension of existing, or the creation of new, industries that may be referred to it by industrial, commercial, or public bodies.'[3] It all sounds very, very familiar. Evidently, having survived the 1920s and lurched into the 1930s, the Government was still no closer to resolving the fundamental problems of capitalism.

Commander Vyner's proposal was very much like Major Blunt's of 1901 – the bright idea of one rich man, with no underlying community support or tangible socio-economic driver. Both the 1901 and 1945 proposals were outliers in the broader history of the long-running campaign for an Ullapool railway. Vyner died as a result of a vehicle accident on his Keanchulish estate in 1989, at the ripe old age of ninety-five; his efforts over the years to make life a little more rewarding for locals and walkers were sorely missed. And, rather sadly, a revived railway from Garve to Ullapool could not be counted among his achievements.

16

'National Duty and National Policy'

The Twenty-first Century

A full 130 years after the original proposals for a railway between Garve and Ullapool, the physical background of the area remains virtually unchanged. The mountains and glens are still bleak in winter, breath-takingly desolate in summer. Of houses or signs of ordinary human life, there is scarcely anything west of Garve until you reach Braemore. Admittedly, Loch Glascarnoch has put in an unexpected appearance; but the estates which lie along the course of the planned railway remain more or less intact, albeit with different owners. The male line of the Fowler family has long gone. Estates have passed into the hands of cider-makers, Dutch businessmen, anonymous trusts and sundry individuals with piles of money; and they remain of much the same size as they did long ago. Ross and Cromarty itself is still one of the emptiest regions in the whole of Scotland. In 1995, around 79 per cent of the area was held in estates larger than 5,000 acres, these being owned by seventy-six individuals or businesses.[1] In terms of the percentage of large estates, only Sutherland outdoes Ross and Cromarty, with figures for 1995 indicating that 80 per cent of the county is covered by fifty-three large estates. In 2012, still 83 per cent of Scotland's countryside was privately owned; 50 per cent of that – so 41 per cent of the total rural area of Scotland – was in the hands of 432 owners.[2] Ownership changes with depressing frequency, but not the overall extent of the estates.

On Lewis, the huge Matheson holding was sold in 1918; the new owner, Lord Leverhulme, having made over Stornoway and the surrounding land (70,000 acres) to a community trust, sold off the rest and abandoned the island in 1925. Despite a recent burst of community buy-outs (a further 130,000 acres), over half of Lewis's 437,000 acres is still divided into a handful of large sporting estates – the four largest accounting in total for almost a third of the whole island. On the mainland, although there have also been some recent community buy-outs in the north-west, inward investment remains a distant dream. Forestry has been pursued to a small degree, but, with local people excluded from ownership, it is questionable whom these forests benefit, and whether they represent anything more than a modern equivalent of the deer forests.[3] There is some tourism, hydro and wind-farm schemes dot the land, fish-farms sporadically set themselves down in the lochs; but in the final analysis Ross and Cromarty remains largely deserted. For lovers of wilderness and the great outdoors, this is not a bad thing; but there is surely a balance to be struck between a man-made wasteland and a discreetly thriving community. One need only look at even the most out-of-the-way rural districts of Europe and Scandinavia to spot the discrepancy.

Of course, the west of Scotland has nothing like the rolling plains and wooded hills of Europe. It is completely unrealistic to suggest that large lumps of mountain could support anything other than ptarmigan and deer, or that rocky coastlines and small islands could offer fertile ground for growing crops or grazing cattle. But in glens and straths at the foot of the mountains, on coastal strips less dominated by rocks, there is land and there is living-space in which communities can support themselves. The livings need not be based on the tilling of the land, the raising of animals or harvesting the seas; this is the twenty-first century, where technology makes possible many other trades and professions, in combination, in true crofting style.

Just imagine if there was also a rail service.

A slow depopulation of the area continues. On Lewis, the 1891 census recorded almost 26,000 people; in 2011, around 19,600; comparative figures for the Loch Broom area suggest around 4,200 in 1891 and 3,300 in 2011. Along much of the line of the proposed Garve to Ullapool railway, people are still few and far between, and their works even more so. Not much to show for more than a century of social progress in the western world. What finally triggered the crofters' and cottars' rebelliousness of the 1880s was not the thoughtless actions of individual landowners; the underlying cause was – and remains – a chronic problem of the ownership and the usage of the land. There are very strong arguments today, as there were almost a century and a half ago, for wide-ranging land reforms to rejuvenate rural Scotland, both in terms of repopulation and of the physical health of the land itself.

In the nineteenth century and the first decades of the twentieth, the fishing grounds off the north and west coasts of Scotland teemed with fish. It was quite possible for thousands of people to make a living from the catching and processing of fish, even if only for part of the year. The railway proposals we have examined stood or fell on how they could support the fisheries, but this justification was less and less persuasive after the years of 'peak herring' in the first decade of the twentieth century. Thereafter, due to a combination of over-fishing and under-investment, the fishing industry began to decline. In 1907, 2.5 million tons of fish were caught; the peak in the interwar years was 1.7 million (1924), dropping to half of that by the start of the Second World War, and not recovering thereafter.[4] Throughout the 1960s, 70s and 80s, total catch figures bounced along the bottom at around half a million tons (in a good year). None of this was helped, of course, by incursions from foreign vessels – both from behind the Iron Curtain and from Europe. In the past decade, the total catch by Scottish vessels has barely reached 0.4 million tons – of which the west coast has delivered over half, in the shape of mackerel.[5] But half a million tons of fish is scarcely a reason to build a railway. Nor is this situation likely to improve: climate change is already affecting what edible things swim in the deep around Scotland, and experience has warned us more than once about the necessity of sustainable fishing.

Not fish, then. But there are other reasons to have a railway reaching the coast: the obvious ones are tourism and general passenger traffic, the transportation of freight, the potential for supplying oil and gas exploration (even if one cannot condone the extraction of yet more fossil fuels), link-ups with the increasing capacity on ferry routes to the isles. But, above all, surely the support and development of coastal and island communities could score high on the list?

The drive to build railways in the west of Scotland – both on the mainland and on the islands – was in part an attempt to skirt nimbly around the thorny issue of the ownership of land, by exploiting and developing the un-owned sea: fisheries provided adequate employment and income. Connect the West Coast fisheries to the urban markets and all those intractable social problems would surely go away. Of course, there were additional benefits, such as easier access for locals to the bustling centres of civilisation – Dingwall, Inverness, Glasgow, Edinburgh – and to better medical and education facilities; and there was always the potential for developing forestry, local industry and tourism. Perhaps, despite the scepticism of some of the commissioners sent to the north-west, the railways really could have gradually improved the lot of ordinary people. But for the common man, as Mr Mackay of the 1918 Commission was at pains to point out, there was little point in having a railway if the fare was unaffordable: any railway would have to be subsidised, in the manner of the Penny Post. Then, and then only, could railways have made a major difference.

The 1890 proposal for a railway between Garve and Ullapool was thwarted largely by a government which was anxious not to spend any more money than necessary in improving the lives of the people of the west coast, and which had still not weaned itself from the 'easy' solutions of emigration and migration. Despite some shining examples of state ownership in Europe, any form of financing or management of railways by the State was anathema to Whitehall. The driving force of the Victorian economy was competition, not collaboration; private and not public interest.

To cap it all, the Garve and Ullapool Railway was also thwarted by the incompetence of several commissions of public servants. In the immortal words of P. Campbell Ross: 'Our people are weary of Commissions, Committees and those sorts of things. I hope we shall have no more bodies of distinguished strangers making enquiries in our midst.'[6] The incompetence of the Scottish Office was perhaps only matched by its tragic ignorance of simple geography, as demonstrated by its publication of several maps. And there was little hope of out-manoeuvring the Highland Railway Company, which had taken obstructionism to a pinnacle of perfection. The Aultbea, Lochinver and Laxford railways suffered much the same fate as the Ullapool one. Three decades later, in 1918, the proposal for a railway to Ullapool was once again frustrated by a government that had better things to do than pay attention to the well-argued recommendations of its own appointees; and by then, in any case, social upheaval and lorries had overtaken dreams and trains. From both 1890 and 1918, the lasting legacy was not so much that no railway was built: it was that, for decades, nothing at all was done to improve transportation and the infrastructure underpinning twentieth-century life in the north-west. It was not until 1973 that the shortest sea route from the mainland to Lewis was served by the new ferry route between Stornoway and Ullapool.

Was the Garve to Ullapool railway, in any of its several manifestations, a viable option? Doubtless, it would still be a very convenient railway for passengers from the Stornoway ferry wishing to travel to the flesh-pots of Inverness and beyond; and for the tourists travelling in the opposite direction wishing to soothe their souls in landscapes of the Outer Isles. Additionally, freight to and from the coast and the islands could be moved rapidly and cleanly. Had the railway been built, Shore Street in Ullapool would be a great deal more cluttered; horses would be startled on a daily basis by the rattling of perhaps antique rolling stock. But that would have been all to the good. A similarly rosy picture obtains for a line between Achnasheen and Aultbea, that seductive line with its three photogenic viaducts and two tunnels.

Could any of these railways have been built? Certainly, the leading railway engineers of the time did not think any of the proposed lines would be inherently difficult to construct. The Laxford and Lochinver lines could well have been the simplest of all; but we will, like any self-respecting nineteenth-century civil servant, ignore them. Both the Ullapool and Aultbea lines contained at least one interesting challenge, but there was nothing insuperable there. If Sir John Fowler thought that a railway could descend from Braemore to Loch Broom, then why should we mortals cast any doubt over the matter? And if Charles Forman could float a railway over Rannoch Moor, then there is no reason to suppose that any engineer with even half of his acumen could not conquer the rugged landscape further north. The likelihood is that construction of lines to Ullapool or Aultbea would have cost far more than predicted – the lines to Mallaig and Kyle both did. It is a truth universally acknowledged that massive construction projects will massively overrun their budgets.

Had any one of the proposed versions of the Garve and Ullapool Railway been built, would it still be operational today? Without a doubt, like most of the railway lines north of Perth, the Ullapool route would have attracted the unwelcome attention of Dr Beeching in 1963. There was no chance that the railway would have been viewed as 'paying its way' with passenger traffic. Amongst Beeching's many targets were the Dingwall to Kyle and Inverness to Wick and Thurso lines, as well as the stopping service on the Mallaig line. However, one of the most gratifying things about the Beeching cuts was that the campaigns of community groups, MPs and others for the preservation of their railway links led to the uninterrupted and quite shameless continuance of those same links. Had the Ullapool line existed, then it too might have been saved.

The principle expressed in Parliament in 1891 and in the 1919 Committee Report, that the public had a right to cheap transport just as they had a right to cheap postage, was – and is – one to be kept to the forefront of the arguments concerning railways.

So let us ask a more difficult question: could a railway from Garve to Ullapool be built now, in the present century? Leaving aside for the moment the social and economic case for such a thing, let us look at the technicalities and costs (for which we now give thanks to modern railway engineers persuaded to dream).[7] We need not look too far for an actual template. In 2015 the 30-mile-long Borders Railway, linking Edinburgh to Galashiels and (almost) Melrose, re-opened after being closed down in 1969. Years of grass-roots campaigning finally led to the passing in 2006 of an Act to authorise the new railway, construction work began in 2012, and – partly because the bulk of the track-bed for the line still existed, inclusive of extremely well-built nineteenth-century viaducts – the first trains were running barely three years later. New life is being breathed into communities along the line, and there is wild talk of extending the line further (the original 'Waverley' line ran all the way to Carlisle). The cost of the reconstruction ran to around £300 million, which is £10 million per mile. Railways are far more complex beasts than they were a century and more ago – there are new and expensive types of signalling, there are major trunk roads to be bridged, there are higher construction, environmental and safety standards to be observed. So a comparison with the nominal £6,000 per mile of 1890 – £600,000 in today's money – is meaningless. What will be more realistic is a comparison with constructing 'perfectly good carriage roads' (for which, see below).

The estimated cost of building the railway to Ullapool, in 2020 values, would be anything between £400 and £850 million – £12 to

£25 million per mile (it is best to leave plenty of slack). More expensive than the Borders line – but remember that this would be a railway built from scratch, with no older works to act as foundations.

The Ullapool Railway, were it to be built today, would largely follow the same line as originally planned, and no doubt would upset a fair few estate owners. There would, however, be some differences and some minor realignments – both at Garve and at Ullapool, but more importantly at Braemore. A proposed solution is set out in more detail in Appendix 10 at the end of this book, with the promise of an enticing timetable (five trains a day, each way!). The changes for a modern-day railway would take advantage of technical advances, but would also create a smoother gradient over the entire length of the line. There would be no level crossings and – rather sadly – still no tunnel. A modern-day civil engineer might ask the same question we have asked: why bother taking the railway down the west side of the descent at Braemore? Why not use the east side which, although possibly steeper in places, is a more direct route? Short of a government commission of inquiry, there may be no answer to that question.

Could a modern railway pay its way? We can only speculate. Arguably, passenger traffic would need to be supplemented by freight traffic – supermarket supplies, machinery, timber, agricultural and industrial materials and equipment. But that brings its own problems, since mixed passenger–freight trains such as would have run in the 1890s are not fashionable – indeed, they do not really exist. One could envisage a freight-only train, timed to meet the regular Stornoway freight ferry which already sails each night, carrying containers to and from the Outer Isles. And that, of course, would require completely different facilities at Ullapool and additional crossing loops all the way to Inverness, thereby increasing construction costs. But the question of 'paying its way' is not the correct one to ask: very few railways in Scotland (or anywhere else) actually pay their way in the twenty-first century. They are heavily subsidised by the taxpayer, and that is because they are recognised as social and national economic assets. Try to put it another way: do trunk roads and expensive bypasses pay their way?

Lest it feels left out, much of the above could also be said to promote a railway between Achnasheen and Aultbea. And maybe even railways on the isles of Lewis and Skye. Why not, after all?

*

And so: what of roads?

The A9 – the principal road link between Inverness and the south, unless you wish to make a lengthy detour via Aberdeen or Fort William – is a road which seems to be blocked by traffic accidents on a weekly basis. In an attempt to make the road safer, and faster, Scottish Government is letting contracts to upgrade 82 miles of road between Perth and Inverness, making it dual carriageway all the way. The budget? A mere £3 billion – which works out at £36 million per mile, or around two to three times the cost of a railway. Of course, the costs could be higher or lower – we simply will not know until the last stretch of tarmac has settled, sometime in 2025. (And, as a footnote, if you choose to avoid the A9 and take the longer route via Aberdeen, you will travel on the main part of the new Aberdeen Western Peripheral Route – 27 miles at about £28 million per mile, barely three times its original estimate.)

Running alongside the A9 from Perth to Inverness is the line built by the Highland Railway between 1861 and 1898. Although 37 miles of the 118-mile railway is double-track, two-thirds of it remains single-track: almost nothing has changed for a century and more. Despite desultory promises made in the past, no civil servant or politician has yet taken active steps to double the track, which would increase the number and speed of passenger trains, or to support regular rail-freight services to ease the congestion, pollution and danger on the roads.

Road traffic continues to make its way around the north-west of Scotland, and has been encouraged to do more of the same with the recent promotion of the North Coast 500 route. That tourist route passes through all four of the termini of the lines which never got built – Laxford, Lochinver, Ullapool and Aultbea. The NC500, for all the increased tourist income it brings, remains a marketing person's dream and a road maintenance person's nightmare. Anyone who has driven or cycled along some parts of that route recently will understand that these roads were never designed for the increased volume of tourist traffic. To bring camper-vans, bicycles and sightseers into conflict with everyday traffic, public transport and lorries, on roads not designed for such a mix, smacks of corporate devilry. Something, sometime, must yield.

*

Although written a hundred years ago, the words of a committee of civil servants still resonate:

> We take the broad view that there is a national duty to provide every community with reasonably convenient means of communication. The fact that people have settled in isolated districts implies no fault on their part; with limited facilities they are endeavouring to utilise the resources of land and sea, and in this they are giving effect to national policy and are entitled to claim the utmost assistance the State can afford. In considering what assistance is possible, it would be too narrow a view to look merely for a direct pecuniary return.[8]

Such means of communication included railways, steamers and roads. Railways might not always be the universal panacea for unsustainable road traffic, emissions and global warming in the modern age; they might not always be a practical lifeline for small communities. But in the late nineteenth century, it was an accepted fact that they were the most efficient method of transport and could also deliver economic and social improvement. Both the Garve and Ullapool Railway and the Loch Maree and Aultbea Railway remain locked in an alternative universe. Just as a Whitehall gentleman had dismissed the proposals as 'quite impossible', a respected railway historian once described these two railways and the other unsuccessful candidates of 1890 as 'pie in the sky lines', the implication being that they had no chance whatsoever of construction.[9] The evidence of several official investigations into the Ullapool proposal suggests otherwise. Difficult of engineering it might have been, but the Victorians were nothing if not good at elegant engineering solutions. And in the late nineteenth century and early years of the twentieth, railway construction was in fact the only logical solution to overland transportation problems. For the moment, we can only admire the efforts of local people – ordinary folk as well as the landowners and the MPs – to have the line to Ullapool built. In terms of a tourist attraction, the helter-skelter descent at Braemore alone would have been worth the fare.

APPENDICES

I TABLE SHOWING CONVERSION OF FARMING LAND TO DEER FOREST

Only some of the land-use figures for each sample estate are shown here.

	Acres in 1853	Acres in 1883
Ross and Cromarty estate of Duke of Sutherland		
Deer forest	17,000	56,500
Large farms	133,500	94,030
Torridon estate		
Deer forest	nil	27,345
Large farms	26,225	80
Gairloch estate		
Deer forest	29,420	38,020
Large farms	87,793	77,648
Achnasheen estate		
Deer forest	nil	15,830
Large farms	19,600	5,415
Lewis estate of Lady Matheson		
Deer forest	15,000	34,747
Large farms	137,000	124,648

2 MEMBERS OF THE NAPIER COMMISSION, 1883

Francis Napier, 10th Lord Napier, 1st Baronet of Ettrick
Sir Kenneth Mackenzie, 6th Baronet of Gairloch
Alexander Nicolson
Donald Cameron of Lochiel, MP
Charles Fraser Mackintosh, MP
Professor Donald Mackinnon
Secretary: Malcolm MacNeill, Esq., Poor Law Commissioner

3 PROMOTERS AND DIRECTORS OF THE GARVE AND ULLAPOOL RAILWAY COMPANY, 1890

Promoters and 'Proprietors':
  Lady Mary Jane Matheson
  Donald Matheson
  Major Duncan Matheson
  Major James Flower Houston
  John Arthur Fowler
Directors:
  All of the above except Lady Matheson
  Earl of Cromartie
Consulting Engineer:
  Sir John Fowler
Honorary Secretary:
  Patrick Campbell Ross

Appendices

4 MEMBERS OF THE WESTERN HIGHLANDS AND ISLANDS COMMISSION, 1890

Spencer Walpole
Formerly an Inspector of Fisheries, then Lt-Governor of the Isle of Man, later Secretary to the Post Office; a grandson of Spencer Perceval, PM

Sir James King
Glaswegian businessman, director of the Clydesdale Bank; later chairman of the Caledonian Railway Company

Dugald Mackechnie
Advocate; prosecution lawyer in 1899 case against William Bury, who was suspected of being Jack the Ripper

Commander Arthur Farquhar
Retired commander-in-chief of Royal Navy establishment in Plymouth

John Wolfe Barry, CE
Designer of the Tower Bridge in London and of the Connel Bridge near Oban

Malcolm MacNeill, Esq.
Erstwhile Secretary to the Napier Commission (see above)

Secretary: George H. Murray, from the Treasury

5 MEMBERS OF THE NORTH-WEST COAST OF SCOTLAND RAILWAYS COMMITTEE, 1891

Major-General Charles Scrope Hutchinson
Formerly of Royal Engineers, Inspector of Railways from 1867 to 1895; promoted to Chief Inspector of Railways in 1892

Rear-Admiral Sir George Nares
Formerly Southern Hemisphere surveyor in the Royal Navy, then leader of a disastrous Arctic expedition in 1875–6; employed as a harbour specialist by the Board of Trade from 1879; promoted to Vice-Admiral in 1892

Henry Tennant
General manager of the North-Eastern Railway Company from 1870 to 1891. From 1895 chairman, then director, of the Central London Railway

Secretary: J. Mauger Nicolle of the Board of Trade

6 PROMOTERS/PROPRIETORS OF THE LOCH MAREE AND AULTBEA RAILWAY, 1892

Sir Kenneth Smith Mackenzie, 6th Baronet of Gairloch
The Earl of Lovelace
Paul Liot-Bankes
Duncan Darroch of Gourock and Torridon
John Henry Dixon
William Ogilvie-Dalgleish of Coulin
Limited Owners:
    Maria Ann Liot-Bankes
    Sir Kenneth Mackenzie
    Osgood Mackenzie
    Hugh Cameron Ross

7 DIRECTORS OF THE HEBRIDEAN LIGHT RAILWAY COMPANY, 1898

Andrew W. Barr, accountant
Harold E. Perrin, accountant
Charles Kemble, solicitor
A. Hanbury Tracey, 'Gentleman J.P.' (later to be found playing polo with Robert Baden-Powell during the siege of Mafeking)
William Godward, accountant
J. W. Hume Williams, 'Director of Railways' (possibly of the Cork and Kinsale Railway)
F. Beaumont Hesseltine, 'Gentleman' (and stockbroker); he married Marion Hood, a famed light opera soprano. He later achieved brief fame by knocking down the Marquess of Queensberry in a fist-fight over the lovely Marion.

8 MEMBERS OF THE RURAL TRANSPORT (SCOTLAND) COMMITTEE, 1918

Sir T. Carlaw Martin, LLD
Editor of the *Dundee Advertiser* and director of the Royal Scottish Museum
H. M. Conacher
Senior official, Board of Agriculture for Scotland
John Ferguson, M.Inst.C.E
Further details unknown
William Haldane, WS
Crown agent for Scotland, and expert on forestry
Sir John Hepburn Milne Home
Forestry expert; sometime vice-president of the Advisory Council, Department of Agriculture for Scotland
George A Mackay
Probably the author of *Practice of the Scottish Poor Law* (1907); member of the Local Government Board for Scotland
Professor W. R. Scott, LLD
Adam Smith Professor of Political Economy at Glasgow University
W. A. Tait, M.Inst.C.E
Member of Board of Trade; expert on water power
Secretary: W. N. MacWilliam of the Board of Agriculture

9 MEMBERS OF THE LOCHBROOM EXECUTIVE/RAILWAY COMMITTEE, 1918

Sir Montague Fowler
Kenneth Cameron, Chairman of Lochbroom Parish Council (and uncle to the late Lord (John) Cameron, senior judge)
Dr D. Wallace, Chairman of the School Board
George Ross (Ullapool)
Roderick Mackenzie (Ullapool)
John Maclean (Aultandhu)
James Stewart (Ullapool)
Secretary: D. S. Ross, Inspector of the Poor, and parish council clerk

10 PROPOSED ROUTE OF A TWENTY–FIRST–CENTURY
RAILWAY LINE

The following proposal is based entirely on suggestions made by David Prescott, consultant railway engineer.

At Garve, some realignment would be necessary to avoid the railway cutting off the primary school from the rest of the village; the railway could only diverge from the Kyle line west of the village centre, and a bridge would be required to go over the A832 road at Gorstan (around NH387625). Thereafter, with the exception of the problem at Braemore, the line would run more or less as originally set out in 1890, closely following the course of the A835 road. At the Ullapool end, from Braes westwards the railway would certainly need to run along a solid embankment built out into the loch: there is very little room to allow road and rail to co-exist safely. A projection into the loch, like the ones at Gourock, Oban or Fort William, would have the additional advantage of permitting the construction of a station of adequate proportions. The pier might have to be realigned to fit. Almost certainly, the presence of such a projection into the loch would be strongly resented by the residents of Shore Street and those living back along the shoreline to the south-east.

But the biggest change would be at the descent from Braemore: here the experts agree with Sir John Fowler – 'no tunnel at all'.

One suggestion for conquering the western side of the strath leading down to Loch Broom is to make the approach from the south more direct and less precipitous. This would require the excavation of a cutting heading north-west from a point at around NH199780, which would pass underneath the A832 road; this cutting (with more than the average drainage installed) would terminate at a viaduct which passes almost directly above the Cuileag Power Station (at NH193789); the viaduct would then curve very gently to bring the railway parallel to the profile of the hillside; a long ledge would be cut into the hill, and down the line would go. Gently. To maintain a steady gradient of 1 in 40, the line would probably lie at a higher elevation than on the original plans. We hope it will not disturb any deer. On reaching a point just behind Inverbroom Lodge (NH182838), the River Broom and the A835 road would both be crossed by a low – but quite lengthy – viaduct: this would continue the relatively gradual slope, and avoid a drop to sea level followed by an immediate ascent. This entire section would cut out about a mile of railway, banish the contentious tunnel to the darker recesses of fantasy, and smooth out all the ascents and descents. Our consultant railway engineer Mr Prescott is convinced that this would work; the author is not inclined to disagree.

Alternatively, it should be possible to make a descent down the east side, keeping above – but very close to – the A835 road, easing through the woods and looping around the back of Inverlael. For this option, another series of bridges and small viaducts would be required. Some pleasant woodland would have to be destroyed; an Ecological Impact Assessment might well prove that this route is undesirable.

Using two separate sets of rolling stock, it would be possible to run five trains each way every day – two of them would be timed to meet the twice-daily Stornoway ferry, and three others would run at times which would facilitate commuting options for work, shopping or study. All would readily link with Inverness trains to and from the south. The journey from Ullapool to Inverness (57 miles) would take around two hours, with stops at Garve, Dingwall and Beauly; this is about thirty minutes less than the journey from Kyle of Lochalsh to Inverness (79 miles), but still slightly longer than the present road-based bus service. There would be a need for minor enhancements to the line between Garve and Inverness, to allow for the increase in traffic.

CHRONOLOGY

April 1882 and following	'Crofters' War' events on Skye
May–October 1883	Napier Commission tours Scotland taking evidence; report published 28 April 1884
December 1884	Representation of People Act extends vote to rural households, with financial restrictions; 60 per cent of Scottish males now have the vote
May 1885	First public proposal for a railway line from Garve to Ullapool
January 1886	Election of Gladstone minority government; five Crofters' Party MPs elected
25 June 1886	Crofters' Holdings (Scotland) Act; creation of Crofters' Commission
July 1886	Election of Conservative government under Lord Salisbury
April 1889	Visit of James Caldwell MP to the west coast and islands
14 May 1889	Joint Committee formed to promote a railway from Achnasheen to Aultbea
8–20 June 1889	Visit of Lord Lothian, Secretary for Scotland, to west coast and islands
April 1890	Major-General Hutchinson inspects proposed level crossings between Garve and Ullapool
April 1890	Great North of Scotland Railway attempts to block Garve and Ullapool's proposed contract with the Highland Railway
April to June 1890	Western Highlands and Islands Commission undertakes a tour

14 August 1890	Passing of the Garve and Ullapool Railway Act
18 August 1890	Report of the Western Highlands and Islands Commission published
4 February 1891	Deputation in support of Aultbea Railway visits Lord Lothian
April 1891	Garve and Ullapool Board meet with the Highland Railway in London
May 1891	Garve and Ullapool invites Great North of Scotland to take over the project
July/August 1891	North-West Coast of Scotland Railways Committee visits west coast and islands
March 1892	Report of the North-West Coast of Scotland Railways Committee published
19 May 1892	Deputation in support of Lochinver Railway visits Lord Lothian
20 May 1892	Deputation in support of Ullapool Railway visits Lord Lothian
31 May 1892	Bill to transfer powers on the Ullapool project to the Great North of Scotland Railway receives its second reading
August 1892	After General Election, minority Liberal government formed by Gladstone, ousting Conservative government of Lord Salisbury. Lord Lothian replaced as Secretary for Scotland by George Trevelyan
September 1892	W. Cospatrick Dunbar, Under-Secretary at Scottish Office, visits areas of all proposed railways
December 1892	Creation of Deer Forest Commission
December 1892	Government announces grant of £45,000 to the Highland Railway towards construction of the line from Strome Ferry to Kyle of Lochalsh
21 April 1893	Private Bill for the Lochmaree and Aultbea Railway receives its second reading
29 June 1893	Highland Railway Act passed to extend Strome Ferry line to Kyle of Lochalsh
24 August 1893	Garve and Ullapool Railway (Abandonment) Act passed
August 1894	Arrival of West Highland Railway at Fort William

August 1895	Conservative government wins General Election and forms coalition with Liberal Unionists; Trevelyan replaced by Lord Balfour as Secretary for Scotland
March 1896	Arthur Fowler asks Highland Railway to construct a light railway to Ullapool
14 August 1896	Passing of the Light Railways Act
November 1897	Completion of Strome Ferry to Kyle extension
August 1897	Creation of the Congested Districts Board for Scotland
April 1901	Completion of Fort William to Mallaig line
November 1901	Major Blunt requests financial assistance from the Congested Districts Board for a tramway from Garve to Isle Martin
February 1906	Landslide victory for Liberals under Campbell-Bannerman
1911	Winding up of Congested Districts Board and Crofters' Commission – powers transferred to Board of Agriculture and Scottish Land Court
1912	Dewar Committee reports on health and medical care in the Highlands
February 1918	Rural Transport (Scotland) Committee appointed; visits west coast and islands from March onwards
June 1918	Rural Transport (Scotland) Committee visits Ullapool
February 1918	Representation of People Act extends vote to all men over twenty-one, and many women over thirty
December 1918	Election of Coalition government (Liberals and Conservatives)
April 1919	Report of the Rural Transport (Scotland) Committee published
August 1919	Ministry of Transport Act
December 1919	Land Settlement (Scotland) Act
1 January 1923	'Big Four' railway companies formed
July 1945	Landslide victory for Labour Party under Attlee
September 1945	Commander Vyner proposes a railway from Garve to Ullapool to the board of the London Midland and Scottish Railway

NOTES

CHAPTER 1

1. Rural Transport (Scotland) Report, paragraph 53.
2. Hansard, House of Commons, 23 March 1891, James Caldwell MP.
3. Napier Commission Report, 1884, vol. 1, p. 657, Q10410.
4. John Thomas, *The West Highland Railway*, pp. 41 and 100.
5. Thomas, *West Highland Railway*, p. 110.
6. Thomas, *West Highland Railway*, p. 81.
7. Hansard, House of Commons, 4 March 1889, James Caldwell MP.

CHAPTER 2

1. Hansard, House of Commons, 4 March 1889, James Caldwell MP.
2. Napier Commission Report, 1884, vol. 1, pp. 658f, Q10420.
3. For more information on the Sutherland clearances, see James Hunter, *Set Adrift Upon the World* (2015).
4. Hunter, *Set Adrift Upon the World*, pp. 369f.
5. See James Hunter, *A Dance Called America*, pp. 194ff.
6. John Murdoch, *For the People's Cause*, p. 99.
7. Napier Commission Report, 1884, vol. 4, p. 3088, Q44463.
8. Napier Commission Report, 1884, vol. 3, p. 2067, Q32488.
9. G. A. Mackay, *Practice of the Scottish Poor Law*, pp. 73ff.
10. G. Nicholls, *A History of the Scotch Poor Law*, pp. 269f.
11. James Hunter, *The Making of the Crofting Community*, p. 110.
12. G. Nicholls, *A History of the Scotch Poor Law*, pp. 244ff.
13. Napier Commission Report, 1884, vol. 5, p. 3.
14. Napier Commission Report, 1884, vol. 3, p. 1822, Q28441.
15. Napier Commission Report, 1884, vol. 3, pp. 1780ff, Q27899ff.
16. See Hunter, *The Making of the Crofting Community*, pp. 53ff; Hunter, *A Dance Called America*, pp. 98f.
17. G. Nicholls, *A History of the Scotch Poor Law*, p. 246f.
18. Napier Commission Report, 1884, vol. 1, p. 197f, Q3823ff.
19. Napier Commission Report, 1884, vol. 1, p. 583f, Q9398.
20. Dewar Report, paragraph 15.

21. Dewar Report, paragraph 11.
22. Dewar Report, paragraph 18.
23. Dewar Report, paragraph 19.
24. Dewar Report, paragraph 22.
25. Napier Commission Report, 1884, vol. 3, p. 1981, Q31084.
26. Dewar Report, paragraph 16.
27. Dewar Report, paragraph 19.
28. Dewar Report, Section III, 8 'Conclusions'.
29. Dewar Report, paragraph 48.
30. Dewar Report, paragraph 136.
31. Napier Commission Report, 1884, vol. 1, p. 657, Q10398f.
32. For the full text of this leaflet, see *The Scotsman*, 22 April 1882, p. 10.
33. Napier Commission Report, 1884, vol. 1, p. 147, Q2804.
34. Napier Commission Report, 1884, vol. 1, pp. 81–2, Q1434 and Q1461.
35. Napier Commission Report, 1884, vol. 1, p. 642, Q10176.
36. Napier Commission Report, 1884, vol. 2, p. 1576, Q41253.
37. *The Scotsman*, 22 April 1882, p. 10.
38. As reported by John Murdoch, Napier Commission Report, 1884, vol. 4, p. 3071, Q44463.
39. Napier Commission Report, 1884, vol. 4, p. 2710, Q25000.
40. Napier Commission Report, 1884, vol. 1, p. 181, Q3528.
41. See J. C. Beckett, *The Making of Modern Ireland 1603–1923*, pp. 335–47.
42. H. D. Gribbon, 'Economic and Social History 1850–1921', in W. E. Vaughan, *A New History of Ireland, Vol. VI*, p. 261.
43. L. P. Curtis, 'Ireland in 1914', in Vaughan, *A New History*, p. 145.
44. David Fitzpatrick, 'Emigration 1871–1921', in Vaughan, *A New History*, p. 638.
45. Beckett, *Making of Modern Ireland*, p. 348.
46. Beckett, *Making of Modern Ireland*, p. 408.
47. Beckett, *Making of Modern Ireland*, p. 310.
48. R. V. Comerford, 'The Land War and the Politics of Distress', in Vaughan, *A New History*, p. 35.
49. Comerford, 'The Land War and the Politics of Distress', in Vaughan, *A New History*, p. 51.
50. The Landlord and Tenant (Ireland) Act 1870, paragraph 2.
51. Beckett, *Making of Modern Ireland*, p. 409.
52. Napier Commission Report, 1884, vol. 1, p. 29, Q507.
53. Napier Commission Report, 1884, vol. 4, p. 2999, Q43750.
54. Napier Commission Report, 1884, vol. 1, p. 165, Q3178.
55. Gribbon, 'Economic and Social History 1850–1921', in Vaughan, *A New History*, p. 310.
56. Napier Commission Report, 1884, vol. 5, appendix A, p. 10.
57. *The Scotsman*, 21 April 1882, p. 3.
58. *The Scotsman*, 18 January 1883, p. 5.
59. *The Scotsman*, 10 February 1883, p. 6.
60. *The Scotsman*, 16 October 1886, p. 8.
61. *The Scotsman*, 21 to 24 July 1886.
62. D. W. Crowley, *The Crofters' Party*, p. 6.
63. As cited in John Murdoch, *For the People's Cause*, p. 199.

64. *Ross-Shire Journal*, 15 April 1892.
65. Caroline Benn, *Keir Hardie*, pp. 61–2.

CHAPTER 3

1. Napier Commission Report, vol. 5, p. v.
2. *Quiz* weekly magazine, Glasgow, 26 October 1883, pp. 6f.
3. *The Scotsman*, 29 June 1883, p. 3.
4. Hansard, House of Lords, 21 November 1884, Duke of Argyll.
5. Murdoch, *For the People's Cause*, p. 190.
6. *The Scotsman*, 5 June 1883, p. 5.
7. Napier Commission Report, vol. 1. p. 1f, Q10 to Q12.
8. Napier Commission Report, vol. 5, appendix A, p. 440.
9. Napier Commission Report, vol. 2, pp. 1557f, Q24792ff; and vol. 5, appendix A, pp. 249–68.
10. Napier Commission Report, vol. 5, pp. 9f.
11. Napier Commission Report, vol. 5, pp. 108–11.
12. Napier Commission Report, vol. 5, p. 102.
13. Napier Commission Report, vol. 1, p. 373, Q6654 (John Macpherson).
14. Napier Commission Report, vol. 5, pp. 63–5.
15. Napier Commission Report, vol. 5, pp. 65.
16. Napier Commission Report, vol. 5, p. 137.
17. Napier Commission Report, vol. 5, p. 133.
18. Napier Commission Report, vol. 5, p. 136.
19. Hansard, House of Lords, 20 May 1885, Duke of Argyll.
20. Crofters Holdings (Scotland) Act, 1886, paragraph 34.
21. Hansard, House of Commons, 19 April 1886, Dr Clark and Dr R MacDonald.
22. For a discussion on the effect of sheep on the land, see R. D. G. Clarke, *Two Hundred Years of Farming*, pp. 188–91, 207.
23. Clarke, *Two Hundred Years of Farming*, p. 160.
24. Napier Commission Report, vol. 1, p. 7, Q68.
25. Napier Commission Report, 1884, vol. 5, appendix A, pp. 434–8.
26. Napier Commission Report, 1884, vol. 4, p. 2773, Q41770.
27. *The Scotsman*, 20 April 1892, p. 6.
28. Napier Commission Report, 1884, vol. 4, p. 2775, Q41788.
29. Napier Commission Report, 1884, vol. 5, appendix C, pp. 530–2.
30. Deer Forest Statistics, 1899, 1902, 1904, 1908 [NRS AF67/294].
31. Secretary for Scotland to J. G. Weir, 6 May 1902 [NRS: AF67/294/11].
32. Hansard, House of Commons, 22 January 1897, James Caldwell MP.
33. Hansard, House of Commons, 8 August 1905, Francis Channing MP.
34. Lord Advocate, 10 August 1905 [NRS: AF67/294/20].
35. Hansard, House of Commons, 22 January 1897, James Caldwell MP.
36. Deer Forest Statistics, 1913 [NRS: AF67/294].
37. Napier Commission Report, vol. 5, p. 53.
38. Napier Commission Report, vol. 2, p. 855, Q13273.
39. Napier Commission Report, vol. 2, p. 1174, Q17836.
40. Napier Commission Report, vol. 2, p. 999, Q15549.
41. Napier Commission Report, vol. 2, p. 947, Q14807.

42. Napier Commission Report, vol. 2, p. 882, Q13754.
43. For more information on this episode, see [NRS: CR11/494].
44. See Hunter, *The Making of the Crofting Community*, p. 162.
45. For all references in the following section, unless otherwise defined, see *Ninth Annual Report of the Fishery Board for Scotland (Part I)*, Edinburgh 1890.
46. R. W. Duff (ed.), *The Herring Fisheries of Scotland*, 1883, p. 5.
47. Napier Commission Report, vol. 5, p. 60.
48. John Anderson to Lord Lothian, 27 May 1889 [NRS: GD40/16/41].
49. Letter from McCombie to W. C. Dunbar, 19 February 1891 [NRS: AF67/199].
50. For this and following reports of events on this matter, see documents in [NRS: AF57/1454].
51. *The Scotsman*, 10 April 1894, p. 3.
52. *The Scotsman*, 21 December 1893, p. 6.
53. Napier Commission Report, vol. 2, p. 1162, Q17708.
54. Letter from C. Fraser-Mackintosh, 20 February 1891 [NRS: AF67/199].
55. Courtesy of David Sutherland. See his Scottish Herring History website: www.scottishherringhistory.uk.
56. For more on this episode, see *The Scotsman*, 4 to 12 June 1883.
57. *The Scotsman*, 2 June 1883, p. 8.
58. *The Scotsman*, 4 June 1883, p. 4.
59. *The Scotsman*, 5 June 1883, p. 5.
60. John Thomas, *The Skye Railway*, pp. 40–2.
61. Statistics of the Scottish Fisheries for the year 1913 [NRS: AF56/738].
62. These figures courtesy of David Sutherland, www.scottishherringhistory.uk.
63. Napier Commission Report, vol. 5, p. 64.

CHAPTER 4

1. *The Scotsman*, 23 May 1889, pp. 6f.
2. *The Scotsman*, 23 May 1889, p. 7.
3. See *The Scotsman*, 8 to 22 June 1889.
4. *The Scotsman*, 21 November 1884, p. 6, and 16 October 1886, p. 9.
5. Hansard, House of Commons, 3 August 1885, Sir Lyon Playfair.
6. For the following information and quotations, see *The Scotsman*, 8 to 22 June 1889.
7. *The Scotsman*, 13 June 1889, p. 6.
8. *The Scotsman*, 19 June 1889, p. 7.
9. A. D. Cameron, *Go Listen to the Crofters*, p. 84.
10. N. S. Robins and D. E. Meek, *The Kingdom of Macbrayne*, p. 95.
11. *The Scotsman*, 19 April 1882, p. 9.
12. Hunter, *The Making of the Crofting Community*, p. 210.
13. *The Scotsman*, 4 June 1883, p. 5.
14. Details of steamers, fares and times taken from Macbrayne's *Summer Tours in Scotland* guide, Glasgow 1890; also from *Guide to Ullapool and Loch Broom*, Ullapool 1903.
15. Hansard, House of Commons, 10 July 1890.
16. *The Scotsman*, 9 January 1891, p. 6.

17. Napier Commission Report, 1884, vol. 2, p. 1696, Q26717.
18. Napier Commission Report, 1884, vol. 3, p. 2106 Q3310; p. 2337 Q37018; p. 2476 Q38694; p. 2497 Q38997.
19. *The Scottish Leader*, 14 May 1889.

CHAPTER 5

1. *The Scotsman*, 8 September 1888, p. 8.
2. *The Scotsman*, 19 June 1889, p. 7.
3. Letter from Major Houston, 27 June 1891 [NRS: AF67/237].
4. *Ross-Shire Journal*, 15, 22 and 29 May 1885.
5. *The Scotsman*, 3 March 1890, p. 9.
6. Letter from J. Fowler to P. C. Ross, 9 April 1889 [NCR: GD40/16/41].
7. File annotation on letter sent by P. C. Ross, 3 January 1889 [NRS: AF67/201].
8. Letter from P. C. Ross, [undated: June?] 1889 [NRS: AF67/199].
9. Letter from Andrew Dougall, 7 February 1889 [NRS: GD40/16/39].
10. Highland Railway Company Minutes, 19 April 1890 [NRS: BR/HR/1/6].
11. Hansard, House of Commons, 4 March 1889.
12. Alexander Mackenzie, *The History and Genealogy of the Mathesons*, p. 61.
13. Mackenzie, *The History and Genealogy of the Mathesons*, p. 45.
14. Napier Commission Report, vol. 3, pp. 1971–3, Q30948ff.
15. Napier Commission Report, vol. 3, pp. 1983f, Q31124.
16. Napier Commission Report, vol. 3, p. 1984, Q31126.
17. T. M. Devine, *Clanship to Crofters' War*, p. 60.
18. Hunter, *The Making of the Crofting Community*, p. 126f.
19. Napier Commission Report, appendix A, p154.
20. For documents and letters relating to this episode, see [NRS: CR11/494].
21. Napier Commission Report, vol. 4, pp. 3078f, Q44463.
22. Hunter, *The Making of the Crofting Community*, pp. 240–3.
23. Hansard, House of Commons, 4 March 1889.
24. *Perthshire Advertiser*, 14 March 1894.
25. Hunter, *The Making of the Crofting Community*, p. 264.
26. Napier Commission Report, vol. 3, p. 1801, Q28222.
27. Hew Scott, *Fasti Ecclesiae Scoticanae*, p. 159.
28. *Guide to Ullapool and Lochbroom*, 1903, p. 39.
29. Letter from P. C. Ross, 13 August 1891 [NRS: AF67/237].
30. See 1891 Population Census; also Napier Commission Report, vol. 5, appendix B, p. 526.
31. Napier Commission Report, vol. 3, p. 1797 Q28181; p. 1835 Q28583; p. 1840 Q28628.
32. Great North of Scotland Railway Company Minutes, 20 November 1889 [NRS: BR/GNS/1/12].
33. Arthur L. Bowley, *Wages in the United Kingdom*, pp. 54ff, 77ff; Michael J. Morris, *A Manly Desire*, p. 292.
34. Dewar Report, paragraph 35.
35. *The Scotsman*, 19 June 1889, p. 7.
36. Petitions from Little Loch Broom, 1 February 1893; from Tanera, 6 March 1893; from P. C. Ross, 21 September 1893 [NRS: AF67/211].

37. See *The Scotsman*, 21, 25 December 1889; 3, 8, 20 January 1890.
38. See petitions May and June 1891 [NRS: AF67/205].
39. *Perthshire Advertiser*, 14 March 1894.
40. *Edinburgh Gazette*, 26 November 1889, p. 1097.
41. Plans and Sections of the Garve & Ullapool Railway, 1890 [NRS: RHP916/1 and RHP14292].
42. Letter from John Fowler to Arthur Fowler, 6 May 1896 [NRS: AF67/214].
43. Letter from M. Paterson to J. Fowler, 9 April 1889 [NRS: GD40/16/41].
44. Letter from John Fowler to W. C. Dunbar, 19 October 1892 [NRS: AF67/208].
45. Alexander Mackenzie, *The History of the Highland Clearances*, p. 152.
46. Napier Commission Report, vol. 3, p. 1811, Q28338.
47. Napier Commission Report, vol. 3, pp. 1835f, Q28599.
48. Napier Commission Report, vol. 3, p. 1840, Q28630.
49. Letter from John Fowler to W. C. Dunbar, 19 October 1892 [NRS: AF67/208].

CHAPTER 6

1. Letters from P. C. Ross to Lord Lothian, January to April 1889 [NRS: AF67/201].
2. See Highland Railway Company Minutes, 6 February, 6 March, 19 April and 26 April 1889 [NRS: BR/HR/1/6].
3. Letter from A. Dougall to P. C. Ross, 7 February 1889 [NRS: GD40/16/39].
4. Letter from Little Loch Broom to Lord Lothian, May 1889 [NRS: AF67/201].
5. Letter from P. C. Ross to J. Fowler, 6 April 1889 [NCR: GD40/16/41].
6. *The Scotsman*, 23 May 1889, p. 7.
7. *The Scotsman*, 23 May 1889, p. 7.
8. Printed document, 'Ullapool versus Aultbea', 11 June 1889 [NRS: GD40/16/42].
9. Napier Commission Report, vol. 5, p. 56.
10. *The Scotsman*, 19 June 1889, p. 7.
11. Letters from Ullapool, 18 June, and P. C. Ross, 24 and 27 June 1889 [NRS: AF67/202].
12. 'Heads of Agreement', signed by J. A. Fowler and A. Dougall, 24 April 1890 [NRS: GD40/16/29].
13. Cited in Roake, *Ross Pies in the Sky*.
14. Garve and Ullapool Railway Act 1890, paragraph 25.
15. Garve and Ullapool Railway Act 1890, paragraph 23.
16. Thomas, *Skye Railway*, p. 18, pp. 46f.
17. Report of the Western Highlands and Islands Commission, 1890, p. 6. [NRS: AF67/404].
18. Second Report on Colonisation, 17 March 1891 [NRS: GD40/16/57].
19. Report of the Western Highlands and Islands Commission, 1890, paragraphs 40–1.
20. Memo by R. W. Cochran-Patrick, 15 May 1889 [NRS: AF67/201].
21. Letter from J. A. Fowler, 5 September 1890 [NRS: AF67/199].
22. Letter from P. C. Ross to George Trevelyan, 4 October 1892 [NRS: AF67/208].
23. Hansard, House of Commons, 23 March 1891.
24. Memorandum of meeting between Garve & Ullapool Railway and Highland Railway, 13 April 1891 [NRS: GD40/16/29].

25. Letter from Mr H. R. Cripps of Dysons & Co., May 1891 [NRS: AF67/237].
26. Letter from W. L. Jackson MP, 24 April 1891 [NRS: GD40/16/29].
27. *The Scotsman*, 27 February 1890, p. 7.
28. Letter from Mr H. R. Cripps to Mr Jackson, May 1891 [NRS: AF67/237].
29. *The Scotsman*, 3 March 1890, p. 9.
30. *The Scotsman*, 22 April 1890, p. 7.
31. Great North of Scotland Railway Company Minutes, 23 April 1891 [NRS: BR/GNS/1/12].
32. Petition from Stornoway to Lord Lothian, 28 May 1891 [NRS: AF67/205].
33. Hansard, House of Commons Private Business, 31 May 1892.
34. Hansard, House of Commons, 31 May 1892.
35. Petition from people of Lewis to Lord Lothian, June 1891 [NRS: AF67/205].
36. Letter from P. C. Ross to R. W. Cochran-Patrick, 10 October 1891 [NRS: AF67/206].
37. Letter from P. C. Ross to Lord Lothian, 24 June 1890 [NRS: AF67/204].
38. Hutchinson Report [NRS: GD40/16/57].
39. Letter from H. R. Simpson of the Treasury to Mauger Nicolle, 26 June 1891 [NRS: AF67/205].
40. *Ross-Shire Journal*, 1 April 1892.
41. Hutchinson Report [NRS: GD40/16/57].
42. Memorandum signed by Major Hutchinson, 29 July 1891 [NRS: AF67/237].
43. Letter from Mr William Gunn, 31 August 1891 [NRS: AF67/237].
44. Letter from Major Houston, 27 June 1891 [NRS: AF67/237].
45. Hansard, House of Commons, 11 August 1892.
46. Hansard, House of Commons, 13 June 1892.
47. *Ross-Shire Journal*, 8 April 1892.
48. *The Scotsman*, 20 April 1892, p. 6.
49. *Ross-Shire Journal*, 15 April 1892.
50. *The Scotsman*, 24 May 1892, p. 5.
51. Letter from P. C. Ross to George Trevelyan, 4 October 1892 [NRS: AF67/208].
52. Andrew Dougall to J. G. Goschen, 1 June 1892 [NRS: AF67/208].
53. Letter from John Fowler to J. A. Fowler, 6 May 1896 [NRS: AF67/214].
54. Reported in Lochbroom Executive Committee Minutes, dated 11 June 1918, p. 7.
55. *The Scotsman*, 21 May 1892, p. 12.
56. Hansard, House of Commons, 10 May, 10 June, 14 June 1892.
57. Hansard, House of Commons, 20 July, 27 July and 5 September 1893.
58. Hansard, House of Commons, 16 September 1893.
59. Letter from P. C. Ross, 2 April 1897 [NRS: AF67/214].
60. Lord Advocate's reply to Dr Farquharson, 1 March 1892 [NRS: AF67/206].
61. *Ross-Shire Journal*, 15 April 1892.

CHAPTER 7

1. See Report of the Western Highlands and Islands Commission, 1890 [NRS: AF67/404], and report by W. C. Dunbar for Trevelyan, November 1892 [NRS: AF67/208].
2. John Fowler to Arthur Fowler, 6 May 1896 [NRS: AF67/214].

3. Charles Forman to W. C. Dunbar, 13 October 1892 [NRS: AF67/208].
4. *Perthshire Advertiser*, 14 March 1894.
5. Source: Office of Rail Regulation, Train Operating Costs report for 2012.
6. Statements by P. Campbell Ross, undated but probably June 1890 [NRS: AF67/199].
7. Contained in report by W. C. Dunbar for Trevelyan, November 1892, appendix A [NRS: AF67/208].
8. See Highland Railway Company Minutes, Half-yearly Statements of Accounts, April 1889 to October 1896 [NRS: BR/HR/1/6; 1/8; 1/9].
9. H. A. Vallance, *The Highland Railway*, p. 78.
10. Thomas, *Skye Railway*, pp. 79 and 127.
11. Letter from Uig on Lewis to Trevelyan, 28 January 1893 [NRS: AF67/210].
12. Memo from W. C. Dunbar to Trevelyan, 23 August 1892 [NRS: AF67/208].
13. Report by W. C. Dunbar for Trevelyan, November 1892 [NRS: AF67/208].
14. Report by W. C. Dunbar for Trevelyan, November 1892, pp. 9–10 [NRS: AF67/208].
15. Letter from Uig on Lewis to Trevelyan, 28 January 1893 [NRS: AF67/210].
16. Letter from P. C. Ross to Trevelyan, 21 September 1893 [NRS: AF67/211].
17. *The Scotsman*, 17 December 1892, p. 8.
18. Telegram from J. G. Weir to Trevelyan, 21 December 1892 [NRS: AF67/209].
19. Correspondence regarding Ullapool Railway, 1 February 1893 [NRS: AF67/211].
20. Highland Railway Company Minutes, 6 April 1898 [NRS: BR/HR/1/9].
21. Thomas, *Skye Railway*, p. 126.
22. Garve and Ullapool Railway (Abandonment) Act 1893, paragraph 3.
23. Record in *Causa* Messrs. Stewart, Rule and Burns, Solicitors, Inverness, against The Garve and Ullapool Railway Company and Others, 15 November 1892 [NRS: CS250/6270].
24. Highland Railway Company Minutes, 3 October 1894 [NRS: BR/HR/1/8].
25. Hansard, House of Commons, 4 May 1893.
26. Letter from Liberal Association of Loch Broom to Trevelyan, 9 March 1893 [NRS: AF67/211].

CHAPTER 8

1. Letter from J. Dixon to G. Goschen, 1 May 1891 [NRS: AF67/236].
2. Alexander Mackenzie, *History of the Mackenzies*, pp. 446–7.
3. Napier Commission Report, vol. 3, p. 1868, Q29040.
4. Napier Commission Report, vol. 3, p. 1889, Q29368.
5. See article by Gavin Strang at www.lyonandturnbull.com/news/article/?i=368
6. Mackenzie, *History of the Mackenzies*, pp. 460 and 619.
7. See W. MacRobbie, *The Lairds and the Clearances*, pp. 45ff.
8. Napier Commission Report, vol. 3, pp. 1860–88, Q28936ff.
9. Napier Commission Report, vol. 4, pp. 2889ff, especially p. 2897, Q42732; also vol. 3, pp. 1902ff, Q29650f.
10. *The Scotsman*, 23 May 1889, p. 7.
11. *The Scotsman*, 6 June 1889, p. 7.
12. *The Scotsman*, 8 March 1890, p. 12.
13. *The Scotsman*, 3 January 1890, p. 6.
14. *The Scotsman*, 17 May 1889, p. 4.

15. Highland Railway Company Minutes, 5 June 1889 [NRS: BR/HR/1/6].

16. *The Scotsman*, 14 November 1889, p. 7.

17. *Inverness Courier*, 23 March 1888.

18. See *The Scotsman*, 25, 31 December 1889, 10 and 20 January 1890.

19. Letter from John Anderson to Scottish Office, 3 May 1889 [NRS: AF67/201].

20. Letter from P. C. Ross, 27 June 1889 [NRS: AF67/202].

21. Letter from P. L. Bankes, 21 November 1889 [NRS: AF67/202].

22. *The Scotsman*, 19 June 1889, p. 7.

23. Letter from J. H. Dixon, 5 February 1890 [NRS: AF67/203].

24. *The Scotsman*, 7 April 1890, p. 10.

25. *The Scotsman*, 27 May 1890, p. 4.

26. File annotation on letter from Sir Kenneth Mackenzie, 20 May 1889 [NRS: AF67/201].

27. Letter and memorandum from J. H. Dixon, 1 May 1891 [NRS: AF67/236].

28. *The Scotsman*, 5 February 1891, p. 5.

29. Letter from Mauger Nicolle to J. H. Dixon, 15 July 1891 [NRS: AF67/236].

30. Letter and 'Epitome' from J. H. Dixon, 3 August 1891 [NRS: AF67/236].

31. Report by W. C. Dunbar to Lord Trevelyan, November 1892 [NRS: AF67/208].

32. Hutchinson Report [NRS: GD40/16/57].

33. Letter from Lovelace to Lord Lothian, 12 May 1892 [NRS: AF67/207].

34. Letter from Durnford & Co. to Lord Lothian, 11 March 1892 [NRS: AF67/207]. Note: Durnford's calculation is based on a distance of 39.5 miles, although the actual surveyed distance was later set at 37.5 miles.

35. *The Scotsman*, 1 December 1892, p. 6. See also *Edinburgh Gazette*, 18 November 1892, p. 1262ff.

36. Bound Plans and Sections, Loch Maree and Aultbea Railway, 1892 [NRS: RHP82306].

37. Meik & Sons: Estimate of Expense for the Railway. Dated 29 December 1892 (archived at Gairloch Museum).

38. Letter from Durnford & Co. to Lord Lothian, 11 March 1892 [NRS: AF67/207].

39. Letter from Durnford & Co. to W. C. Dunbar, 16 December 1892 [NRS: AF67/209].

40. Letter from Andrew Dougall to Trevelyan, 5 January 1893 [NRS: AF67/209].

41. Letter from Durnford & Co. to W. C. Dunbar, 25 January 1893 [NRS: AF67/210].

42. Letter from Treasury to Durnford & Co., 27 January 1893 [NRS: AF67/210].

43. *The Scotsman*, 22 April 1893, p. 9.

44. See Thomas, *Skye Railway*, p. 124.

CHAPTER 9

1. Napier Commission Report, vol. 2, p. 1694, Q26671.

2. Napier Commission Report, vol. 2, p. 1696, Q26716.

3. Letters and petitions to Lord Lothian, 3 January, 10 and 13 March 1890 [NRS: AF67/203].

4. Letter to Lord Salisbury, 7 April 1890 [NRS: AF67/203].

5. Report of the Western Highlands and Islands Commission, 1890, p. 10 and p. 14.

6. Petition from Laxford, 12 February 1891 [NRS: AF67/205].

7. Letter to Lord Lothian, 9 November 1891 [NRS: AF67/206].

8. Letter to Lord Lothian, 11 December 1891 [NRS: AF67/206].

9. Report of meeting with Lord Lothian, 25 May 1892 [NRS: AF67/208].

10. Letter to Trevelyan, 14 January 1893 [NRS: AF67/210].

11. Cited in letter from William Mackay to Trevelyan, 14 January 1893 [NRS: AF67/210].

12. Highland Railway Company Minutes, 31 March 1896 [NRS: BR/HR/1/8].

13. Highland Railway Company Minutes, 5 January 1897 [NRS: BR/HR/1/9].

14. Letter to Lord Balfour, 12 August 1896 [NRS: AF67/210].

15. Highland Railway Company Minutes, 1 September 1896 [NRS: BR/HR/1/9].

16. Hunter, *Set Adrift Upon the World*, pp. 376–94.

17. Report of the Western Highlands and Islands Commission, 1890 [NRS: AF67/404].

18. Petition sent to Scottish Office, 9 June 1892 [NRS: AF67/208].

19. Letter to Trevelyan, 16 January 1893 [NRS: AF67/210].

20. Hutchinson Report, pp.5f [NRS: GD40/16/57].

21. Minute of meeting with Lord Lothian, 19 May 1892 [NRS: AF67/208].

22. Highland Railway Company Minutes, 27 October 1896 [NRS: BR/HR/1/9].

23. Highland Railway Company Minutes, 5 January 1897 [NRS: BR/HR/1/9].

24. Highland Railway Company Minutes, 3 March 1897 [NRS: BR/HR/1/9].

25. Thomas, *West Highland Railway*, pp. 25–6.

26. *The Scottish Leader*, 14 May 1889.

27. Letter from William Munro, 18 June 1889 [NRS: AF67/201].

28. Letter from J. Struthers, 2 February 1891 [NRS: AF67/205].

29. *Glasgow Herald*, 2 September 1891.

30. Letter from H. T. Humphreys, 4 January 1890 [NRS: AF67/203].

31. For more information, see http://nzetc.victoria.ac.nz/tm/scholarly/tei-Gov13_09Rail-t1-body-d4.html.

32. Letters from Charles Forman to W. C. Dunbar, 13 and 22 October 1892 [NRS: AF67/208].

33. Thomas, *West Highland Railway*, p. 81.

CHAPTER 10

1. Light Railways Act, 1896, paragraph 5.

2. Light Railways Act, 1896, paragraph 7, subsection 4.

3. Regulation of the Railways Act, 1868, paragraph 28.

4. For further details, see David Spaven and Julian Holland, *Mapping the Railways*, p. 164.

5. Hansard, House of Commons, 3 August 1894.

6. Hansard, House of Commons, 26 August 1895.

7. Hansard, House of Commons, 24 April 1896.

8. Highland Railway Company Minutes, 31 March 1896 [NRS: BR/HR/1/8].

9. Letter and petition from Ullapool, 9 August 1895 [NRS: AF67/212].

10. Letters from P. C. Ross to Balfour, 12 and 29 May 1896 [NRS: AF67/213].

11. Letter from P. C. Ross, 2 April 1897 [NRS: AF67/214].

12. Letter from Balfour, 10 May 1897 [NRS: AF67/214].

13. Letter from P. C. Ross, 28 June 1897 [NRS: AF67/214].
14. Highland Railway Company Minutes, 7 September 1898 [NRS: BR/HR/1/10].
15. Letter from J. G. Weir, 12 April 1899 [NRS: AF67/214].
16. Highland Railway Company Minutes, 1 March and 5 April 1899 [NRS: BR/HR/1/10].

CHAPTER 11

1. *The Scotsman*, 11 June 1889, p. 5.
2. *The Scotsman*, 12 June 1889, p. 7.
3. Highland Railway Company Minutes, 6 October 1896 [NRS: BR/HR/1/9].
4. Highland Railway Company Minutes, 28 April 1897 [NRS: BR/HR/1/9].
5. Highland Railway Company Minutes, 6 April 1898 [NRS: BR/HR/1/9].
6. Board of Trade documents held at National Archives, Kew: ref – BT31/7845/56157.
7. *Northern Weekly*, 21 April 1898, p. 1.
8. National Archives, Kew: ref MT54/100.
9. *The Scotsman*, 28 April 1898, p. 9.
10. *The Scotsman*, 3 May 1898, p. 8.
11. *Edinburgh Evening News*, 6 May 1898.
12. Highland Railway Company Minutes, 7 June and 2 August 1899 [NRS: BR/HR/1/10].
13. *The Scotsman*, 23 May 1889, p. 7.
14. See *The Scotsman*, 17 January 1888, p. 5; and 20 January 1888, p. 5.
15. See *The Scotsman*, 16, 18 and 22 June 1889.
16. *The Scotsman*, 9 January 1891, p. 6.
17. Report by W. C. Dunbar for Trevelyan, November 1892 [NRS: AF67/208].
18. For almost all the details concerning this road, I am indebted to the research notes kindly offered to me by Jack Kernahan.
19. Minutes of Lewis District Committee of County Council of Ross and Cromarty, 13 March 1891.
20. Minutes of Lewis District Committee, 10 November 1892.
21. Highland Railway Company Minutes, 3 February 1897 [NRS: BR/HR/1/9].
22. North British Railway Company Minutes, 29 July 1897 [NRS: BR/NBR/1/46].
23. Minutes of the Directors Board of the North British Railway, 21 October 1897 [NRS: BR/NBR/1/46].
24. See *Dictionary of Irish Architects* at https://www.dia.ie/architects/view/270/.
25. *Northern Weekly*, 5 May 1898, p. 5.
26. *The Scotsman*, 7 May 1898, p. 11.
27. *The Scotsman*, 2 May 1898, p. 9.
28. *The Scotsman*, 6 May 1898, p. 5.
29. *The Scotsman*, 10 May 1898, p. 11.
30. *Northern Weekly*, 5 May 1898, p. 5.
31. *Edinburgh Evening News*, 6 May 1898.
32. North British Railway Company Minutes, 19 May and 14 July 1898 [NRS: BR/NBR/1/46].
33. North British Railway Company Minutes, 9 March 1899 [NRS: BR/NBR/1/48].

34. Highland Railway Company Minutes, 7 June 1899 [NRS: BR/HR/1/10].
35. National Archives, Kew: ref – MT6/833/7.
36. National Archives, Kew: ref – BT31/7845/56157.
37. Annual Report of the Congested Districts Board, 1897–1898, p. 5.
38. Annual Report of the Congested Districts Board, 1899–1900, p. xxvii.
39. Annual Report of the Congested Districts Board, 1903–1904, p. 8 and p. 15.
40. *The Scotsman*, 7 September 1912, p. 10.
41. *The Scotsman*, 9 September 1912, p. 6.

CHAPTER 12

1. Hansard, House of Commons, 2 August 1897.
2. See Annual Reports of the Congested Districts Board, 1899–1910.
3. Hansard, House of Commons, 7 May 1901.
4. *The Scotsman*, 11 August 1911, p. 10.
5. Letter from E. W. Blunt to the Congested Districts Board, 24 November 1901 [NRS: AF42/1026].
6. Letter from E. W. Blunt to the Congested Districts Board, 4 April 1901. [NRS: AF42/846].
7. *Ross-Shire Journal*, 27 November 1903, p. 5.
8. See https://broompowerblog.wordpress.com/2016/07/31/history-of-hydro-in-lochbroom/, with thanks to Peter Newling.
9. Establishment of the Strathpeffer and Dingwall Electric Company Limited, 1909 [NRS: BT2/7111].
10. *North Star*, 2 December 1903.

CHAPTER 13

1. Courtesy of Scottish Herring History website, www.scottishherringhistory.uk.
2. For more details, see Leah Leneman, *Land Settlement in Scotland after World War I*.
3. For more details on Leverhulme and Lewis, see Roger Hutchinson, *The Soap Man*.
4. Figures from Office for National Statistics – see www.ons.gov.uk/employment andlabourmarket/peopleinwork/employmentandemployeetypes/articles/thehistoryofstrikesintheuk/2015-09-21.
5. *The Scotsman*, 29 September 1919, p. 6.
6. *The Scotsman*, 9 August 1920, p. 7. See also John Maclean's own report at: www.marxists.org/archive/maclean/works/1920-highland.htm
7. E. H. Whetham, cited by Leneman in *Land Settlement in Scotland after World War I*, p. 54.
8. Land Settlement (Scotland) Act, 1919, paragraph 28.
9. Cited in Dewar Report, paragraphs 9 and 10.
10. Dewar Report, paragraph 1.
11. Dewar Report, paragraphs 2 to 7.
12. Dewar Report, paragraphs 13, 14, 26, 33.
13. For more details see https://wartimememoriesproject.com/greatwar/battles/view.php?pid=4898.
14. Hutchinson, *The Soap Man*, pp. 79–80.

CHAPTER 14

1. Rural Transport (Scotland) Report, p. 5.
2. *The Scotsman*, 26 May 1919, p. 6.
3. Rural Transport (Scotland) Report, paragraph 54.
4. Rural Transport (Scotland) Report, paragraph 61.
5. For this and subsequent references to the minutes, see unpublished Lochbroom Executive Committee Minutes.
6. *Sydney Morning Herald*, 1 November 1913, p. 4.
7. See *The Scotsman*, 17 July 1917, p. 3.
8. This information is courtesy of Peter Newling.
9. *The Scotsman*, 30 June 1933, p. 6.
10. Lochbroom Executive Committee Minutes, p. 7.
11. Letter from D. S. Ross, 24 June 1918 [NRS: GD305/2/519].
12. Mackenzie, *History of the Mackenzies*, pp. 511–12.
13. Rural Transport (Scotland) Report, paragraph 245.
14. Rural Transport (Scotland) Report, paragraph 271.
15. Rural Transport (Scotland) Report, paragraph 234.
16. Rural Transport (Scotland) Report, pp. 45–6.
17. Rural Transport (Scotland) Report, p. 46.
18. Rural Transport (Scotland) Report, paragraph 252.
19. See letter from W. N. MacWilliam to John McCaskill of Gairloch estate, 15 February 1921 (archived in Gairloch Museum).
20. Rural Transport (Scotland) Report, appendix 2.
21. Printed petition concerning the Garve to Ullapool Railway, [undated; post-April] 1919 [NRS: GD305/2/541].
22. Letter from Montague Fowler, [undated] 1919 [NRS: GD305/2/519].
23. Hansard, House of Commons (Home-Grown Timber Committee), 15 March 1917.
24. *The Times*, 1 October 1919, p. 8.
25. Ministry of Transport Act, August 1919, paragraph 2.
26. Cited in the Rural Transport (Scotland) Report, paragraph 147.

CHAPTER 15

1. See Valuation Roll for Ross and Cromarty, 1945/46 [NRS: VR115/90].
2. LMS Railway Company, Scottish Committee Minutes, 18 September 1945 [NRS: BR/LMS/1/142].
3. Hansard, House of Commons, 1 April 1936, Sir Godfrey Collins.

CHAPTER 16

1. Andy Wightman, *Who Owns Scotland?*, p. 159.
2. Andy Wightman, *The Poor Had No Lawyers*, pp. 142–66.
3. See Andy Wightman, *Forest Ownership in Scotland*, 2012, at http://www.forest policygroup. org/wp-content/uploads/2014/08/Forest-Ownership-In-Scotland-Feb-2012.pdf.
4. See http://www.scottishherringhistory.uk/statistics/AnnualExport.html.

5. See statistics published by Scottish Government at: https://www2.gov.scot/Topics/Statistics/Browse/Agriculture-Fisheries/PubFisheries.

6. Letter from P. C. Ross to George Trevelyan, 4 October 1892 [NRS: AF67/208].

7. With thanks to David Prescott, Chris Lees and David Spaven, who contributed their thoughts to this section.

8. Rural Transport (Scotland) Report, 1919, paragraph 22.

9. Thomas, *Skye Railway*, pp. 109–23.

BIBLIOGRAPHY

BOOKS AND ARTICLES REFERENCED

Anon, *Guide to Ullapool and Lochbroom* (Ullapool: n.p., 1903)

Beckett, J. C., *The Making of Modern Ireland 1603–1923* (London: Faber & Faber, 1981)

Benn, Caroline, *Keir Hardie* (London: Hutchinson, 1997)

Bowley, Arthur L., *Wages in the United Kingdom in the Nineteenth Century* (Cambridge: Cambridge University Press, 1900)

Cameron, A. D., *Go Listen to the Crofters* (Stornoway: Acair, 1986)

Clarke, Reay D. G., *Two Hundred Years of Farming in Sutherland* (Isle of Lewis: Islands Book Trust, 2014)

Crowley, D. W., 'The Crofters' Party – 1885 to 1892', *Scottish Historical Review*, vol. 35, 1956

Duff, R. W. (ed.), *The Herring Fisheries of Scotland* (London: W. Clowes, 1883)

Hunter, James, *A Dance Called America* (Edinburgh: Mainstream, 1999)

Hunter, James, *The Making of the Crofting Community* (Edinburgh: Birlinn, 2010)

Hunter, James, *Set Adrift Upon the World* (Edinburgh: Birlinn, 2015)

Hutchinson, Roger, *The Soap Man: Lewis, Harris and Lord Leverhulme* (Edinburgh: Birlinn, 2003)

Leneman, Leah, 'Land Settlement in Scotland after World War I', *Agricultural History Review*, vol. 37, Part 1, pp. 52–64, 1989

Mackay, George A., *Practice of the Scottish Poor Law* (Edinburgh: W. Green, 1907)

Mackay, John Charles, *Light Railways for the United Kingdom, India, and the Colonies: A Practical Handbook* (London: C. Lockwood, 1896)

Mackenzie, Alexander, *The History and Genealogy of the Mathesons* (Inverness: A. & W. Mackenzie, 1882)

Mackenzie, Alexander, *The History of the Mackenzies* (Inverness: A. & W. Mackenzie, 1894)

Mackenzie, Alexander, *The History of the Highland Clearances*, 2nd edn (Glasgow: P. J. O'Callaghan, 1914)

MacRobbie, William, *The Lairds and the Clearances* (Gairloch: n.p., 2001)

Morris, Michael J., 'A Manly Desire to Learn: The Teaching of the Classics in 19th-Century Scotland', PhD thesis, Open University, 2009

Murdoch, John, *For the People's Cause*, ed. James Hunter (Edinburgh: HMSO, 1986)

Nicholls, G., *A History of the Scotch Poor Law* (London: John Murray, 1856)

Roake, John, 'Ross Pies in the Sky – II: The Garve and Ullapool Railway', *Highland Railway Journal*, vol. 3, no. 46 (1998), pp. 15–21.

Robins, N. S. and Meek, D. E., *The Kingdom of Macbrayne* (Edinburgh: Birlinn, 2006)

Scott, Hew, *Fasti Ecclesiae Scoticanae: The Succession of Ministers in the Church of Scotland from the Reformation* (Edinburgh: Oliver & Boyd, 1928)

Spaven, David and Holland, Julian, *Mapping the Railways* (London: Times Books, 2011)

Thomas, John, *The West Highland Railway* (Newton Abbot: David St John Thomas, 1984)

Thomas, John, *The Skye Railway* (Nairn: David St John Thomas, 1990)

Vaughan, W. E. (ed.), *A New History of Ireland, Vol. VI* (Oxford: Oxford University Press, 1989)

Vallance, H. A., *The Highland Railway* (Colonsay: House of Lochar, 1996)

Wightman, Andy, *Who Owns Scotland?* (Edinburgh: Canongate, 1996)

Wightman, Andy, *The Poor Had No Lawyers* (Edinburgh: Birlinn, 2015)

GOVERNMENT ACTS AND REPORTS REFERENCED

Congested Districts Board for Scotland – Annual Reports, 1899–1910

Congested Districts Board for Scotland – Correspondence, 1901 [NRS – references AF42/846 and AF42/1026]

Crofters' Holdings (Scotland) Act, 1886

'Dewar Report': Highlands and Islands Medical Service Committee Report, 24 December 1912

Edinburgh Gazette, 1889 and 1892

Fishery Board for Scotland, Ninth Annual Report, 1890

Garve and Ullapool Railway Act, 1890

Bibliography

Garve and Ullapool Railway (Abandonment) Act, 1893

Garve & Ullapool Railway, correspondence 1918–1919 [NRS – references GD305 /2/519 and GD305/2/541]

Hansard reports between 1888 and 1917

Highland railways archives 1889–99 [NRS – references AF67/199 to AF67/237]

'Hutchinson Report': Report of a Special Committee appointed to Inquire into Certain Schemes for the Improvement of Railway Communication on the Western Coast of Scotland, 1891

Light Railways Act, 1896

Marquess of Lothian's Collected Papers 1889–1892 [NRS – references GD40/16/ 29 to GD40/16/57]

'Napier Commission Report': Report of the Commission of Inquiry into the Conditions of the Crofters and Cottars in the Highlands and Islands of Scotland, 1884

Population Census of the United Kingdom, April 1891

Regulation of the Railways Act, 1868

Rural Transport (Scotland) Committee Reports, 1919/1920

'Second Report on Colonisation': Second Report of Her Majesty's Commissioners appointed to carry out a scheme of Colonisation in the Dominion of Canada, of Crofters and Cottars from the Western Highlands and Islands of Scotland, 7 February 1891

Western Highlands and Islands Commission Report 1890 [NRS – reference AF67 /404]

OTHER ARCHIVES CONSULTED

Garve and Ullapool Railway, Bound Plans and Sections and Books of Reference, 1890 [NRS – references RHP916/1, RHP916/2 and RHP14292]

Great North of Scotland Railway Company Minutes 1886–1891 [NRS – reference BR/GNS/1/12]

Highland Railway Company Minutes 1896–1899 [NRS – references BR/HR/1 /6 to BR/HR/1/10]

Lochbroom Executive Committee Minutes, 1918/1919 [Ullapool Museum, ref: ULM 1997.097]

Loch Maree and Aultbea Railway, Bound Plans and Sections and Book of Reference, 1892 [NRS – reference RHP82306]

London, Midland and Scottish Railway Company, Scottish Committee Minutes 1945 [NRS – reference BR/LMS/1/142]

North British Railway Company Minutes 1897–1899 [NRS – references BR/
   NBR/1/46 to /48]
The North Star and Farmers' Chronicle, 1903
Ross-Shire Journal, 1885
The Scotsman, 1882–1933

FURTHER RECOMMENDED READING

Devine, T. M., *Clanship to Crofters' War* (Manchester: Manchester University
   Press, 1994)
Devine, T. M., *The Scottish Clearances* (London: Allen Lane, 2018)
Hunter, James, *Insurrection: Scotland's Famine Winter* (Edinburgh: Birlinn, 2019)
Hutchinson, Roger, *Martyrs: Glendale and the Revolution in Skye* (Edinburgh:
   Birlinn, 2015)
Miller, James, *The Dam Builders* (Edinburgh: Birlinn, 2002)
Simms, Frederick Walter, *Practical Tunnelling: Explaining in Detail, the Setting Out of
   the Works; Shaft-sinking, and Heading Driving; Ranging the Lines, and Levelling
   Under Ground; Sub-excavating, Timbering; and the Construction of the Brickwork of
   Tunnels: with the Amount of Labour Required For, and the Cost of the Various Portions
   of the Work etc* (London: Troughton & Simms, 1877)

USEFUL WEBSITES

https://hansard.parliament.uk/   Parliamentary reports for House of Commons
   and Lords
https://maps.nls.uk/   Ordnance Survey maps and Admiralty charts for Scotland
   1795–1963
www.ambaile.org.uk   Old photographs of, and articles on, north-west Scotland
www.biodiversitylibrary.org/   Fishery Board Annual Reports
www.irishstatutebook.ie/   Irish Government Acts (Westminster and Dublin)
   1801–present
www.legislation.gov.uk/   UK Government Acts 1801–present
www.scottishherringhistory.uk/   Historical and statistical information on Scottish
   fisheries
www.uhi.ac.uk/en/research-enterprise/cultural/centre-for-history/research/
   the-napier-commission/ Online copies of the five volumes of the Napier
   Report.

INDEX

Index